Women through Women's Eyes

Women through Women's Eyes

Latin American Women in Nineteenth-Century Travel Accounts

Edited by June E. Hahner

SR BOOKS

Lanham • Boulder • New York • Toronto • Oxford

Published by SR Books
An imprint of Rowman & Littlefield Publishers, Inc.
A wholly owned subsidary of The Rowman & Littlefield Publishing Group, Inc.
4501 Forbes Boulevard, Suite 200
Lanham, MD 20706

PO Box 317
Oxford
OX2 9RU, UK

Copyright © 1998 by Scholarly Resources, Inc.
First Rowman & Littlefield edition 2005

British Library Cataloguing in Publication Information Available

Library of Congress Cataloging-in-Publication Data

Women through women's eyes : Latin American women in nineteenth-century
    Travel accounts / edited by June E. Hahner.
        p. cm. — (Latin American silhouettes)
    Includes bibliographical references.
    ISBN 0-8420-2633-9 (cloth : alk. paper) ISBN 0-8420-2634-7 (paper : alk. paper)
        1. Women—Latin America—Social conditions. 2. Women—Latin America—
History—19th century. 3. Women travelers—Latin America—History—19th century.
I. Hahner, June Edith, 1940—   .
II. Series.
HQ1460.0. W65 1998
305.4'098'09034—dc21   97-43639

Printed in the United States of America

⊖™ The paper used in this publication meets the minimum requirements of American National Standard for Information Sciences—Permanence of Paper for Printed Library Materials, ANSI/NISO Z39.48-1992.

To the memory of my mother

Acknowledgments

Without the assistance of many others, this book would not have been possible. My greatest debt is owed to Roderick J. Barman and Mary Karasch, who gave generously of their time and talents, reading the entire manuscript and offering critical insights and valuable suggestions. The book benefited enormously from their efforts. Dolores B. Schmidt, who also read the manuscript with great care and attention, helped to improve it in many ways. Additional thanks are due to Jean Barman, Asunción Lavrin, Dauril Alden, William French, Lea Fletcher, Judith Ewell, and William H. Beezley for their suggestions. Gerald Zahavi and Marianne E. Simon's help and patience with a nontechnologically minded person such as myself is deeply appreciated. The services of the interlibrary loan office of the State University of New York at Albany were essential in obtaining needed travel accounts, and the assistance of Lic. Rogelio García Espinosa, director of the Museo Regional de Guanajuato, Alhóndiga de Granaditas, Mexico, was the key to gaining access to the photographs that appear on the cover of the paperback edition of this volume.

About the Editor

June E. Hahner is professor of history at the State University of New York at Albany. Her previous books include *Emancipating the Female Sex: The Struggle for Women's Rights in Brazil, 1850–1940* (1990); *Poverty and Politics: The Urban Poor in Brazil, 1870–1920* (1986); *Women in Latin American History: Their Lives and Views* (1976; rev. ed., 1980); and *Civilian-Military Relations in Brazil, 1889–1898* (1969).

Contents

Introduction

Travelers from Europe and the United States journeyed to Latin America in increasing numbers during the nineteenth century, sometimes writing detailed accounts of their adventures. Although most of those foreign travelers were men, a small but growing number of female voyagers also portrayed the places and people they encountered. Their books, produced for the enlightenment and entertainment of their contemporaries, still allow readers a century and more later to witness Latin America and its people firsthand. These travel writings serve both as a genre of literature and as a source for social history. They yield insights into gender relations in Latin America as well as in the authors' own societies.[1]

The nineteenth century was a period of peak popularity for travel literature. In countries such as Great Britain and the United States, these writings appealed to a large public, providing readers with both education and vicarious adventure. Such firsthand accounts could be as entertaining as novels while also abounding in sound information. Travel writing for an expanding marketplace even afforded a living for a few authors. Although some produced only one or two narratives, the more prolific of them competed for audiences. But their intended readership remained that located within their own homeland and culture.

The political independence of Latin America, like the growth of European empires in Africa and Asia, fostered both foreign travel and the related writing. Loosening travel restrictions, which accompanied Latin American political independence early in the nineteenth century, led to a notable increase in the number of foreign visitors at a time of European economic expansion and rising investments. As transportation and communication improved and international trade and commerce grew, the numbers of foreign visitors increased steadily, with travelers frequently following paths traced by their countries' economic investment. At the same time, the European reading public welcomed knowledge of the lands with which their countries had commercial or political dealings. Companies owned by European investors often sent agents to Latin

women aren't, in fact, homogeneou

America to search out sources of exploitable wealth or to make contact with local elites, and thus provided information on investment opportunities and local conditions. Merchants were joined by naturalists, explorers, mineralogists, engineers, agronomists, and military men. During the early nineteenth century, the British response to commercial opportunities led the United Kingdom to dominate the wave of foreign visitors to South America. But during the second half of the century, travelers from Great Britain more frequently followed the trail of their empire to Asia and Africa, even though British investments in such areas as mining and railroads continued to pour into South America, especially Argentina.

Travelers from the United States, who also included scientists, missionaries, military men, and merchants, seemed more likely to venture southward to Latin America rather than head east or west, although pleasure-seeking U.S. citizens often took a European Grand Tour. Other Europeans—such as the French and Germans, whose businessmen also fixed their eyes on Latin America—crossed the Atlantic and left written records of their adventures. Mexico and Brazil, the largest and most populous Latin American countries, proved the principal centers of attraction for foreigners, male and female alike, followed by Argentina and Peru. Cuba, due primarily to its geopolitical location, also drew many visitors from the United States. By the end of the nineteenth century, the construction of railroad lines running from the United States southward to Mexico City would facilitate commercialized tourism undertaken for recreation. Tour packages complete with guides and hotel reservations (invented by Thomas Cook for early nineteenth-century British visitors to southern Europe) were provided in the New World as well, with tours to Mexico filling entire coaches of private trains.

Prior to the nineteenth century, travel writing about Latin America was an overwhelmingly male activity. Thus it is extremely difficult to find any earlier accounts written by women.[2] In the nineteenth century, foreign male travel writers on Latin America far outnumbered their female counterparts, in a total ratio of roughly 10 to 1.[3] However, the proportion of female to male authors increased over the course of the century as travel became safer and more foreigners ventured abroad. With the decline of sailing ships—subject to shipwreck and piracy—and the rise of regularly scheduled service by faster and cheaper steamships, increasing numbers of travelers (usually members of the middle and upper classes with leisure time) headed across the Atlantic. So did masses of immigrants, who did not anticipate an immediate return home to Europe and who rarely had the time or education needed to write accounts of their journeys. By the late nineteenth century, travelers could expect less danger, difficulty, and delay. Nonetheless, female travel writers remained a minority among authors of travelogues everywhere, and fewer women wrote travel narratives about Latin America than about areas such as the Middle East.[4]

motives

Women's motivation for embarking on journeys might or might not parallel men's. Certainly we find women other than the stereotypical eccentric Victorian spinster or the indomitable individual seeking an escape from conventional women's roles. Men tended to travel in their occupational capacities, venturing to Latin America not only as missionaries, merchants and businessmen, scientists, engineers, and military men but also as diplomats, journalists, artists, and adventurers. In contrast, many women traveled as wives and helpmates accompanying and aiding their diplomat, military, engineer, or scientist husbands and, as in the cases of Elizabeth Cabot Cary Agassiz and Anne Cary Morris Maudslay,[5] wives of scientist husbands, keeping the diaries that became the basis of "coauthored" travel books. However, some women also went to Latin America to teach school, serve as missionaries, pursue artistic endeavors, recover their health or spirits, seek self-fulfillment, or alleviate financial distress, as in the case of Flora Tristán, who went to Peru to attempt to collect an inheritance (Chapter 2).

limitations in travel

The subordinate position of women in Europe and the United States, particularly in the early nineteenth century, could not but limit their ability to see the world and restrict their opportunities to write and publish. Matrimonial restraints, a paucity of legal rights, circumscribed education, and the physical difficulties and dangers of travel all imposed boundaries on their behavior. The serious constraints under which they labored while traveling, with the necessity for proper dress and conduct, not only limited their experiences but also the type of books that they could produce. Through their trips or publications, women might appear to be intruding into largely male, public areas of activity. Many female travelers might feel obliged to write primarily about subjects considered suitable for their participation and comment, such as scenic rides, shopping, and social encounters. Chronicles of topics considered unseemly for women would not win favor with publishers or the reading public. Women's accounts tended to be presented as the *examples of conforming to society?* (handwritten marginalia)

by-products of travel. At least the authors often disavowed intentions of publication, thereby conforming to contemporary standards of femininity and proving their modesty by claiming that they had never intended to expose their writings to the common gaze. However, toward the end of the nineteenth century, with improvements not only in transportation but also in some women's education and legal, social, and economic status, more women openly traveled with the intention of publishing tour memoirs.

Far fewer female travelers ventured abroad unaccompanied as did Ina von Binzer, a German schoolteacher (Chapter 7); Emília Serrano García del Forel, Baronesa de Wilson, a Spanish aristocrat residing in Paris;[6] Mary Lester, an English expatriate, writer, and would-be teacher in Central America;[7] Ida Pfeiffer, a mid-century German who pursued her youthful dreams to become a world traveler;[8] or Flora Tristán herself. Even reporter Nellie Bly (real name, Elizabeth Cochrane Seaman), in 1887, at the beginning of her journalistic career, traveled to Mexico with her mother,[9] though two years later she did go alone on her famous voyage around the world in less than eighty days. However, five years prior to that famous trip, Lillian Leland, a New Yorker in her mid-twenties, undertook a voyage around Cape Horn to California, ostensibly for health reasons; she then extended her travels around the globe, covering almost 60,000 miles in two years. Her book, entitled *Traveling Alone. A Woman's Journey Around the World* and supposedly drawn from letters sent home to family and friends who suggested their publication, appeared the same year as Nellie Bly's book. In her concluding chapter, Leland noted the relative ease with which she accomplished her journey on comfortable steamships and trains as compared with the hardships suffered by Ida Pfeiffer half a century earlier.[10]

Family ties combined with political events, such as those in midnineteenth-century Mexico and the United States, to produce a different, less common set of travel accounts. Authors of such works include a former Confederate wife whose family left Louisiana for the Texas-Mexican border and later ran a sugar plantation in Cuba,[11] the American wife of a Prussian officer and soldier of fortune who fought first for the Union army and then for Emperor Maximilian in Mexico,[12] a then-teenaged American girl living in Paris who was sent to join her family in Mexico during Maximilian's reign,[13] and an Austrian countess who served as a lady-in-waiting to Empress Carlota.[14] These women often expressed more concern with their own tribulations and sufferings than with the customs of the countries through which they passed, and they detailed their own political activities and attempts to further their personal social and political positions rather than describing local women's activities.

By the late nineteenth century, the ranks of female foreign travelers included more tourists as well as travel writers. Some participants in the popular train excursions from the United States to Mexico, including a few Britons who extended their American sojourns southward, published their letters home just for the entertainment of friends and relatives.[15] Magazines and newspapers such as *Harper's Bazaar* and the *New York Tribune* printed travel sketches by female as well as male authors, including Alice Le Plongeon, who also published her Mexican sketches in book form.[16] Like Mexico, Cuba, situated at the crossroads of the principal sea-lanes of the Caribbean and the Gulf of Mexico, attracted many foreign visitors. Some of these indulged in instant authorship, as did Adelaide Rosalind Kirchner, who converted a one-week trip into an entire book, *A Flag for Cuba, Pen Sketches of a Recent Trip Across the Gulf of Mexico to the Island of Cuba*, appealing for Cuban independence.[17] To their lists of destinations and subjects, well-traveled European authors and adventurers such as Lady Florence Dixie might add Latin America, or, in her case, Patagonia, the isolated southern tip of South America.[18] Similarly, the determined world traveler Ida Pfeiffer included Latin America on her midnineteenth-century round-the-world voyages, undertaken when, like some later Victorian women travelers, she was finally freed from family obligations and inherited funds that could be used for travel.

Although women who journeyed abroad undertook their voyages for a variety of reasons ranging from altruism to business, health, pleasure, curiosity, adventure, and family ties, most traveled because of family obligations, not independent decisions. A few women traveled alone, but most accompanied a husband or other family member or were part of a group, occupying subordinate or dependent positions. While some travel writers spent years, or at least months, in Latin America, others stayed only a few weeks, recording just scenery and street life, not social interactions. Status, location, and activities also helped determine which Latin American women they met and could write about. The socioeconomic differences between a diplomat's wife in the capital and a Protestant missionary on the Mexican frontier would lead them to associate with different classes of Mexican women. In a mining town in northern Mexico, an English engineer's wife might encounter no other foreign women. Nor would such a town provide anything resembling the rounds of social calls paid by upper-class women—including cultivated foreign visitors—in large urban centers such as Mexico City or Rio de Janeiro, or the leisurely promenades in open coaches enjoyed by wealthy visitors to Havana. However, the need to run a household and deal with market women and domestic servants—in the United States, as in Europe, upper- and upper-middle-class women automatically employed servants and discussed their relations with them—could provide readers with depictions of poorer Latin American women and cross-class as well as cross-national female relationships that many other foreign travelers did not experience or describe.

Despite the differences among them, whether of class, nationality, religion, or location, foreign observers had much in common. They remained outsiders. Unlike so many of their subjects, they were all literate and sufficiently educated to keep diaries or write letters or narratives. They might speak some of the languages of Latin America or, if well-polished, chat in French with educated members of the upper classes, although most could only converse in their own tongue. Like their male counterparts, female travelers could be superficial and careless chroniclers or shrewd, attentive observers. They could be racist, since few foreign visitors could escape the influence of the ideologies of the time, or sometimes open-minded. In their books, these largely well-to-do, educated, and secure (although dependent) women tended to propagate the gender and class assumptions of their societies. They were most likely to have voice if they upheld the status quo. Nonetheless, the more careful travel accounts, despite the powerful constraints of gender, race, and class, do tell us much about Latin American societies and the women living in them.

Following the formats employed by men, women's travel writings could take the form of diary entries, letters (a form less frequently employed by men), or autobiographical or third-person narratives. In those sometimes sentimental or romanticized accounts, the author might make herself the protagonist of the tale, as did Flora Tristán. Although some authors drew on an older tradition of survival narratives, fewer female than male accounts dwelt on the trials and tribulations of travel or celebrated the journey and its hardships, portraying them as obstacles to overcome. Few women, after all, traveled by themselves, or were forced to interact with the harsh realities of life in Latin America, as was Mary Lester. This British expatriate, engaged as the schoolmistress for what turned out to be a fraudulent colonization scheme in Central America, journeyed some two hundred miles by mule over the mountains of Honduras. In a first-person story published in part to recoup her travel expenses, she described with relative good humor the poor food, lack of sleep, crazed mules, swollen rivers, and sullen innkeepers she faced.[19] Other authors dwelt on personal problems and frustrations, such as in running a household in Mexico,[20] or, like Melinda Rankin, detailed labors as a missionary on the Mexican frontier.[21] But many wealthier female travelers easily avoided difficult journeys or the necessity of dealing directly with various people around them. Two such women were Gertrude Layard, who sailed on a comfortable steamship to the West Indies and enjoyed the hospitality of the British colonists—generally avoiding even the need for hotels[22]—and Lady Mary Carbutt, whose party sometimes rode in private cars on Mexican trains arranged for by English railway personnel, rather than just in Pullman cars as they did in the United States.[23]

Female foreign travelers' observations of Latin American women tended to be based on models of femininity in their own countries. The ways in which they observed gender relations generally conformed to such relations in their own societies, where women did not occupy dominant positions. Women authors measured Latin American systems of gender relations, sexuality, and family against Northern European and U.S. systems, which they generally assumed to be superior. They frequently lamented the relative lack of education or freedom accorded women in Latin America as compared to that found in their homelands, or commented on customs that they found unusual or unpleasant, such as women frequently smoking. Hence, their observations also inform us about the authors' own countries and cultural and personal values, including their notions of proper female behavior. Gender, after all, is neither timeless nor independent of place, race, and class.[24]

Not all male foreign travelers' accounts ignored women, and not all female accounts dealt extensively with them. Only Emília Serrano de Wilson placed women, particularly literary figures, at the center of her account.[25] Nevertheless, few female travel writers on Latin America completely ignored women, in contrast to their total exclusion from the accounts of many male travelers.[26] Female visitors often demonstrated more concern with other women, courtship, marriage, household management, and family life than did men. Many aspects of social life in Latin America were sexually segregated. Foreign women could enter some domestic and other settings to which foreign men had more difficulty in gaining access, such as convents (see Chapter 3, from the account of Fanny Calderón de la Barca). Like Maria Graham, these visitors might converse more freely with elite women than could foreign men and absorb "a good deal of information on subjects that only women attend to."[27] A few male foreign travelers were received in Latin American homes, but in contrast to women's accounts, the narratives they wrote rarely included descriptions of houses. Only a few men, such as artist Samuel Hazard in Cuba or naturalist Herbert E. Smith in Brazil, fixed their trained eyes on domestic arrangements.[28]

The treatment women travelers received differed from that accorded men. Male visitors would not be subjected to blatant attempts at sexual conquest by Latin American men, like those recounted by Adèle Toussaint-Samson, a Parisian in Brazil (Chapter 5). No male foreign traveler could ever personally experience the restrictions placed on women of his own class or the condescending treatment accorded them, as did the extremely well-educated Elizabeth Agassiz when a Brazilian plantation owner tried to replace a novel she was perusing with a book of moral sayings more "suitable" to women (Chapter 6). Female travelers might also comment on mistress-slave or mistress-servant relationships, as did Fanny Gooch (Chapter 8), something that Latin Americans, female or male, were unlikely to describe. Women seemed less likely than many male authors to repeat and perpetuate the stereotype of the passive and secluded upper-class woman, and more apt to describe individual women and specific social encounters. Yet some women's accounts largely ignored private life, concentrating instead on public events or on their own political position, while others, such as the books by Maria Graham, Fanny Calderón de la Barca, or Flora Tristán, recorded both public events and private aspects of some Latin American women's lives.

Not only did some female travel writers do more than describe scenery or social visits but they also engaged in activities abroad similar to those pursued at home—activities that might help expand their own spheres of action or aid them in acquiring political voice in their own countries. Like charity workers, social reformers, abolitionists, or other female investigators in their homelands, some women, especially those remaining in Latin America for longer periods of time, such as Tristán, Graham, and Calderón de la Barca, visited orphanages, hospitals, convents, and prisons. The Swedish novelist Fredrika Bremer investigated conditions on slave plantations (Chapter 4). These explorations and institutional critiques were not mere exercises in personal taste or complaints about living habits that differed from those of their own societies; they also contain accurate and insightful commentaries. However, some modern critics view these activities as attempts to exercise a civilizing mission or even as female imperial authority and intervention.

In any case, the cultural, class, and racial boundaries separating foreign travelers from their subjects could not be easily breached. The Latin Americans whom foreigners tended most to meet and write about were members of the upper classes. The visitors' interactions with the poor were largely limited to street sellers, servants, or slaves. Foreigners might easily remain unaware of the complexity of class, ethnic, and gender relations in Latin America, let alone systems of race or race relations that differed from those in their own countries, although longer stays sometimes heightened awareness. Moreover, few female travel writers, aside from some scientists' wives such as Elizabeth Agassiz and Anne Cary Maudslay, ventured deep or long into rural regions or dealt with Indian women, or, like Adèle Toussaint-Samson, resided on plantations run with slave labor. Far more foreigners, such as those on train trips to Mexico, viewed the countryside at a distance and stopped only in cities.

The reception accorded women's travel accounts in their home countries or in Latin America (for those that were translated) is difficult to determine but seems to have varied widely. Some books intended only for family or local consumption, such as descriptions of Mexican train trips, sank into obscurity. Others, such as the journals of Maria Graham, met with great popularity in her homeland of Great Britain (Chapter 1). Perhaps Graham's initial success was facilitated by the relative novelty of travel accounts in the early nineteenth century. During the second half of the century, when travel writing had to possess an element of originality or the unusual to command success, women found it more difficult than less-constrained male travelers to provide this ingredient of the exotic.

Latin American sensibilities were easily offended by foreign criticisms or less than favorable comparisons with European conditions and behavior. Keenly aware of European publications concerning their countries and resentful of the patronizing tone of many travel accounts, Latin American elites remained highly sensitive to writings that highlighted their countries' imperfections. The publication of some of Fanny Calderón de la Barca's letters in a Mexico City newspaper, even though her stinging sketches of President Antonio López de Santa Anna were omitted, caused a political uproar. Nineteenth-century Peruvians protested Flora Tristán's account. Although this advocate of women's and workers' rights was largely forgotten following her death in 1844, she would be reclaimed by twentieth-century feminists in both Europe and Peru. By the late twentieth century, books such as those by Graham and Calderón de la Barca would win respect in Latin America and be seen as classics in the countries they described as well as in the authors' homelands.

In the twentieth century, travel writings are viewed both as a genre of literature and as a source for social history. For decades, much of the travel literature was just celebratory, recapitulating the adventures of intrepid explorers or dedicated scientists. This largely biographical approach long focused on the more numerous male writers, at times considered more truthful and serious than female authors. The tradition of treating women's writing as trivial or marginal to the mainstream also clearly existed with travel literature, when accounts by women were ignored or stereotyped as just records by eccentric spinsters of the Victorian period. Although some feminist scholars today do study women travel writers, they tend to employ a biographical approach or analyze the texts using the methods of autobiography.

In recent years, the development of colonial discourse analysis has focused new attention on travel writing, often seen as one of the intellectual supports of empire, and scholars have combined ideological and cultural critiques with studies in genre.[29] Travel writings can figure in the analysis of the cultural and intellectual processes inherent in imperialism. Authors concerned with relations of domination and subordination often viewed travel books—that is, writings about colonized societies, with their demonstrations of European and North American superiority—as having served as instruments promoting their nations' interests and imperialist expansion. They then analyze discursive shifts in travel writing together with the relations between this type of writing and the processes of European economic and political expansionism. Such critics tend to see travel accounts not as representations of reality but as illustrative of various discourses that are much more revealing about the authors' own cultures than about those countries they visited.

One could view female foreign travelers to Latin America as falling within this frame of reference, although the places those women visited—with the major exception of Cuba—were nominally independent nations, no longer European colonies. However, North Atlantic commercial expansion and domination did produce economic dependence, and the travelers themselves tended to display superior airs when visiting Latin America just as they did on trips to Asia, Africa, or even southern Europe. Travel writings could provide the authors' contemporaries with proof of European superiority. Female travel writers remained women of their own class and society, producing their books under the power of both "patriarchy" and "colonialism." Today's readers, who sometimes also see their culture as superior, must therefore not accept these authors' viewpoints uncritically.

While the literary scholarship on travel writing has concentrated on the authors far more than on their subjects, historians have taken the opposite approach. If practitioners of discourse analysis and postmodern theory tend to separate text from context, historians focusing on the context can forget the text. Over the years, many historians have drawn on travel accounts for information about the places and people portrayed while largely ignoring the authors of those accounts.[30] Modern ethnohistorians and historical anthropologists have also used travelers' narratives as a source of raw ethnographic data and are paying increasing attention to the accounts' rhetorical conventions and styles of text construction.[31]

Scholars in the expanding field of Latin American women's history generally neglect travel writings, even those by women, relying instead on such sources as notarial and trial records or wills and testaments. They neither examine the foreign traveler as historical actor nor analyze foreign female perceptions of Latin American women in the nineteenth century. Yet feminist scholars from different disciplines, insisting on the importance of the female experience, do seek to listen to women's voices and to recover women's lives. For some scholars, a woman telling the story of her life, and thereby creating herself through that story, stands at the center of the feminist enterprise. The growing interest in women's testimonial literature (oral narratives generally told to editors who then present them to the world) partly reflects this concern.[32] Whether produced by women or men, this genre, which has its roots in events of the 1960s, is widely recognized as a source of insights into Latin American society, just as travel writing was long admired for its informational value. However, the contemporary popularity of testimonial literature has not yet approached that of travel literature in the nineteenth century.

When historians use travel writings, they must do so carefully, reading against the grain. Although these works can complement and enrich other sources—fleshing out quantitative data, for example—it is necessary to be cautious and read between the lines. Generalizations can be subjected to even more intense questioning than individual experiences. Descriptions of physical appearances and actions may prove more accurate than those of social institutions or personal relations. Historians need not interpret the incidents relayed by travelers in the same light as did those travelers themselves. Foreigners provide an angle of vision different from that of a country's inhabitants and can bring the advantages of a comparative perspective. Of course, travelers carried their cultural prejudices and racial, gender, and class biases with them, and these in turn could obstruct their vision. But historians should be able to determine the travelers' points of cultural references as well as examine the intersections between observers and those being observed. As outsiders and portrayers of the other, foreign visitors tended to note that which was novel or different from things at home and which was accepted by local inhabitants as natural or not subject to comment, including female activities and behavior. Travel writings are firsthand accounts, possessing an immediacy like that of the testimonial literature so prized today.

The selections in this book are drawn from ten of the more insightful accounts by female visitors to Latin America in the nineteenth century. Organized chronologically, they range in time from the independence period to the end of the century and extend across Latin America from the Caribbean to Chile, with the greatest concentration on Mexico and Brazil, the principal centers of attraction for foreign visitors, female and male alike. The more perceptive and less patronizing accounts, such as those by Flora Tristán and Ina von Binzer, were written by women who not only spent longer periods of time in Latin America but also had to deal with Latin American women on a level of equality or even dependence. By the end of the century, as demonstrated by the final selections in this volume by Helen Sanborn and Marguerite Dickens, the increasing number of female (and male) foreign visitors who enjoyed greater possibilities of and ease of travel to Latin American countries tended to pass through those nations more quickly and recorded more superficial encounters with or observations of members of local societies. Their narratives were inclined to be more conventional and condescending.

The following accounts document Latin American women's domestic activities, their public presence, and class, racial, ethnic, and geographic differences. The selections also allow readers to gauge change, or lack thereof, over time in the lives of some women, especially in the growing urban centers, whether in matters such as marriage and education or activities pursued outside the home. Some foreigners commented directly on certain changes apparent in the lives of upper-class women, as did Alice Humphries. This American visitor to Brazil recalled that when she "went first to Rio in 1884 it was not proper for a woman to go into the street without some man to take care of her. She certainly could not go to shop alone in the Ouvidor [Rio's principal shopping and socializing street] as she sometimes does now [at the turn of the century]. . . . Now she is verily a new woman, being far less restricted."[33]

Through the eyes of female foreign travelers, a diversity of Latin American women come into focus: nuns, laundresses, market women, slaves, plantation workers, camp followers, courting couples, the wives and daughters of landowners and politicians, feuding mistresses and servants, and even a heroine of the independence movement. These firsthand accounts shed light on questions of gender difference, family life, religion, and women's labor and education. They help reveal attitudes, customs, practices, and interrelationships between men and women within the structure of Latin American societies as well as cross-cultural relations between Latin Americans and foreign visitors. These writings provide a window into nineteenth-century Latin America.

The selections help us understand how gender relations in nineteenth-century Latin America differed from those in Northern Europe and the United States. We can learn how female foreign travelers presented and depicted themselves, not just other women. *Women through Women's Eyes* permits readers to ponder both contrasts and commonalities among women in Latin America while witnessing those women and their societies close up. Through these writings, we can discern something of the specificities of gender

—intertwined with race and class—within the complex world of Latin America.

Notes

1. Several bibliographies on travel accounts, usually limited to specific Latin American countries or to visitors from an individual country, can be found, including: Paulo Berger, *Bibliografia do Rio de Janeiro de viajantes e autores estrangeiros, 1531–1900* (Rio de Janeiro: Livraria São José, 1964); Garold Cole, *American Travelers to Mexico, 1821–1972: A Descriptive Bibliography* (Troy, NY: Whitston Publishing Co., 1978); Pablo Macera Dall'Orso, *La imagen francesa del Perú (Siglos XVI–XIX)* (Lima: Instituto Nacional de Cultura, 1976); Bernard Naylor, *Accounts of Nineteenth-Century South America. An Annotated Checklist of Works by British and United States Observers* (London: The Athlone Press, 1969); S. Samuel Trifilo, *La Argentina vista por viajeros ingleses: 1810–1860* (Buenos Aires: Ediciones Gure, 1959); and Gilda Maria Whitaker Verri, *Viajantes franceses no Brasil. Bibliografia* (Recife: Editora Universtária UFPE, 1994).

2. One that has been published is Mrs. Nathaniel Edward Kindersley, *Letters from the Island of Teneriffe, Brazil, the Cape of Good Hope, and the East Indies* (London: J. Hourse, 1777).

3. The ratio of male to female travel authors varied according to time period and authors' nationality. Perhaps the largest percentage of female authors occurred among U.S. visitors to Mexico during the late nineteenth century. In contrast, only one female author is included among the approximately one hundred French travel writers visiting Brazil in the nineteenth century who are listed in Verri, *Viajantes franceses no Brasil.*

4. For British travel writers to the Middle East, see Billie Melman, *Women's Orients: English Women and the Middle East, 1718–1918. Sexuality, Religion, Work* (Ann Arbor: University of Michigan Press, 1995). Other literary studies concentrating on British women travelers, but basically excluding those venturing to Latin America, include: Catherine Barnes Stevenson, *Victorian Women Travel Writers in Africa* (Boston: Twayne Publishers, 1992); Shirley Foster, *Across New Worlds, Nineteenth-Century Women Travellers and Their Writings* (New York: Harvester Wheatsheaf, 1990); Dorothy Middleton, *Victorian Lady Travelers* (London: Routledge and Kegan Paul, 1965); and Dea Birkett, *Spinsters Abroad. Victorian Lady Explorers* (Oxford: Basil Blackwell, 1989).

5. Anne Cary Maudslay and Alfred Percival Maudslay, *A Glimpse at Guatemala and Some Notes on the Ancient Monuments of Central America* (London: John Murray, 1899).

6. Emília Serrano García del Forel, Baronesa de Wilson, *América y sus mujeres* (Barcelona: Tipografia de Fidel Giró, 1890).

7. Mary Lester (pseud. María Soltera), *A Lady's Ride Across Spanish Honduras* (Edinburgh: William Blackwood and Sons, 1884).

8. Ida Pfeiffer, *A Woman's Journey Round the World, from Vienna to Brazil, Chili, Tahiti, China, Indostan, Persia and Asia Minor* (London: Office of the National Illustrated Library, 1850), and *A Lady's Second Journey Round the World: From London to the Cape of Good Hope, Borneo, Java, Sumatra, Celebes, Ceram, the Moluccas, etc., California, Panama, Peru, Ecuador, and the United States* (New York: Harper, 1856).

9. Nellie Bly, *Six Months in Mexico* (New York: American Publishers Corp., 1888).

10. Lillian Leland, *Traveling Alone. A Woman's Journey Around the World* (New York: American News Co., 1890).

11. Eliza Moore McHatton-Ripley, *From Flag to Flag. A Woman's Adventures and Experiences in the South During the War, in Mexico, and in Cuba* (New York: D. Appleton and Co., 1889).

12. Princess Felix Salm-Salm, *Ten Years of My Life*, 2 vols. (London: Richard Bentley and Son, 1876).

13. Sara Yorke Stevenson, *Maximilian in Mexico. A Woman's Reminiscences of the French Intervention, 1862–1870* (New York: Century Co., 1899).

14. Countess Paula Kollonitz, *The Court of Mexico*, trans. J. E. Ollivant (London: Saunders, Otley and Co., 1867).

15. See, for example, S. M. Lee, *Glimpses of Mexico and California* (Boston: Geo. H. Ellis, 1887).

16. Alice D. Le Plongeon, *Here and There in Yucatán. Miscellanies* (New York: J. W. Bouton, 1886).

17. Adelaide Rosalind Kirchner, *A Flag for Cuba. Pen Sketches of a Recent Trip Across the Gulf of Mexico to the Island of Cuba* (New York: Mershon Co., 1897).

18. Lady Florence Dixie, *Across Patagonia* (New York: R. Worthington, 1881).

19. Lester, *A Lady's Ride Across Spanish Honduras.*

20. Annie Sampson Poole, *Mexicans at Home in the Interior* (London: Chapman and Hall, 1884).

21. Melinda Rankin, *Among the Mexicans, A Narrative of Missionary Labor* (Cincinnati: Chase and Hall, 1875).

22. Mrs. Granville (Gertrude) Layard, *Through the West Indies* (London: Sampson Low, Marston, Searle, and Rivington, 1887).

23. Mary Carbutt (Lady), *Five Months' Fine Weather in Canada, Western U.S., and Mexico* (London: Sampson Low, Marston, Searle, and Rivington, 1889).

24. A key discussion of the concept of gender is that by Joan W. Scott, "Gender: A Useful Category of Analysis," *American Historical Review* 91, no. 15 (December 1986): 1053–75.

25. Serrano de Wilson, *América y sus mujeres.*

26. One male author who did describe women in detail was Charles Expilly, *Le Brésil tel qu'il est* (Paris: Charlieu et Huillery, 1862). This sometimes caustic account by a Frenchman who spent several years working in midnineteenth-century Brazil, and who expressed strong antislavery sentiments, contains descriptions of women in various sectors of society.

27. Maria Dundas Graham (Lady Maria Calcott), *Journal of a Voyage to Brazil and a Residence There, During Part of the Years 1821, 1822, 1823* (London: Longman, Hurst, Rees, Orme, Brown, and Green, and J. Murray, 1824), 224.

28. Samuel Hazard, *Cuba with Pen and Pencil* (Hartford, CT: Hartford Publishing Co., 1871); and Herbert E. Smith, *Brazil. The Amazons and the Coast* (New York: Charles Scribner's Sons, 1879). Illustrations from their books are included in this volume, as are drawings by the French artist Jean Baptiste Debret. His watercolors, painted in Rio de Janeiro in the early 1820s and published in various books, included domestic scenes.

29. See Mary Louise Pratt, *Imperial Eyes. Travel Writing and Transcultur-ation* (London: Routledge, 1992). Sara Mills sets British travelers within the co-lonial context and discourse, using Foucault's work as the frame for *Differences of Discourse. An Analysis of Women's Travel Writing and Colonialism* (London: Routledge, 1991).

30. One of the first historians of Latin America to make extensive use of travel literature was Gilberto Freyre in one of his early publications, "Social Life in Brazil in the Middle of the Nineteenth Century," *Hispanic American Histori-cal Review* 5 (November 1922): 597–630. Although long out of favor in some academic circles, Freyre's books continue to reach a broad reading public in Bra-zil and to be cited in United States scholarship devoted to comparative slave societies. Often forgotten is that Freyre was one of the first historians of Latin America to draw attention to women's roles and activities. Recently, with cul-tural history seen by some as providing new insights into the imperatives of so-cial development, there has been a revival of interest in Freyre. His seminal work served as a subject for analysis in the *American Historical Review*: Jeffrey D. Needell, "Identity, Race, Gender, and Modernity in the Origins of Gilberto Freyre's *Oeuvre*," *AHR* 100 (February 1995): 51–77.

31. See the special issue on travel literature, ethnography, and ethnohistory of *Ethnohistory* 33, no. 2 (1986).

32. Perhaps the best-known examples of testimonial literature by Latin American women are Rigoberta Menchu, *I, Rigoberta Menchú, An Indian Woman in Guatemala* (London: Verso, 1984); and Domitila Barrios de Chungara, *Let Me Speak! Testimony of Domitila, A Woman of the Bolivian Mines* (New York: Monthly Review Press, 1978). For a discussion of Latin American testimonial literature, including changes in its critical reception, see George M. Gugelberger, ed., *The Real Thing. Testimonial Discourse and Latin America* (Durham, NC: Duke Uni-versity Press, 1996).

33. Alice R. Humphrey, *A Summer Journey to Brazil* (New York: Bonnell, Silver and Co., 1900).

1

MARIA GRAHAM England

Life among the Elite in Brazil and Chile

Maria Dundas Graham (1785–1842), best known during her life-time as the author of the popular *Little Arthur's History of England*, loved books and travel. The well-educated and independent-minded daughter of Rear Admiral and Commissioner of the Admiralty George Dundas, she spent nine years at a fine girls' school in the south of England before entering fashionable and intellectual circles in England and Scotland, and then, at the age of twenty-one, suf-·fering her first bout of tuberculosis, the same disease that had killed her mother. In 1808 she sailed with her father on a voyage to India, during which she studied Persian and became romantically linked to Thomas Graham, an officer of the Royal Navy, whom she mar-ried the following year. The couple's experiences led to her first book, *Journal of a Residence in India*, which appeared in 1812, with a second edition published the following year. A second book, *Letters on India*, followed in 1814. In 1819, after several years in England where she pursued her intellectual interests and suffered another bout of tuberculosis, Graham traveled to Italy with her husband, who had been appointed to the Foreign Service. This trip yielded *Three Months Passed in the Mountains East of Rome*. Then, Captain

From Maria Dundas Graham (Lady Calcott), *Journal of a Voyage to Brazil, and Residence There, During Part of the Years 1821, 1822, 1823* (London: Longman, Hurst, Rees, Orme, Brown, and Green, and J. Murray, 1824), 135–37, 271–73, 284–85, 292–94, and 305–6; and *Journal of a Residence in Chile During the Year 1822 and a Voyage from Chile to Brazil in 1823* (London: Longman, Hurst, Rees, Orme, Brown, and Green, and J. Murray, 1824), 117–20, 140–44.

Graham was given a new command, the HMS *Doris*, a forty-two-gun frigate, under orders to patrol the coast of Brazil.

On July 31, 1821, the Grahams sailed for South America, where the independence movements from Portugal and Spain were nearing completion and British economic interests were growing rapidly. After six months in Brazil, the Grahams left for Chile. But Captain Graham died in his wife's arms en route to Valparaiso, where Maria Graham remained for almost a year under the protection of Lord Thomas Cochrane, a Scottish officer hired to command the navies of the Chilean and then the Brazilian independence forces and a family friend who shared her fascination with science and nature. She then returned to Brazil for seven months before setting sail for England. All the while this disciplined author kept the diaries upon which she would draw for her books *Journal of a Voyage to Brazil, and Residence There, During Part of the Years 1821, 1822, 1823* and *Journal of a Residence in Chile During the Year 1822 and a Voyage from Chile to Brazil in 1823*, both published in London in 1824, shortly after her return to England. After a brief home stay she sailed back to Brazil to serve as governess to Princess Maria da Gloría, eldest child of Emperor Pedro I, only to return to England shortly afterwards, perhaps as a consequence of court intrigues. In London she met and married Augustus Calcott, a popular landscape painter, and they set off on a long and rigorous honeymoon through Europe in 1827. Back in England she oversaw the publication of her history of Spain, translated a history of Turkey, and in 1835, after she had become a chronic invalid, published her English schoolroom classic, *Little Arthur's History of England*, which would go through some seventy editions over the course of the following century. She succumbed to tuberculosis in 1842.

At the time the Grahams had sailed for South America the independence movements from Spain and Portugal were nearing their conclusion. The Portuguese royal family's departure for Brazil in 1807, escaping the conquering French armies of Napoleon, helped set Brazil on a path toward political independence (declared in 1822) different from that followed in the Spanish empire. Not only did the Portuguese empire in America—unlike that of Spain—resist disintegration but it also suffered little bloodshed or devastation and emerged as an independent monarchy and relatively stable state, ruled by Emperor Pedro I, son of the king of Portugal. However, the political postindependence quarrels in Chile witnessed by Graham would, a decade after her departure, be succeeded by a durable and adaptable constitutional order and many years of political stability.

Graham's published journals display her wide-ranging interests, extending from botany to manufacturing, art, and politics. She recorded political life and personalities in Brazil and Chile, not just dramatic scenery or domestic activities. In fact, this advocate of independence prefaced her published journals with accounts of the independence struggle, based in large part on conversations with notable political figures such as Bernardo O'Higgins, the leader of the Chilean independence movement, to whom she had easy access. As an urban-based upper-class woman, Graham participated in the rounds of visiting undertaken by women of her station. And at the end of her stay in Brazil she entered into the life of the imperial court in Rio de Janeiro. However, she also peered into the dwellings of rural workers and joined them at meals, visited sugar mills and slave markets, took a ride on the first steamship ever to navigate the Pacific, and even attempted to make pottery in a poor artisan village. Although she sought to be tolerant, especially as a Protestant in Roman Catholic countries, she anchored many of her descriptions in comparisons with English customs and behavior, often citing their superiority. Yet she also criticized the English merchant colony in Bahia for its concentration on trade, ignorance of its Brazilian surroundings, and disregard for a woman in search of knowledge. She praised the librarians at the national library in Rio de Janeiro, where she was given a reading room for studying Brazilian history, "a kindness and attention to a woman and a stranger that I was hardly prepared for."* Above all, Graham sought to be precise and accurate in describing events, and she succeeded. She also tried not to quote from personal conversations or letters, unlike many other travel writers. She learned to speak Spanish and Portuguese, besides being able to converse in French with the better-educated members of the elite, both male and female. But

*Maria Dundas Graham (Lady Calcott), *Journal of a Voyage to Brazil, and Residence There, During Part of the Years 1821, 1822, 1823* (London: Longman, Hurst, Rees, Orme, Brown, and Green, and J. Murray, 1824), 301.

some contemporary British critics commented on aspects of her published journals which dealt with matters they considered unfemi-
nine. Perhaps she would have been given a better contemporary
reception had she not discussed political events, venturing into what
was perceived as a masculine realm. However, scholars today appreciate her accuracy and strengths of observation.

The following selections from Graham's Chilean and Brazilian
journals record parties, marriage arrangements, pottery making, a
meeting with a heroine of the Brazilian independence struggle who
had fought dressed as a man, and, of course, visits to upper-class
homes. These include her early, unflattering portrait of well-to-do
Portuguese women living in Bahia, drawn at a time when, as she
admitted, she knew little of local society. But the women she depicted as slovenly and unkempt had been surprised by Graham and
a British friend at an hour far earlier than the accustomed time for
social visits in Bahia. Graham's views changed with time and knowledge. Following her Chilean sojourn, when she had learned Spanish and Portuguese and was a more experienced observer, she
found much to admire among elite women in Rio de Janeiro. There
she also noted the effects of the opening of Brazil's ports to trade
with foreign nations and of increased contact with Europeans upon
elite modes of behavior. After all, Maria Graham herself added to
the large foreign presence in the capital, which included not only
the fourteen thousand Portuguese who had accompanied the royal
family to Brazil but also European merchants, scientists, and other
visitors, together with members of foreign diplomatic missions accredited to the court.

Salvador, Bahia (Brazil), October 1821

Friday, 19*th*.—I accompanied Miss Pennell* on a tour of visits to
her Portuguese friends. As it is not their custom to visit or be visited in the forenoon, it was hardly fair to take a stranger to see
them. However, my curiosity, at least, was gratified. In the first
place, the houses, for the most part, are disgustingly dirty: the lower
story usually consists of cells for the slaves, stabling &c.; the stair-

---

*Daughter of the British consul in Salvador—Ed.

cases are narrow and dark; and, at more than one house, we waited in a passage while the servants ran to open the doors and windows of the sitting-rooms, and to call their mistresses, who were enjoying their undress in their own apartments. When they appeared, I could scarcely believe that one half were gentlewomen. As they wear neither stay nor bodice, the figure becomes almost indecently slovenly, after very early youth; and this is the more disgusting, as they are very thinly clad, wear no neck-handkerchiefs, and scarcely any sleeves. Then, in this hot climate, it is unpleasant to see dark cottons and stuffs, without any white linen, near the skin. Hair black, ill combed, and dishevelled, or knotted unbecomingly, or still worse, *en papillote,** and the whole person having an unwashed appearance. When at any of the houses the bustle of opening the cobwebbed windows, and assembling the family was over, in two or three instances, the servants had to remove dishes of sugar, mandioc, and other provisions, which had been left in the best rooms to dry. There is usually a sofa at each end of the room, and to the right and left a long file of chairs, which look as if they never could be moved out of their place. Between the two sets of seats is a space, which, I am told, is often used for dancing; and, in every house, I saw either a guitar or piano, and generally both. Prints and pictures, the latter the worst daubs I ever saw, decorate the walls pretty generally; and there are, besides, crucifixes and other things of the kind. Some houses, however, are more neatly arranged; one, I think belonging to a captain of the navy, was papered, the floors laid with mat, and the tables ornamented with pretty porcelain, Indian and French: the lady too was neatly dressed in a French wrapper. Another house belonging to one of the judges was also clean, and of a more stately appearance than the rest, though the inhabitant was neither richer nor of higher rank. Glass chandeliers were suspended from the roof; handsome mirrors were intermixed with the prints and pictures. A good deal of handsome china was displayed round the room; but the jars, as well as the chairs and tables, seemed to form an inseparable part of the walls. We were every where invited, after sitting a few moments on the sofa, to go to the balconies of the windows and enjoy the view and the breeze, or at least amuse ourselves with what was passing in the street. And yet they did not lack conversation: the principal topic, however, was praise of the beauty of Bahia; dress, children, and diseases, I think, made

*Paper hair curlers—Ed.

A Brazilian woman of the elite and her slave attendants, who are making lace, as depicted by the French artist Jean Baptiste Debret, circa 1823. *Courtesy of the Biblioteca Nacional do Rio de Janeiro*

up the rest; and, to say the truth, their manner of talking on the latter subject is as disgusting as their dress, that is, in a morning: I am told they are different after dinner. They marry very early, and soon lose their bloom. I did not see one tolerably pretty woman to-day. But then who is there that can bear so total a disguise as filth and untidiness spread over a woman?

Monday 22nd.—This evening there was a large party, both Portuguese and English, at the consul's. In the well-dressed women I saw to-night, I had great difficulty in recognising the slatterns of the other morning. The senhoras were all dressed after the French fashion: corset, fichu, garniture, all was proper, and even elegant, and there was a great display of jewels. Our English ladies, though quite of the second rate of even colonial gentility, however, bore away the prize of beauty and grace; for after all, the clothes, however elegant, that are not worn habitually, can only embarrass and cramp the native movements; and, as Mademoiselle Clairon remarks, "she who would *act* a gentlewoman in public, must *be* one in private life."

The Portuguese men have all a mean look; none appear to have any education beyond counting-house forms, and their whole time

[handwritten marginalia: what are socialburdges? ntways?]

[handwritten marginalia: value of education]

is, I believe, spent between trade and gambling: in the latter, the ladies partake largely after they are married. Before that happy period, when there is no evening dances, they surround the card tables, and with eager eyes follow the game, and long for the time when they too may mingle in it. I scarcely wonder at this propensity. Without education, and consequently without the resources of mind, and in a climate where exercise out of doors is all but impossible, a stimulus must be had; and gambling, from the sage to the savage, has always been resorted to, to quicken the current of life. On the present occasion, we feared the younger people would have been disappointed of their dance, because the fiddlers, after waiting some time, went away, as they alleged, because they had not their tea early enough; however, some of the ladies volunteered to play the piano, and the ball lasted till past midnight.

[handwritten marginalia: what is now savage? can savagery be found in upper class?]

Rio de Janeiro, 1823

[handwritten marginalia: less self postulating]

August 15th.—The feast of Our Lady of the Assumption, called here Nossa Senhora da Glória, the patroness of the Emperor's* eldest child, is celebrated to-day, and of course the whole of the royal family attended Mass in the morning and evening. I was spending the day with Mrs. May, at her pleasant house on the Glória hill, and we agreed to go in the afternoon to see the ceremony. The church is situated on a platform, rather more than half way up a steep eminence overlooking the bay. The body is an octagon of thirty-two feet diameter; and the choir, of the same shape, is twenty-one feet in diameter. We entered among a great crowd of persons, and placed ourselves within the choir; and shortly afterwards the Imperial party entered, and I was not disagreeably surprised at being most pleasantly recognised. The salutation, as this evening's service is called, was well performed as to music, and very short: after it, for the first time, I heard a Portuguese sermon. It was of course occasional. The text, 1 Kings, chap. ii, ver. 19.— "And the king rose up to meet his mother, and bowed himself unto her, and sat down on his throne, and caused a seat to be set for the king's mother, and she sat on his right hand." The application of this text to the legend of the Assumption is obvious, and occupied the first division of the discourse. The second part consisted in an application of the history

[handwritten marginalia: women are men's first hand? (right)]

---

*Pedro I. The son of João VI of Portugal, Dom Pedro was the first emperor (1822–1831) of an independent Brazil—Ed.

of the early part of Solomon's reign to the present circumstances of Brazil; the restoration of the kingdom, the triumph over faction, and the institution of laws, forming the grounds of comparison. The whole people of Brazil were called upon to join in thanksgiving and prayers to the Virgin of Glory: thanksgiving that she had given to her people, as rulers, the descendants of the Emanuels, the Johns, and the Henrys of Portugal, and of the Maria Theresas of Austria; and prayers that she would continue her gracious protection, and that most especially to the eldest hope of Brazil, named after her and dedicated to her. The whole was gravely and properly done, with as little of the appearance of flattery to the illustrious persons present as possible, and did not last above fifteen minutes. On this occasion, the veadors, and other persons attendant on the Imperial family, wore white silk surplices, and bore torches in their hands.

I went in the evening to a ball and concert at the Baronesa de Campos: on entering, I was met by the young ladies of the family, and led up to their grandmother; and after paying my compliments to her, I was placed among the division of the family where I had most acquaintance. There were only two Englishwomen besides Lady Cochrane and myself, and these were the wives of the consul and the commissioner for the slave business. A foreign gentleman present remarked, that though we were but four, we hardly conversed together. This was perfectly true: I like, when I am in foreign society, to talk to foreigners; and think it neither wise nor civil to form coteries with those of one's own nation in such cases. Several rooms were open for cards; the stakes, I fancy, were high. The tea-room was no sooner full, than tea was handed round; and I perceived that some of the older servants, with great respect indeed, spoke to such of the guests as they were acquainted with. After tea, I had the pleasure of again hearing Dona Rosa sing, and almost grudged my gayer companions their ball, which broke in upon that "sober certainty of waking bliss," which music inspires into all, and especially to those who have known sorrow. I am no musician; but sweet sounds, especially those of the human voice, whether in speaking or singing, have a singular power over me.

After the first dance was over, we walked all about the house, and found a magnificent dining-room as to size, but scarcely furnished to correspond with the rest of the house; the bed-rooms and dressing-rooms of the ladies are neat and elegantly fitted up with English and French furniture; and all as different as possible from the houses I saw in Bahia. I am told that they are likewise as different from what they were here twenty years since, and can well believe it; even during the twelve months of my absence from Rio, I see a wonderful polishing has taken place, and every thing is gaining an European air.

I took the liberty of remarking to one of the ladies, the extreme youth of some of the children who accompanied their mothers this evening; and saying, that in England we should consider it injurious to them in all respects. She asked me what we did with them. I told her that some of them would be in bed, and others with their nurses and governesses. She said we were happy in that: but that here, there were no such persons, and that the children would be left to the care and example of the slaves, whose manners were so depraved, and practices so immoral, that it must be the destruction of the children; and that those who loved their children must keep them under their own eyes, where, if they were brought too forward in company, they at least could learn no ill. I love to collect these proofs of the evils of slavery—even here where it exists in a milder form than in most countries.—I left the dancers busily engaged at twelve o'clock, and I heard that they continued the ball until three. There is no peculiarity in the dancing here; the ladies of Rio being like ourselves, the pupils of the French, in that branch of the fine arts.

August 23rd.—After breakfast, we rode along the causeway that crosses the plain of Santa Cruz [some forty miles from Rio de Janeiro], to the Indian aldea of San Francisco Xavier de Itaguahy, commonly called Taguahy, formed by the Jesuits* not very long before their expulsion. The situation of the aldea and church is extremely fine; on the summit of a hill overlooking a rich plain, watered by a navigable river, and surrounded by mountains. We entered several of the huts of the Indians, whom I had understood to be of the Guaranee nation. I enquired of one of the women, in whose hut I sat down, if she knew whence her tribe came: she said no; she had been brought, when a mere child, from a great distance to Taguahy, by the fathers of the company; that her husband had died when she was young; that she and her daughters had always lived there; but her sons and grandsons, after the fathers of the company went, had returned to their fathers, by which she meant that they had resumed

*This Roman Catholic religious order, the Society of Jesus, was expelled from the Portuguese empire in 1759—Ed.

their savage life. This is not surprising. The Indians here must work for others, and become servants; a state they hardly distinguish from slavery. Besides, slaves are plentiful; and as the negro is hardier than the Indian, his labour is more profitable; therefore, a willing Indian does not always find a master. The produce of his little garden, or his fishing, is rarely sufficient for his family; and without the protection of the priest, whose chief favour was procuring constant occupation, the half-reclaimed savage droops, and flies again to the liberty of his forest, to his unrestrained hunting and fishing. The Chilian Indians rarely or never return to their forests when their villages are once formed; but that depends on circumstances, which have nothing in common with the state of Brazil. Many of the Indian women have married the creole Portuguese; intermarriages between creole women and Indian men are more rare. The children of such couples are prettier, and appear to me to be more intelligent, than the pure race of either. The Indian huts at Taguahy are very poor; barely sufficient in walls and roof to keep out the weather, and furnished with little besides hammocks and cooking utensils; yet we were every where asked to go in and sit down: all the floors were cleanly swept, and a log of wood or a rude stool was generally to be found for a seat for the stranger, the people themselves squatting on the ground. . . .

August 29th.—To-day I received a visit from Dona Maria de Jesús, the young woman who has lately distinguished herself in the war of the Reconcave.* Her dress is that of a soldier of one of the Emperor's battalions, with the addition of a tartan kilt, which she told me she had adopted from a picture representing a highlander, as the most feminine military dress. What would the Gordons and MacDonalds say to this? The "garb of old Gaul," chosen as a womanish attire!—Her father is a Portuguese, named Gonsalvez de Almeida, and possesses a farm on the Rio do Pex, in the parish of San José, in the Certão,† about forty leagues in-land from Cachoeira. Her mother was also a Portuguese; yet the young woman's features, especially her eyes and forehead, have the strongest characteristics of the Indians. Her father has another daughter by the same wife; since whose death he has married again, and the new wife and the young children have made home not very comfortable to

*Recóncavo is a large fertile area surrounding the city of Salvador on the coast of Bahia—Ed.

†Sertão, the back country, especially of Brazil's Northeast—Ed.

Dona Maria de Jesús. The farm of the Rio do Pex is chiefly a cattle farm, but the possessor seldom knows or counts his numbers. Senhor Gonsalvez, besides his cattle, raises some cotton; but as the Certão is sometimes a whole year without rain, the quantity is uncertain. In wet years he may sell 400 arobas,* at from four to five milrees;† in dry seasons he can scarcely collect above sixty or seventy arobas, which may fetch from six to seven milrees. His farm employs twenty-six slaves.

The women of the interior spin and weave for their household, and they also embroider very beautifully. The young women learn the use of fire-arms, as their brothers do, either to shoot game or defend themselves from the wild Indians.

Dona Maria told me several particulars concerning the country, and more concerning her own adventures. It appears, that early in the late war of the Reconcave, emissaries had traversed the country in all directions, to raise patriot recruits; that one of these had arrived at her father's house one day about dinner time; that her father had invited him in, and that after their meal he began to talk on the subject of his visit. He represented the greatness and the riches of Brazil, and the happiness to which it might attain if independent. He set forth the long and oppressive tyranny of Portugal; and the meanness of submitting to be ruled by so poor and degraded a country. He talked long and eloquently of the services Don Pedro‡ had rendered to Brazil; of his virtues, and those of the Empress: so that at the last, said the girl, "I felt my heart burning in my breast." Her father, however, had none of her enthusiasm of character. He is old, and said he neither could join the army himself, nor had he a son to send thither; and as to giving a slave for the ranks, what interest had a slave to fight for the independence of Brazil? He should wait in patience the result of the war, and be a peaceable subject to the winner. Dona Maria stole from home to the house of her own sister, who was married, and lived at a little distance. She recapitulated the whole of the stranger's discourse, and said she wished she was a man, that she might join the patriots. "Nay," said the sister, "if I had not a husband and children, for one half of what you say I would join the ranks for the Emperor." This was enough.

---

*The arroba was a Portuguese measure of weight, equivalent to about 15 kg.—Ed.

†The mil-réis was the Brazilian monetary unit—Ed.

‡Dom Pedro I—Ed.

Maria received some clothes belonging to her sister's husband to equip her; and as her father was then about to go to Cachoeira to dispose of some cottons, she resolved to take the opportunity of riding after him, near enough for protection in case of accident on the road, and far enough off to escape detection. At length being in sight of Cachoeira, she stopped; and going off the road, equipped herself in male attire, and entered the town. This was on Friday. By Sunday she had managed matters so well, that she had entered the regiment of artillery, and had mounted guard. She was too slight, however, for that service, and exchanged into the infantry, where she now is. She was sent hither, I believe, with despatches, and to be presented to the Emperor, who has given her an ensign's commission and the order of the cross, the decoration of which he himself fixed on her jacket.

She is illiterate, but clever. Her understanding is quick, and her perceptions keen. I think, with education she might have been a remarkable person. She is not particularly masculine in her appearance, and her manners are gentle and cheerful. She has not contracted any thing coarse or vulgar in her camp life, and I believe that no imputation has ever been substantiated against her modesty. One thing is certain, that her sex never was known until her father applied to her commanding officer to seek her.

There is nothing very peculiar in her manners at table, excepting that she eats farinha* with her eggs at breakfast and her fish at dinner, instead of bread, and smokes a segar after each meal; but she is very temperate. . . .

Sept. 26th.—A marriage in high life engages many of the talkers of Rio. A fidalgo,† an officer distinguished under Beresford,‡ Don Francisco ——, whose other name I have forgotten, is fortunate enough to have obtained one of the loveliest grand-daughters of the Baroness de Campos, *Maria de Loreto*; whose extraordinary likeness to our own Princess Charlotte of Wales is such, that I am sure no English person can have seen her without being struck with it. Here, no unmarried women are allowed to be present at a marriage; but the ceremony is performed in the presence of the nearest

*Farinha is manioc meal—Ed.

†A nobleman—Ed.

‡During the Peninsular campaigns (1808–1813) of the Napoleonic Wars, General Beresford commanded Anglo-Portuguese forces fighting the French—Ed.

Portrait of Maria de Jesús, who fought in the Brazilian independence struggle. From Maria Dundas Graham, *Journal of a Voyage to Brazil, and Residence There, During Part of the Years 1821, 1822, 1823* (London: Longman, Hurst, Rees, Orme, Brown, and Green, and J. Murray, 1824), n.p.

relations, being married, on both sides. The mother of the bride sends notice to court, if she be of rank to do so, afterwards to other ladies, according to their degree, of the marriage of her daughter. The bride then goes to court; after which the ladies visit her, and proceed to congratulate the other members of the family. It is said this match is one in which the lawful lord of such things, *i.e.* Master Cupid, has had more to do than he is usually allowed to have in Brazil, even since it was independent; and truly a handsomer couple will not often be seen. I am glad of it. Surely free choice on such an important subject is as much to be desired as on any other. On this occasion,

> The god of love, who stood to spy them,
> The god of love, who must be nigh them,
> Pleased and tickled at the sight,
> Sneezed aloud; and at his right
> The little loves that waited by,
> Bow'd and bless'd the augury;

as my favourite [Abraham] Cowley says; and I hope we shall have more such free matches in our free Brazil, where, hitherto, the course of true love is apt not to run smooth, that is, if my informants on the subject are in the right. Seriously, perhaps there has not hitherto been refinement enough for the delicate metaphysical love of Europe; which, because it is more rational, more noble, than all others, is less easily turned aside into other channels.

~

Valparaiso (Chile), 1822

May 10*th.*—Thanks to my friends both ashore and in the frigate, I am now pretty comfortably settled in my little *home.* Every body has been kind; one neighbour lends me a horse, another such furniture as I require: nation and habits make no difference. I arrived here in need of kindness, and I have received it from all.

I have great comfort in strolling on the hill behind my house; it commands a lovely view of the port and neighbouring hills. It is totally uncultivated, and in the best season can afford but poor browsing for mules or horses. Now most of the shrubs are leafless, and it is totally without grass. But the milky tribe of trees and shrubs are still green enough to please the eye. A few of them, as the lobelia, retain here and there an orange or a crimson flower; and there

are several sorts of parasitic plants, whose exquisitely beautiful
blossoms adorn the naked branches of the deciduous shrubs, and
whose bright green leaves, and vivid red and yellow blossoms shame
the sober grey of the neighbouring olives, whose fruit is now rip-
ening. The red soil of my hill is crossed here and there by great
ridges of white half marble, half sparry stone; and all its sides bear
deep marks of winter torrents; in the beds of these I have found
pieces of green stone of a soft soapy appearance, and lumps of quartz
and coarse granite. One of these water-courses was once worked
for gold, but the quantity found was so inconsiderable, that the proprietor was glad to quit the precarious adventure, and to cultivate
the CHACRA or garden-ground which joins to mine, and whose
produce has been much more beneficial to his family.

I went to walk in that garden, and found there, besides the fruits
common to my own, figs, lemons, and pomegranates, and the hedges
full of white cluster roses. The mistress of the house is a near relation of my landlady, and takes in washing, but that by no means
implies that either her rank or her pretensions are as low as those of
an European washerwoman. Her mother was possessed of no less
than eight chacras;* but as she is ninety years old, that must have
been a hundred years ago, when Valparaiso was by no means so
large a place, and consequently chacras were less valuable. However, she was a great proprietor of land; but, as is usual here, most
of it went to portion off a large family of daughters, and some I am
afraid to pay the expenses of the gold found on the estate.

The old lady, seeing me in the garden, courteously invited me
to walk in. The veranda in front of the house is like my own, paved
with bricks nine inches square, and supported by rude wooden pil-
lars, which the Chileno architects fancy they have carved hand-
somely; I found under it two of the most beautiful boys I ever saw,
and a very pretty young woman the grandchildren of the old lady.
They all got up from the bench eager to receive me, and show me
kindness. One of the boys ran to fetch his mother, the other went to
gather a bunch of roses for me, and the daughter Joanita, taking me
into the house gave me some beautiful carnations. From the garden
we entered immediately into the common sittingroom, where, according to custom, one low latticed window afforded but a scanty
light. By the window, a long bench covered with a sort of coarse
Turkey carpet made here, runs nearly the length of the room, and

*Small farms—Ed.

before this a wooden platform, called the *estrada*, raised about six inches from the ground, and about five feet broad, is covered with the same sort of carpet, the rest of the floor being bare brick. A row of high-backed chairs occupies the opposite side of the room. On a table in a corner, under a glass case, I saw a little religious baby work,—a waxen Jesus an inch long, sprawls on a waxen Virgin's knee, surrounded by Joseph, the oxen and asses, all of the same goodly material, decorated with moss and sea shells. Near this I observed a pot of beautiful flowers, and two pretty-shaped silver utensils, which I at first took for implements of worship, and then for inkstands, but I discovered that one was a little censer for burning pastile, with which the young women perfume their handkerchiefs and mantos, and the other the vase for holding the infusion of the herb of Paraguay, commonly called matte,* so universally drank or rather sucked here. The herb appears like dried senna; a small quantity of it is put into the little vase with a proportion of sugar, and sometimes a bit of lemon peel, the water is poured boiling on it, and it is instantly sucked up through a tube about six inches long. This is the great luxury of the Chilenos, both male and female. The first thing in the morning is a matte, and the first thing after the afternoon siesta is a matte. I have not yet tasted of it, and do not much relish the idea of using the same tube with a dozen other people.

I was much struck with the appearance of my venerable neighbour; although bent with age she has no other sign of infirmity; her walk is quick and light, and her grey eyes sparkle with intelligence. She wears her silver hair, according to the custom of the country, uncovered, and hanging down behind in one large braid; her linen shift is gathered up pretty high on her bosom, and its sleeves are visible near the wrist: she has a petticoat of white woollen stuff, and her gown of coloured woollen is like a close jacket, with a full-plaited petticoat attached to it, and fastened with double buttons in front. A rosary hangs round her neck, and she always wears the manto or shawl, which others only put on when they go out of doors, or in cold weather. The dress of the granddaughter is not very different from that of a French woman, excepting that the manto supersedes all hats, caps, capotes, and turbans. The young people, whether they fasten up their tresses with combs, or let them hang

*Yerba mate, the drink made from the dried leaves of the *Ilex paraguariensis*—Ed.

down, are fond of decorating them with natural flowers, and it is not uncommon to see a rose or a jonquil stuck behind the ear or through the earring. . . .

Friday, May 31*st.*—To-day I indulged myself with a walk which I had been wishing to take for some days, to an obscure portion of the Almendral,* called the Rincona, or nook, I suppose because it is in a little corner formed by two projecting hills. My object in going thither was to see the manufactory of coarse pottery, which I supposed to be established there, because I was told that the *ollas*, or jars, for cooking and carrying water, the earthen lamps, and the earthen brassiers, were all made there. On quitting the straight street of the Almendral, a little beyond the rivulet that divides it from my hill, I turned into a land, the middle of which is channelled by a little stream which falls from the hills behind the Rincona, and after being subdivided and led through many a garden and field, finds its way much diminished to the sand of the Almendral where it is lost. Following the direction, though not adhering to the course of the rill, I found the Rincona beyond some ruined but thick walls, which stretch from the foot of the hills to the sea, and which were once intended as a defence to the port on that side: they are nothing now. I looked around in vain for any thing large enough either to be a manufactory, or even to contain the necessary furnaces for baking the pottery; nevertheless I passed many huts, at the doors of which I saw jars and dishes set out for sale, and concluded that these were the huts of the inferior workmen. However on advancing a little farther I found that I must look for no regular manufactory, no division of labour, no machinery, not even the potter's wheel, none of the aids to industry which I had conceived almost indispensable to a trade so artificial as that of making earthenware. At the door of one of the poorest huts, formed merely of branches and covered with long grass, having a hide for a door, sat a family of manufacturers. They were seated on sheep-skins spread under the shade of a little penthouse formed of green boughs, at their work. A mass of clay ready tempered† lay before them, and each person according to age and ability was forming jars, plates, or dishes. The work-people were all women, and I believe that no man

---

*A suburb of Valparaiso—Ed.

†The clay is very fine and smooth, and found about nine inches or a foot from the surface; it requires little tempering, and is free from extraneous matter; the women knead it with their hands.

condescends to employ himself in this way, that is, in making the small ware: the large wine jars, &c. of Melipilla are made by men. As the shortest way of learning is to mix at once with those we wish to learn from, I seated myself on the sheep-skin and began to work too, imitating as I could a little girl who was making a simple saucer. The old woman who seemed the chief directress, looked at me very gravely, and then took my work and showed me how to begin it anew, and work its shape aright. All this, to be sure, I might have guessed at; but the secret I wanted to learn, was the art of polishing the clay, for it is not rendered shining by any of the glazing processes I have seen; therefore I waited patiently and worked at my dish till it was ready. Then the old woman put her hand into a leathern pocket which she wore in front, and drew out a smooth shell, with which she first formed the edges and borders anew; and then rubbed it, first gently, and, as the clay hardened, with greater force, dipping the shell occasionally in water, all over the surface, until a perfect polish was produced, and the vessel was set to dry in the shade.

Sometimes the earthenware so prepared is baked in large ovens constructed on purpose; but as often, the holes in the side of the hill, whence the clay has been dug, or rather scraped with the hands, serve for this purpose. The wood chiefly used for these simple furnaces is the espinella or small thorn, not at all the same as the espina or common firewood of the country, which is the mimosa, whose flowers are highly aromatic. The espinella has more the appearance of a thorny coronilla. It is said to make the most ardent fire of any of the native woods. The pottery here is only for the most ordinary utensils; but I have seen some jars from Melipilla and Penco which in shape and workmanship might pass for Etruscan. These are sometimes sold for prices as high as fifty dollars, and are used for holding water. They are ornamented with streaks, and various patterns, in white and red clay, where the ground is black; and where it is red or brown, with black and white. Some of the red jars have these ornaments of a shining substance that looks like gold dust, which is, I believe, clay having pyrites of iron; and many have grotesque heads, with imitations of human arms for handles, and ornaments indented on them; but, excepting in the forming of the heads and arms, I do not recollect any Chileno vase with raised decorations.

It is impossible to conceive a greater degree of apparent poverty than is exhibited in the potters' cottages of the Rincona. Most, however, had a decent bed; a few stakes driven into the ground, and laced across with thongs, form the bedstead; a mattress of wool, and, where the women are industrious, sheets of coarse homespun cotton and thick woollen coverlets form no contemptible resting-place for the man and wife, or rather for the wife, for I believe the men pass the greater part of every night, according to the custom of the country, sleeping, wrapped up in their ponchos, in the open air. The infants are hung in little hammocks of sheepskins to the poles of the roof; and the other children or relations sleep as they can on skins, wrapped in their ponchos, on the ground. In one of the huts there was no bed; the whole furniture consisted of two skin trunks; and there were eleven inhabitants, including two infants, twins, there being neither father nor man of any kind to own or protect them. The natural gentleness and goodness of nature of the people of Chile preserve even the vicious, at least among the women, from that effrontery which such a family as I here visited would, and must, have exhibited in Europe. My instructress had a husband, and her house was more decent: it had a bed; it had a raised bench formed of clay; and there were the implements of female industry, a distaff and spindle, and knitting needles formed of the spines of the great torch-thistle from Coquimbo, which grow to nine inches long.* But the hamlet of the Rincona is the most wretched I have yet seen. Its natives, however, pointed out to me their beautiful view, which is indeed magnificent, across the ocean to the snow-capped Andes, and boasted of the pleasure of walking on their hills on a holiday evening: then they showed me their sweet and wholesome stream of water, and their ancient fig-trees, inviting me to go back "when the figs should be ripe, and the flowers looking at themselves in the stream." I was ashamed of some of the expressions of pity that had escaped me.—If I cannot better their condition, why awaken them to a sense of its miseries?

Leaving the Rincona, instead of going directly to the Almendral, I skirted the hill by the hamlet called the Pocura, where I found huts of a better description, most of them having a little garden with cherry and plum trees, and a few cabbages and flowers. In the veranda of one of them a woman was weaving coarse blue cloth. The operation is tedious, for the fixed loom and the *shuttle* are unknown; and next to the weaving of the Arab hair-cloths, I should conceive that in no part of the world can this most useful operation

---

*The more delicate spines of the lesser torch-thistle serve here for pins.

"beauty is in the eye of the beholder"
(!)
The chooses to see beauty in places

be performed so clumsily or inconveniently. At the further part of the Pocura an English butcher has built a house that looks like a palace here, to the great admiration of the natives. Immediately above, on a plain which may be from 80 to 100 feet above the village, is the new burying ground or pantheon, the government having wisely taken measures to prevent the continuance of burying in or near the town. The prejudices, however, naturally attached to an ancient place of sepulture prevents this from being occupied according to the intention of the projectors. Separated from this only by a wall, is the place at length assigned by Roman Catholic superstition to the heretics as a burial ground; or rather, which the heretics have been permitted to purchase. Hitherto, such as had not permission to bury in the forts where they could be guarded, preferred being carried out to sea, and sunk;—many instances having occurred of the exhumation of heretics, buried on shore, by the bigotted natives, and the exposure of their bodies to the birds and beasts of prey.

2

FLORA TRISTÁN

France (handwritten)
feminist (handwritten)

Peregrinations of a Self-Proclaimed Pariah

courageousness in these political views? (handwritten)

A prominent pre-Marxist socialist and fighter for workers' and women's rights in France during the late 1830s and early 1840s, Flora Tristán (1803–1844) was quickly forgotten in Europe following her death. But by the late twentieth century she would be hailed in Europe, and her father's native Peru, as a feminist precursor. She is also sometimes recalled as the grandmother of the painter Paul Gauguin.

financial limitations due to men (handwritten, left margin)

Born in 1803 to a Frenchwoman married to the son of a wealthy Peruvian family from Arequipa, Flora Tristán y Moscozo was thrust into a life of poverty in France at an early age by the death of her father, who had never registered his marriage or made a will. Still in her teens, Tristán went to work in a printmaker's studio in Paris and then married its owner at the urgings of her mother. But the marriage proved disastrous, and she finally left her husband only to fall back into poverty and wage a vicious lifelong battle with him over custody of their two surviving children. In 1833 she sailed to Peru in a desperate attempt to gain financial security by claiming an inheritance from her father's family, but without success. Her relatives may have received her warmly, but her uncle, Pio Tristán, the family head and a leading royalist during the independence struggles, refused her the legacy, promising her only a small allowance instead. Yet Tristán remained with her relatives in Peru over a

From Flora Tristán, *Peregrinations of a Pariah, 1833–1834*, trans. and ed. Jean Hawkes (Boston: Beacon Press, 1986), 100–102, 179–81, 293–96, 300–305. Reprinted by permission of Little, Brown and Co.

year, keeping the journals that would serve as the basis for her first full-length book, *Peregrinations of a Pariah, 1833–1834*. Her Peruvian experiences marked the beginning of her career as a social critic and activist. She would spend the remaining ten years of her life writing and agitating in France and England for workers' rights, women's emancipation, and the peaceful transformation of society. Her health was never robust, but she pushed on through headaches, fevers, and bouts of dysentery until she succumbed to typhoid fever on November 14, 1844.

In *Peregrinations of a Pariah*, Tristán employed the autobiographical narrative to present herself as the protagonist of her travels and her life. She portrayed herself as a fearless truth-teller and isolated martyr determined to write about people of all classes, not just the ruling elite. She also demonstrated her supreme self-confidence and a tendency toward self-dramatization. Her book's arrival in Lima several months after its publication in France met with a hostile reception from Peru's conservative and privileged upper classes, who resented her lecturing them on their shortcomings. Not until the midtwentieth century would Spanish, and later English, translations appear.

At the time of Tristán's visit, Peru was suffering from the political strife and economic depression that accompanied formal independence from Spain, an event that had not shaken the old conservative and caste-ridden social order. Peru would remain a deeply divided nation, with an oppressed Indian majority concentrated in the Andean highlands and a Spanish-speaking minority living largely on the coast. Not only did Tristán describe the political intrigues and struggles of the post-independence period in which her family participated but she also investigated institutions such as slavery and plantation society. She detailed her dealings with her family and demonstrated an increasing concern with women, as shown in the following selections from her book. No doubt Tristán's own bitter marital experiences and gender-related loss of property and inheritance informed and influenced her description of her widowed cousin Carmen's unhappy life as an upper-class wife in Arequipa, a story that could be used to criticize the situation of women in France and the limitations that marriage and family placed on women. As Tristán indicates, the only choice for women of the elite in the early nineteenth century seemed to be—just as in colonial days—marriage or the convent, and she viewed both as prisons.

Tristán found much to admire in the upper-class women of Lima. Their distinctive dress, which largely hid the face while fitting tightly over parts of the body, permitted considerable mobility and freedom. The dress of these *tapadas** actually scandalized some male foreign visitors. Among these were Jorge Juan and Antonio de Ulloa, two young Spanish naval officers and participants in the French scientific expedition of geographer Charles Marie de La Condamine of the 1730s and 1740s, to whom "at first coming it appears extremely indecent."[†] However, by the midnineteenth century, according to some female foreign visitors to Lima, the dress was somewhat modified, fitted less closely over the body but with the mantle still covering most of the face, so that only one eye could be seen when the women passed freely on city streets.[‡]

Tristán's relationship to, and, therefore, descriptions of, women outside the world of the urban elite was not as personal or intimate, as we see with the fierce *rabonas*, "camp followers," who were in reality support personnel who bravely struggled to supply the transportation and provisions on which the roaming armies depended. Tristán closes her account with a dramatic description of her encounter with a powerful, ambitious woman, Doña Pencha (wife of Agustín Gamarra, Peru's president from 1829 to 1833) at the moment of "La Presidenta's" defeat, possibly as proof of women's capacities and strength, or perhaps as a demonstration of Tristán's own superiority and valor.

It is the custom in Peru when women of the upper class arrive in a town where they are unknown to stay at home and receive visits for the whole of the first month, after which they return all the visits

---

*Luis Martin, *Daughters of the Conquistadores. Women of the Viceroyalty of Peru* (Albuquerque: University of New Mexico Press, 1983), includes a discussion of the *tapadas* (see especially 299–309).

†Jorge Juan and Antonio de Ulloa, *A Voyage to South America*, trans. John Adams (New York: Alfred A. Knopf, 1964), 196.

‡Emmelline Stuart Wortley, *Travels in the United States, etc., During 1849 and 1850* (New York: Harper and Brothers, 1851), 382–83; and Madeleine Vinton Dahlgren, *South Sea Sketches, A Narrative* (Boston: James R. Osgood and Co., 1881), 39–40.

they have received. My cousin Carmen, who is a stickler for etiquette, told me how I should behave, in the belief that I attached the same importance to convention as she did and would conform to it in every detail; but in this respect the yoke of custom appeared too heavy to me, and I took it upon myself to shake it off. My cousin, who disliked receiving visits as much as I did, applauded the brisk way I dispensed with them, though she was incapable of such boldness herself.

Before I go on with my story, I think I should introduce the reader to my cousin Doña Carmen Pierola de Florez, who would have been between thirty-eight and forty when I met her. If I am to be truthful, I am afraid I have to admit that my poor cousin's ugliness amounts almost to deformity, as her face is cruelly ravaged by smallpox. But it is not God's will that His most disadvantaged creatures should be entirely deprived of charms, for my cousin Carmen has the prettiest feet, not only in Arequipa, but perhaps in all Peru, and what is even more extraordinary, although she is extremely thin, her feet and legs are plump and dimpled. Her coloured stockings are of the finest silk and she wears her skirts very short: she is right to do so, for her feet are too admirable to be hidden away. She is very fond of clothes and dresses with taste, but in a style rather too young for her age.

My cousin has a very remarkable character: she never had an education, but has educated herself and understands everything with admirable intelligence. The poor woman lost her mother when she was a child, and that was when her misfortunes began. Raised by a strict unloving aunt, she was so unhappy that as her only means of escape was marriage or the cloister, she decided to marry the son of one of my father's sisters. He had asked for her hand, drawn by the attraction of a rich dowry. This cousin was exceptionally good-looking and very agreeable, but he was also a gambler and a rake who squandered his fortune and that of his wife in every kind of debauchery. The proud Doña Carmen had to suffer every torture imaginable during the ten years that the marriage lasted. She loved her husband, but he brutally rejected her devotion and lived only to gratify his senses. Several times he left her to live openly with mistresses, and these women would parade beneath Doña Carmen's window, staring boldly at her and insulting her to her face. In the early days of her marriage the young woman ventured to complain to her husband's family or their mutual friends, but she was told that she should stop complaining and think herself lucky to have

[margin note: focus on "intelligence"]

such a good-looking man for a husband. People found in the ugliness of the wife and the beauty of the husband sufficient justification for the plundering of her fortune and the constant indignities to which she was subjected. Such is the morality which proceeds from the indissolubility of marriage! After that Doña Carmen never uttered a murmur of complaint, but, adopting an exaggerated view of human wickedness, she banished all affection from her heart and admitted in its place only sentiments of hatred or disdain. She sought to deaden the pain she felt by entering society, and although she had neither beauty nor wealth, her wit made her the centre of an admiring circle.

After ten years of marriage, her husband, who was by then thirty, returned to her. He had dissipated both their fortunes, was heavily in debt and was afflicted with a horrible malady that no doctor could identify. She received him, not with affection, for nothing could revive this sentiment in her heart, but with the secret pleasure people like her obtain from displaying their superiority in the exercise of a noble vengeance. Her unhappy husband paid dearly for the disorders of his life: he spent sixteen months confined to his bed suffering the cruellest tortures. All that time his wife never left him for a moment: she was his nurse, his doctor and his confessor. She had a couch placed next to his sickbed, and day and night she was there, ready to give him every assistance. She bore with admirable patience the caprices, rebuffs and despairing moods of the dying man. His long illness used up the last of my unfortunate cousin's resources, and after his death she was forced to take her only child, a daughter, and return once more to live with her aunt.

When I arrived in Arequipa she had been a widow for twelve years, leading an uneventful life and hiding her real poverty beneath an appearance of opulence. Six months of every year she spent at her aunt's place, a sugar refinery not far from my uncle's, at Camana. She intensely disliked living in the country, but she had no choice, and it was an unforeseen circumstance which had kept her in town. She and I saw it as an act of Providence, for had she not stayed in Arequipa I would have found nobody to receive me at my uncle's house.

If at first my poor cousin's unprepossessing countenance and dry manner produced a disagreeable effect on me, I soon discovered a kind of nobility and superiority in the depths of her soul which won my sympathy. From the beginning she showed me much affection and it was thanks to her that I learned Spanish so quickly. In the morning she would send for me to breakfast with her, and in the afternoon at about three o'clock I would go and dine with her. She was always intending to invite a few friends as company for me, but I preferred to stay alone with her as I found in her conversation an endless source of information on both people and things. . . .

The *rabonas* are the camp-followers of South America. In Peru each soldier takes with him as many women as he likes: some have as many as four. They form a considerable troop, preceding the army by several hours so that they have time to set up camp, obtain food and cook it. To see the female avant-garde set out gives one an immediate idea of what these poor women have to suffer and the dangerous life they lead. The *rabonas* are armed; they load onto mules their cooking-pots, tents and all the rest of the baggage, they drag after them a horde of children of all ages, they whip their mules into a gallop and run along beside them, they climb high mountains, they swim across rivers, carrying one or even two children on their backs. When they arrive at their destination, they choose the best site for the camp, then they unload the mules, erect the tents, feed the children and put them to bed, light the fires and start cooking. If they chance to be near an inhabited place, they go off in a detachment to get supplies; they descend on the village like famished beasts and demand food for the army. When it is given with a good grace they do no harm, but when they are refused they fight like lionesses and their fierce courage overcomes all resistance. Then they sack the village, carry their loot back to the camp and divide it among themselves.

These women, who provide for all the needs of the soldier, who wash and mend his clothes, receive no pay and their only reward is the freedom to rob with impunity. They are of Indian race, speak the native language, and do not know a single word of Spanish. The *rabonas* are not married, they belong to nobody and are there for anybody who wants them. They are creatures outside society: they live with the soldiers, eat with them, stop where they stop, are exposed to the same dangers and endure far greater hardships than the men. When the army is on the march it is nearly always on the courage and daring of these women four or five hours ahead of them that it depends for its subsistence, and when one considers that in leading this life of toil and danger they still have the duties of motherhood to fulfil, one is amazed that any of them can endure it. It is worth observing that whereas the Indian would rather kill himself than be a soldier, the Indian women embrace this life *voluntarily*, bearing its fatigues and confronting its dangers with a courage of which the men of their race are incapable. I do not believe it possible to adduce a more striking proof of the superiority of woman in primitive societies; would not the same be true of peoples at a more advanced stage of civilisation if both sexes received a similar education? We must hope that some day the experiment will be tried.

Several able generals have sought to find a substitute for the service the *rabonas* provide and prevent them from following the army, but the soldiers have always revolted against any such attempt and it has been necessary to yield to them. They are not at all sure that the military administration would be able to provide for their needs, and that is why they refuse to give the *rabonas* up.

These women are horribly ugly, which is understandable when one considers the kind of hardships they endure. In fact they have to withstand extremes of climate ranging from the burning sun of the pampas to the icy summit of the Cordilleras, so their skin is burnt and wrinkled, their eyes red-rimmed; their teeth, however, are very white. Their only clothing is a little woollen skirt which reaches only to their knees, and a sheepskin cover with a hole in the middle for their head to go through, while the two sides cover their chest and back; their feet, arms and head are always bare. They seem to get on fairly well together, though their jealous scenes sometimes lead to murders; as there is nothing to restrain their passions, such happenings should occasion no surprise. There is no doubt that if an equal number of men were freed from all control and forced to lead the life of these women, murders would be far more frequent. The *rabonas* adore the sun but do not observe any religious practices.* . . .

There is no place on earth where women are so *free* and exercise so much power as in Lima. They seem to have absorbed for their use alone what little energy the warm, heady climate allows the fortunate inhabitants. In Lima the women are as a rule taller and better built than the men. At eleven or twelve they are fully

*The sun was an important part of pre-Columbian religious beliefs in the Andes. The sun was believed to protect and mature crops. The sun god Inti was the special patron deity of the Incas, believed to be the divine ancestor of the Inca dynasty—Ed.

developed; nearly all of them marry at about this age and are very fertile, commonly producing from six to seven children. They have healthy pregnancies, give birth easily, and are quick to recover. Nearly all of them nurse their babies, but they are always helped by a wet nurse, a custom which comes to them from Spain, where the children in well-to-do families always have two women to feed them.

The women of Lima are not as a rule beautiful, but there is something irresistibly attractive about their faces; there is no man whose heart does not beat faster at the sight. They are not dark-skinned, as many Europeans believe; on the contrary, the majority are very white, while the rest are different shades of brown according to their diverse origins, but their skin is always smooth as velvet and their complexion glowing with vitality. Their colouring is rich: bright red lips, lovely black hair which curls naturally, admirably shaped black eyes, and an expression of mingled wit, pride and languor hard to define, but in which lies all their charm. They express themselves with great facility and their gestures are no less eloquent than their words.

Their costume is *unique*. Lima is the only city in the world where it has ever appeared. People have consulted the most ancient chronicles, but in vain; nobody has yet discovered its origin. It has nothing in common with the various Spanish costumes, and it is quite certain that it was not brought from Spain. It was found on this spot at the time Peru was discovered, and it is at the same time common knowledge that it has never existed in any other South American city. This costume, called the *saya*, is a skirt, worn with a sort of sack called a *manto*, which envelops the shoulders, arms and head. I can hear our elegant Parisiennes protesting at the simplicity of this style of dress; little can they imagine the advantage it gives to the coquette. It is only in Lima that you can have it made; the women there claim that only a woman born in Lima is capable of making it, and that a woman from Chile, or even from Arequipa or Cuzco could never acquire the art of *pleating the saya*.

To make an ordinary *saya* it takes between sixteen and eighteen yards of satin and some lightweight silk or cotton fabric for the lining. In exchange the seamstress brings you a narrow skirt which reaches from waist to ankles and is so tight that it allows just enough room to put one foot in front of the other and to take very little steps. Thus you are encased in this skirt like a sword in a sheath. It is entirely pleated from top to bottom with very narrow pleats so finely worked that it is impossible to see the stitches. However, these pleats are so firmly made and give the skirt such elasticity that I have seen fifteen-year-old *sayas* which were still flexible enough to reveal the whole shape of the body and to give with every movement of the wearer.

The *manto* is pleated in the same way, but as it is made in a very light material it is not as durable as the skirt, and the pleats cannot stand up to the constant movements of the wearer and the humidity of her breath. Women in good society have their *sayas* made in black satin, while fashionable ladies also have them in less common colours such as violet, maroon, bright green or deep blue, but never in light shades, as these are favoured by prostitutes. The *manto* is always black. It completely covers the bust and most of the head, leaving only one eye uncovered. The women of Lima always wear a little bodice, of which only the sleeves are ever seen, and whether they are short or long, this bodice is made of some rich fabric such as velvet, coloured satin or tulle; although in fact most women have their arms bare in all seasons. Their footwear is elegant enough to catch every eye: they wear pretty embroidered satin slippers in every colour, with ribbons in some contrasting shade, and fine silk stockings in various colours with richly embroidered clocks.

The women of Lima wear their hair parted in the middle and falling in two immaculate tresses tied in a big bunch of ribbons. However, this is not the only style, as some women wear their hair like Ninon de Lenclos, in long clusters of ringlets right down to their bosom, which in accordance with the custom of the country they nearly always leave bare. A few years ago the fashion for wearing big embroidered crêpe-de-Chine shawls was introduced. This has made their costume more decent by hiding their nakedness and any part of their bodies which was a little too prominently outlined. A further luxury they affect is to carry an exquisite embroidered handkerchief trimmed with lace. Oh! how enchanting they are, with their beautiful black *saya* shining in the sun; how graceful the movements of their shoulders are, as first they draw their *manto* right over their face, then slyly draw it aside! What fine supple figures they have, and how sinuously they sway as they walk! How pretty their tiny feet are, and what a pity they are just a little too plump!

Put such a woman in a Paris gown, and she is no longer the same person: one looks in vain for the seductive woman one encountered that morning in the church of St. Mary. For in Lima foreigners go to church not to hear the monks sing mass but to admire these unique women in their national costume. A number of foreigners have told me what a magical effect the sight of these women produced on their imagination. They fancied they had landed in Paradise, and that it was to compensate them for the hardship of a long voyage that God had set them down in this enchanted land. These flights of fancy are not implausible when one sees the follies and extravagances that these beautiful women lead foreigners to commit. Men follow them out of a burning desire to see their features, which they so carefully hide from view; but it takes an expert to follow a woman in a *saya*, as the costume tends to make all women look alike. I can say without fear of contradiction that if a lovely form and a magnetic glance were sufficient to ensure women the supremacy they are destined to possess, the women of Lima in their *sayas* would be proclaimed queens of the earth; but while this kind of beauty may excite the senses, only spiritual, moral and mental qualities can prolong its reign.

For God has endowed woman with a heart more loving and devoted than that of man; and if, as there can be no doubt, it is through love and devotion that we honour the Creator, then woman has an incontestable superiority over man, but she must cultivate her intelligence and exercise her self-control in order to retain it. Only on those conditions can she acquire the influence which comes from the power God has given her. But when she fails to recognise her mission, when, instead of being the inspiration of man and improving his character, she seeks only to seduce him, her authority disappears together with the desire she has aroused. Thus, when these enchanting women of Lima, who have never directed their lives towards any noble purpose, first electrify the imagination of young foreigners and then proceed to show themselves as they really are, heartless, uncultivated, shallow, and above all, mercenary, the powerful fascination produced by their charms is immediately destroyed.

For all that, the women of Lima dominate the men because they are so far above them in intelligence and will-power. But the stage of civilisation the Peruvians have reached is still far behind ours in Europe. Nowhere in Peru is there any institution for the education

→ she does not want to dominate men?

of either sex: the intelligence can develop only through its native resources. Thus the pre-eminence of Lima's women, however inferior they may be to European women from a moral aspect, must be attributed to the superior intelligence with which God has endowed them.

However, I must point out how much their style of dress has contributed to the great freedom and powerful influence they enjoy. If they should ever abandon it, they would have to adopt an entirely different set of values. To prove my point I will touch briefly upon one or two customs of Lima society so that the reader will be able to appreciate the justice of my observation.

The *saya*, as I have said, is the national costume; all women wear it whatever their rank, and it is respected as part of the culture of the country just as the Muslim woman's veil is in the Orient. At all times of the year the women of Lima go out in this disguise, and if anybody ever dared to lift the *manto* which covers the whole of her face except one eye, public indignation would be aroused and that person would be severely punished. It is accepted that *every woman may go out alone*; the majority have a negress following behind, but they are not obliged to do so. This costume so alters a woman—even her voice, since her mouth is covered—that unless she is very tall or very short, lame, hunchbacked or otherwise conspicuous, it is impossible to recognise her. I am sure it needs little imagination to appreciate the consequences of this time-honoured practice which is sanctioned or at least tolerated by law. A woman breakfasts with her husband in her little French *peignoir*, her hair pinned up exactly like a Parisienne's; and later on, if she wants to go out, she slips on her *saya*—without a corset, as the underskirt is quite tight—lets down her hair, puts on her *manto* and goes wherever her fancy takes her; she meets her husband in the street, and he does not recognise her; she flirts with him, leads him on, lets him offer her ices, fruit, cakes, gives him a rendezvous, leaves him, and immediately starts a new conversation with an officer passing by. She can let this new adventure go as far as she pleases without ever taking off her *manto*; then she goes to visit friends, takes a walk, and is back in time for dinner. Her husband does not ask where she has been, for he knows perfectly well that if it suits her better to hide the truth from him, she will lie, and as he has no means of restraining her, he takes the wisest course, which is not to worry. So these ladies go out alone to the theatre, to bullfights, to

[margin top, handwritten: no school system?]
[margin right, handwritten: Peru women are naturally more intelligent?]
[margin left, handwritten: Is her freedom in anonymity? How is there power in this?]

public gatherings, to balls, to churches and to pay visits; and they are accepted everywhere they go. If they wish to speak to anybody they do so, then take their leave, so that they remain free and independent in the midst of the crowd, far more so than the men. This costume has the enormous advantage of being at the same time economical, very clean, comfortable, ready to put on immediately, and never in need of the slightest attention.

There is one further custom I must not omit to mention: when the women of Lima want to make their disguise even more complete, they put on an old bodice, an old *manto*, and an old *saya* which is falling into rags and losing its pleats; but to show that they come from good society they wear immaculate shoes and stockings and carry one of their finest handkerchiefs. This is a recognised form of disguise and is known as *disfrazar*. A *disfrazada* is looked upon as eminently respectable, so nobody ever accosts her; indeed, people are very timid about approaching her, and it would be improper and even *dishonourable* to follow her. It is supposed, and rightly, that if she has disguised herself it is because she has important reasons for doing so, and consequently nobody should claim the right to investigate her movements.

From what I have just written about the costume and customs of the women of Lima it is easy to understand that they must have a completely different outlook from European women, who from their earliest childhood are the slaves of laws, morals, customs, prejudices, fashions and everything else whereas beneath their *sayas* the women of Lima are *free*, enjoying their independence and confident in that genuine strength which all people feel within them when they are able to act in accordance with their needs. In every situation the woman of Lima is always *herself*; never does she submit to any constraint. When she is young she escapes the domination of her parents through the freedom her costume allows her; when she marries she does not take her husband's name but keeps her own; when she is tired of staying in, she puts on her *saya* and goes out, in the same way as a man does when he takes up his hat. Freedom of action characterises everything she does.

In their more intimate relationships, whether these are casual or serious, the women of Lima always preserve their dignity, although their conduct in this regard is certainly very different from ours. Like all women they measure the strength of the love they inspire by the scale of the sacrifice their lovers are prepared to make; but just as ever since their country was discovered, only its gold has had the power to lure Europeans so far from home, gold alone, to the exclusion of talent and virtue, has always been the sole object of consideration, the sole motive for every action; and the women of Lima, consistent in their conduct and acting on the same principle, recognise no proof of love except the masses of gold they are offered, and their vanity is satisfied in proportion to the size of the sum or the cost of the gift. When anybody wants to give some idea of the violent love a gentleman feels for a lady, the expression used is always: "He gave her gold by the sackful!" just as we would say: "He killed himself for love of her!" So the wealthy woman always accepts money from her lover, even if she ends up giving it to her servants, for to her it is a *proof of love*, the only thing which can convince her that she is loved. The vanity of foreign travellers blinds them to this truth, and when anyone told us about the success he had had with the women of Lima he did not mention that it had cost him a small fortune, right down to the valuable keepsake he gave his beloved when he left. These customs are very strange, but they are real enough: I saw several ladies in high society wearing men's rings, watches and chains. . . .

The women of Lima spend little time on their households, but as they are very energetic, this is sufficient to keep everything in order. They have a marked inclination for politics and intrigue; it is they who find posts for their husbands, sons and all the men who take their fancy, and there is no obstacle they cannot overcome to achieve their ends. Men do not meddle in this sort of business, and they are right: they would not acquit themselves nearly as well. The women are very fond of pleasure and festivities, and love social gatherings, where they gamble for high stakes and smoke cigars. They go riding, not side-saddle like English women, but in breeches like the men. They have a passion for sea-bathing and swim extremely well. As for their accomplishments, they play the guitar, sing rather badly (though a few are good musicians) and dance their native dances with a charm it is impossible to describe. These women have no education as a rule, they do not read at all, and they are ignorant of everything that is happening in the world. They have much natural wit, a quick understanding, a good memory and a surprising amount of intelligence.

I have described the women of Lima exactly as they are and not as certain travellers depict them; it has hurt me to do so, as I was deeply grateful for their generous hospitality, but my rôle of conscientious traveller made it my duty to tell the whole truth. . . .

vain to include this →
Flora, too, likes being
recognized

34   *Women through Women's Eyes*

Señora Gamarra* appeared on deck [on board an English vessel in Callao harbor, on the way to exile in Chile]. "Ah! Señorita Florita, how happy I am to see you! I am impatient to make your acquaintance. Do you know, you beautiful young lady, that you have made a conquest of our dear Escudero? He never stops talking to me about you and quotes your opinion on every subject. As for your uncle, everything he does is *inspired by you*. It was very naughty of you to leave Arequipa just two days before I arrived. To think that you were so curious to see San-Roman, the bogeyman of Arequipa, but not curious enough to see Doña Pencha, the terror of all Peru! I am sure I deserve a place in your journal as much as he does!"

So saying, she conducted me to the end of the poopdeck, made me sit beside her, and dismissed with a wave of her head anybody importunate enough to wish to follow us. Though a prisoner, Doña Pencha was still the president's wife: her spontaneous gesture revealed a consciousness of her superiority. Not a single person remained on the poop, though as the awning had been put up, it was the only place sheltered from the burning sun; everybody stayed below. She examined me intently, and I looked at her with no less interest; everything about her revealed a being as exceptional for her will-power as for her intelligence. She was between thirty-four and thirty-six, of medium height and wiry frame, though she was very thin. Her face was assuredly not beautiful by accepted standards, but to judge from the effect it produced, it possessed something more than conventional beauty. She had a long, slightly turned-up nose and a large but very expressive mouth; her whole face was long, with prominent cheekbones and muscles, while her skin was very brown but full of vitality. She had an enormous head adorned with a mass of thick long hair which hung over her brow; it was a dark chestnut colour, with a lustrous and silky texture. Her voice was heavy, harsh, imperious; she spoke in an abrupt and jerky manner. Her movements were graceful enough, but they could not hide the tenor of her thoughts. Her fresh, elegant and distinguished toilette formed a strange contrast with the harshness of her voice, the austere dignity of her look and the gravity of her person. She was wearing a gown of heavy Indian silk the colour of bird-of-paradise, embroidered in white silk, with the finest pink silk stockings and white satin slippers. A brilliant red crêpe-de-Chine shawl

*Pencha Gamarra, wife of Agustín Gamarra, president of Peru from 1829 to 1833 and from 1839 until his death in 1841—Ed.

embroidered in white, the most beautiful I ever saw in Lima, was thrown carelessly over her shoulders. She had rings on every finger, diamond ear-rings, and a superb necklace of fine pearls, beneath which hung a worn and dirty scapular. Seeing my surprise as I contemplated her, she said in her brusque manner: "You must find me very ridiculous in this grotesque costume, my dear Florita, you dress so simply yourself; but now you have passed judgment on me, you probably realise that these clothes are not mine. It was my poor sister who persuaded me to wear them, to please her and my mother and all the rest of them; these good people imagine that my luck will change if I consent to wear European clothes. So I yielded to their entreaties and put on this gown which hampers my movements, these stockings which feel cold to my legs, this big shawl which I am afraid of burning with the ash from my cigar. I like clothes which are comfortable for riding, clothes which will stand up to the strains of campaigning, visiting camps and barracks, and going aboard Peruvian ships: those are the only clothes that suit me. For years I have been travelling all over the country in breeches of the coarse cloth they make in my native Cuzco, a great-coat of the same material embroidered in gold, and boots with gold spurs. I love gold, it is the precious metal which gives the country its reputation, the finest ornament a Peruvian can have. I have a long cloak as well, a little heavy, but very warm; it was my father's and it has been very useful in the snow of our mountains. You are admiring my hair," continued this alarming woman with the eagle eye, "well, my dear Florita, in a career where my strength has often fallen short of my courage, my position has been threatened more than once, and to compensate for the weakness of our sex I have had to retain its attractions and exploit them as need arose in order to enlist the support of men."

"So," I could not stop myself crying out, "this strong soul, this superior intelligence, has had to yield to brute force in order to gain domination."

"Child," retorted the ex-president's wife, crushing my hand in an iron grip and giving me a look I shall never forget, "child, let me tell you that it is precisely because I have never been able to submit my invincible pride to brute force that you see me a prisoner here, driven into exile by the very men I commanded for three years. . . ."

In that moment I penetrated her mind; my soul took possession of hers. I felt stronger than she was and dominated her with the power of my gaze. She perceived this and grew pale; the colour

awks

drained from her lips, and with a sudden movement she flung her cigar into the sea and ground her teeth. Her expression would have made the boldest tremble, but she was under my spell and I read distinctly all that was passing inside her. In my turn, taking her hand which was cold and bathed in sweat, I said to her in a grave tone:

"Doña Pencha, the Jesuits* said: Who desires the ends desires the means; and the Jesuits ruled the mighty of the earth . . ."

She looked at me for a long time without speaking: she too sought to penetrate my soul . . . She broke the silence in tones of irony and despair.

"Ah! Florita, your pride is leading you astray; you think you are stronger than I am; you are mad! You know nothing of the never-ending struggle I have had for the past eight years, the humiliations I have had to endure! I have begged, flattered, lied: I have tried everything and stopped at nothing . . . and yet it was not enough. I thought that at last I had reached the point where I could reap the harvest of eight years of pain and sacrifice, but then the infernal blow struck and I saw myself driven out, lost, lost, Florita! . . . I shall never return to Peru. Ah! glory, how dearly you are bought! What folly to sacrifice the joy of living, the whole of life, to obtain you! Glory is nothing but a flash of light, a puff of smoke, a cloud, an illusion; and yet, Florita, the day I lose all hope of living enveloped in that cloud, there will be no more sun to light me, no more air for me to breathe, and I shall die."

These last words were uttered in a prophetic tone which matched the sombre expression of Doña Pencha's face; she gazed at the serene blue sky above our heads in rapt contemplation of her celestial vision and seemed no longer to belong to this world. I bowed before this superior being who had suffered all the torments reserved for natures such as hers in their passage on earth. I was about to continue the conversation, but she rose abruptly, and darting to the other end of the deck, she called her sister and two other ladies, saying, "Come quickly, I feel ill." . . .

[The next day], I went into the captain's cabin which was large and very handsome, and there I found Doña Pencha, half-dressed, lying on a mattress upon the floor. She gave me her hand and I sat beside her.

*Members of the Society of Jesus, the powerful Roman Catholic religious order that was expelled from the Spanish empire in 1767—Ed.

"No doubt you know that I suffer from a terrible disease, and . . ."

"I know," I interrupted her, "but is there no medicine which will cure it, or have you no confidence in the relief it offers?"

"I have consulted all the doctors and done exactly as they prescribed; but their remedies have been unsuccessful; the older I get, the worse the disease becomes. It has done me great harm in everything I have undertaken; any strong emotion brings on an immediate attack, so you can judge what an obstacle it has been to my career. Our soldiers are so badly trained and our officers so cowardly that in every serious engagement I had to take command myself. For the past ten years, long before I had any hope of getting my husband nominated president, I have taken part in every battle to accustom myself to fire. Often when the fight was fiercest I would grow so angry at the apathy and cowardice of the troops under my command that I would foam with rage, and then I would have one of my attacks. I had only enough time to throw myself to the ground; several times I was trampled by the horses and carried off for dead by my servants. Well, Florita, would you believe it, my enemies used my cruel illness to discredit me with the army; they gave out that *fear*, the noise of the cannon and the smell of gunpowder were attacking my nerves and making me faint away like some little lady of fashion! I confess it is slanders like these that have made me hard. I wanted to make them see that I was not afraid of blood or of death. Each reversal makes me more cruel, and if . . ."

She stopped, and raising her eyes to heaven, she seemed to be communicating with some being that she alone could see; then she said: "Yes, I am leaving my country never to return, and before two months are up, I shall be with you . . ." Only some presence not of this world could have given her features the expression they wore as she spoke these words. I looked at her then: how changed I found her since the day before, with her wasted cheeks, livid complexion, pale lips, cold hands, and glittering sunken eyes! Life seemed about to abandon her. I dared not speak to her for fear of making her worse. I was leaning over her; one of my tears fell upon her arm and this had the effect of an electric spark upon the unfortunate woman. She came out of her trance, turned abruptly towards me, fixed me with her burning gaze and said in sepulchral tones: "Why do you weep? Is it out of pity at my fate? Do you think I am banished for ever, lost, as good as dead?" I could find no words to reply; she had thrust me away, so I was now on my knees before her. I clasped my hands together in a mechanical gesture and continued to weep as I gazed at her. There was a long silence; she seemed to grow calmer and said in a voice that wrung my heart: "So, you weep, do you? Ah! God be praised! You are young, there is still life in you; weep for me, I am finished, I am dead. . . ."

A lady who was born in Cuzco and had known Doña Pencha since childhood told me various particulars about this extraordinary woman which I think cannot fail to interest the reader.

Doña Pencha was the daughter of a Spanish officer who had married an extremely wealthy young lady from Cuzco. During her childhood she stood out among her companions by reason of her proud, bold, melancholy disposition. She was very devout: from the age of twelve it was her desire to enter a convent and become a nun, but her poor health did not permit her to realise her intention. When she was seventeen her parents made her return home so that she could receive the care and attention she needed. Her father's house was frequented by many officers, several of whom sought her hand, but she declared that she did not wish to marry, being resolved to return to her convent at the earliest opportunity. Her father arranged for her to travel, in the hope of restoring her to health; he took her to Lima, brought her out in society, and provided her with every distraction, but she remained melancholy and seemed insensitive to the pleasures normally associated with youth. She spent two years in travel, and soon after her return to Cuzco, she gave up all idea of becoming a nun and chose as her husband an ugly, stupid little officer, the least distinguished of all her suitors. She married Señor Gamarra, a simple captain. Although she was still in poor health and nearly always pregnant, she followed her husband wherever the war took him, and the constant exertion so strengthened her constitution that she was soon capable of covering enormous distances on horseback. For a long time she managed to conceal the cruel infirmity which afflicted her, and which was steadily growing worse. It was only when, as wife of the president, her life came under investigation, that the public got to know about it through her enemies. Her solicitation and intriguing had raised her husband to the presidency. . . .

When she succeeded General de la Mar* to [effective] power, the republic was in the most deplorable state; the country was rent

*José de la Mar, president of Peru from 1827 to 1829—Ed.

asunder by civil war, there was not a single piastre in the treasury, soldiers sold their services to the highest bidder—in short, it was anarchy with all its horrors. Yet this woman, raised in a convent, without education, but gifted with a strong moral sense and an uncommonly powerful will, governed a people even Bolívar* had found ungovernable with such success that in less than a year order was restored, rival factions were tamed, trade flourished, the army regained confidence in its leaders; and even if parts of Peru were still unsettled, most of the country enjoyed peace.

With such a character, Doña Pencha seemed destined to continue the work of Bolívar for many years to come, and she would certainly have done so had not her all too feminine exterior stood in her way. She was beautiful, she could be very gracious when she chose, and she had the power to inspire great passion. Her enemies spread the vilest slanders about her and, finding it easier to attack her morals than her political actions, attributed various vices to her to console themselves for her superiority.

Doña Pencha was too ambitious to take love seriously. Several officers in her retinue fell in love with her and others feigned love in order to advance their fortunes, but she repulsed them all, not with the indulgence a woman feels towards a love she cannot share, but with the anger and contempt of outraged pride. However, she did not stop there: she conceived a violent hatred for them, ceased to trust them, and missed no opportunity of insulting them, even in public. Once when she was inspecting the troops she caught sight of a colonel who, it was said, had boasted of having once been her lover. She pounced upon him, tore off his epaulettes, struck him three or four times across the face with her riding-whip, and pushed him so roughly that he fell off his horse. Then she cried in ringing tones: "This is the way I shall punish anyone who dares to slander the President's wife."

On another occasion she invited four officers to dinner, was perfectly agreeable throughout the meal, then turned to one of them during dessert and said: "Is it true, captain, that you told these three gentlemen you were tired of being my lover?" The unfortunate man turned pale and looked in terror at his comrades, who remained silent. "What!" she continued, "Have you lost your tongue? Answer me! If it is true I will have you whipped by your comrades; if

*Simón Bolívar, renowned independence leader, the liberator of northern South America—Ed.

they have maligned you, the two of us will make them pay for their cowardice." It was only too apparent that the rash young man was indeed guilty of the remark in question, so she summoned four enormous negroes, had the doors locked, and made the three other officers thrash their comrade with birch-rods.

Such conduct was not in accordance with the morals of the country she governed and was bound to antagonise public opinion, because in a country where there is complete independence between the sexes, people do not think of virtue, in the conventional sense of the word, in connection with women, and the Peruvians considered themselves insulted by the arrogant behaviour of the president's wife. Not that Doña Pencha had any more concern for virtue than any other woman in Peru; in private life she would not have been in the least offended at the homage paid to her charms, and she would have been as indifferent to gossip about the number of lovers she had as any other lady in Lima. But she was intoxicated by her power and convinced that she belonged to a superior order of creation. Ministers had to submit every act of congress to her scrutiny; she struck out any passages which did not suit her and substituted her own, so that in the end she became an absolute ruler within a constitutional republic.

Señora Gamarra had all the virtues necessary for the exercise of power at this stage of Peru's development, yet she had great difficulty in serving her full three-year term of office. Her despotism had been so harsh, her yoke so heavy, she had wounded so many people's self-esteem, that a strong opposition rose against her. When she saw that she would not be able to get her husband reelected, she resorted to a trick. Señor Gamarra declared in the Senate that his health did not permit him to continue in public life; Señora Gamarra wished to have one of her creatures nominated as president, a slave obedient to her will. So she and her husband transferred their support, and that of their friends, to Bermúdez;* but Orbegoso† won the day. . . .

To conclude the story of Doña Pencha: when she reached Valparaiso she rented a splendid furnished house where she installed herself . . . and her numerous retainers; but not one lady in the town

---

*Pedro Pablo Bermúdez, whose election President Gamarra, legally barred from a second successive term, tried to secuure in 1833—Ed.

†Luis José Orbegoso, chosen president by Congress in December 1833—Ed.

went to call on her. All the foreigners she had offended joined in the outcry against her, and barely a handful of her former comrades-in-arms had the courtesy to go and see her. This proud and haughty woman must have suffered cruelly from the abandonment and isolation in which hatred kept her confined. To be condemned to inactivity was like being buried alive for one of her restless spirit. . . . Seven weeks after she left Callao, she died.

3

FANNY CALDERÓN DE LA BARCA *Scotland*

Women's Lives in Midnineteenth-Century Mexico

The author of *Life in Mexico*, one of the best-known foreign travel accounts of that country, was born Frances Erskin Inglis in Edinburgh on December 23, 1804. Her father was a well-born, well-to-do landowner and a Writer to the Signet, a specialized branch of the Scottish legal profession; her mother was a member of another distinguished Scottish family whose prosperity derived from a thriving distillery. The fifth of their ten children, Fanny, as she was always called, received a good education and enjoyed periods of travel in Italy. But in 1828 her father was forced into bankruptcy, dying two years later. The next year, 1831, several female members of the family, including Fanny, emigrated to the United States and established a school in Boston. Their establishment enjoyed distinguished patronage, and their affairs appeared to go well for several years until the publication of an anonymous pamphlet—rumored to be the work of Fanny and an admirer—that caricatured a number of prominent Bostonians. Although Fanny's unsuccessful suitor claimed sole responsibility, victims who had daughters in the family's school withdrew them, and competition from other schools also caused difficulties. In 1837, Fanny and her mother moved to New Brighton on Staten Island, then a fashionable resort enjoyed

From Frances Calderón de la Barca, *Life in Mexico During a Residence of Two Years in That Country* (Boston: Little, Brown and Co., 1843), 151–54, 202–19, 232–36, 441–43, 453–54.

by Southerners and foreign diplomats escaping sweltering Washington summers. Among those diplomats was Angel Calderón de la Barca, Spain's minister plenipotentiary to the United States. Studious and cautious, a man of varied interests, Calderón had been sought out by the historian William H. Prescott in his efforts to obtain source materials from Spain. Fanny was also a friend of Prescott's.

On September 24, 1838, Angel Calderón de la Barca and Fanny Inglis were married in New York. A year later they left for Mexico, as Calderón had received the important appointment as Spain's first envoy to an independent Mexico. After two years in Mexico the Calderóns returned to the United States, where Fanny prepared her book on Mexico for publication. Following a sojourn in Europe, Calderón's reappointment as Spanish minister to the United States brought them back to Washington in 1844, where they remained for nine years and where Fanny was received into the Roman Catholic faith. Then they returned to Europe and experienced diplomatic advancement, political upheavals, exile, and a return to Spain, where Calderón died in 1861. Not long afterwards, Queen Isabel II requested the widowed Fanny to undertake the education of her eldest daughter, the Infanta Isabel. The rest of Fanny's life was spent among the royal family at the palace, in exile, and then back at the palace. In 1873 she was accorded the title of Marquesa de Calderón de la Barca. Active till the end, she died in Madrid on February 6, 1882, at the age of seventy-seven.

The Mexico to which this intelligent, spirited, and sophisticated Scotswoman traveled in 1838 was still suffering from the economic chaos, political turmoil, and heavy loss of life that had accompanied the war for independence. Mexico, in contrast to other areas of the former Spanish empire, had experienced attempts at social revolution, which delayed the establishment of formal independence until 1821. The country would remain politically turbulent and economically weakened for decades afterward. Religious questions sharply separated Mexico's liberals and conservatives, and their disputes over the proper place of the Roman Catholic Church could turn bloody. During her two-year stay in Mexico, Fanny Calderón de la Barca witnessed the overthrow of General Antonio López de Santa Anna in July of 1840 and then the brief presidential tenure of Valentín

Gómez Farías. The latter sought to restrict the secular power and influence of the wealthy Church and its servants, who were possessors of rural estates and urban properties accounting for half the total value of the nation's real estate. But the liberals' reforms, including the abolition of compulsory tithes, efforts to secularize education, and granting members of religious orders the option of retracting their vows, were annulled when Santa Anna returned to power a year later. The struggle between liberals and conservatives then continued.

Fanny Calderón de la Barca's *Life in Mexico* was published in 1843 to far more favorable comment in Boston or even in London than it received in Mexico a few months later. There a Mexico City newspaper started to serialize a few selections but abandoned the effort under the force of a government-sponsored newspaper's attacks on Fanny and her book. English-language reissues continued to appear in the nineteenth and twentieth centuries, with the first full-length Spanish translation published in 1920. Today the book is as highly regarded in Mexico as elsewhere.

Although the preface to *Life in Mexico* by William H. Prescott (who, in his *Conquest of Mexico*, would draw heavily on Fanny's descriptions of the country he never visited) states that the book comprises letters written to relatives and is not intended for publication, it seems that much of the material came from journals this Scotswoman kept. She certainly reorganized and revised material, deleting passages or comments likely to cause serious offense or about which she had changed her mind, and she sought to conceal the identities of many living people.* But men like General Santa Anna would still not be pleased by her descriptions. She vividly depicted not only the elite's political dissension and Mexico's instability but also the country's poverty, terrain, festivals, society, mines, haciendas, and banditry. Tales of robberies and murders mingle with expressions of appreciation for Mexican hospitality and human warmth. The turmoil of politics did not extend into the elite's

*The most recent, and very well illustrated, edition of *Life in Mexico*, carefully annotated by Howard T. Fisher and Marion Hall Fisher (Garden City, NY: Doubleday and Co., 1996), not only gives the names deleted in the original edition but also includes material from Fanny Calderón de la Barca's private journals.

family lives. In the following selections, she gives her uncomplimentary opinions of Mexican servants, details the elaborate festivities and ceremonies held for nuns taking the veil (the fact that she was still a Protestant at this time no doubt affected her perceptions of convent life), depicts foundling hospital nurses and women jailed for murdering their husbands, and sympathetically describes the circumscribed lives of upper-class women in Mexico, including their personal modesty and warmth and the negligible education they received.

April 24, 1840

The Archbishop has not only granted me permission to visit the convents, but permits me to take two ladies along with me, of course I have been informed by the Minister, Señor C—o, in a very amiable note just received, enclosing one from Señor Posada, which I translate for your edification.

> *To His Excellency, Señor Don J. De D. C—o.*
> *April 24th*, 1840.

My dear Friend and Companion:

The Abbess and Nuns of the Convent of the Encarnación are now prepared to receive the visit of our three pilgrims, next Sunday, at half-past four in the afternoon, and should that day not suit them, let them mention what day will be convenient.

Afterwards we shall arrange their visit to the Concepcion, Enseñanza Antigua, and Jesús María, which are the best, and I shall let you know, and we shall agree upon the days and hours most suitable. I remain your affectionate friend and *Capellan*,

MANUEL POSADA.

April 27, 1840

Accordingly, on Sunday afternoon, we drove to the *Encarnación*, the most splendid and richest convent in Mexico, excepting perhaps la Concepción. If it were in any other country, I might mention the surpassing beauty of the evening, but as except in the rainy season, which has not yet begun, the evenings are always beautiful, the weather leaves no room for description. The sky always blue, the air always soft, the flowers always blossoming, the birds

always singing; Thomson never could have written his "Seasons"
here. We descended at the convent gate, were admitted by the
portress, and received by several nuns, their faces closely covered
with a double crape veil. We were then led into a spacious hall,
hung with handsome lustres, and adorned with various Virgins and
Saints magnificently dressed; and here the eldest, a very dignified
old lady, lifted her veil, the others following her example, and introduced herself as the *Madre Vicaria*; bringing us many excuses
from the old abbess, who having an inflammation in her eyes, was
confined to her cell. She and another reverend mother, and a group
of elderly dames, tall, thin, and stately, then proceeded to inform
us, that the archbishop had, in person, given orders for
our reception, and that they were prepared to show us the whole
establishment.

The dress is a long robe of very fine white casimere, a thick
black crape veil, and long rosary. The dress of the novices is the
same, only that the veil is white. For the first half-hour or so, I
fancied, that along with their politeness, was mingled a good deal
of restraint, caused perhaps by the presence of a foreigner, and especially of an Englishwoman. My companions they knew well; the
Señorita having even passed some months there. However this may
have been, the feeling seemed gradually to wear away. Kindness or
curiosity triumphed; their questions became unceasing; and before
the visit was concluded, I was addressed as *"mi vida"* (my life), by
the whole establishment. Where was I born? Where had I lived?
What convents had I seen? Which did I prefer, the convents in
France, or those in Mexico? Which were largest? Which had the
best garden? etc., etc. Fortunately, I could, with truth, give the pref-
erence to their convent, as to spaciousness and magnificence, over
any I ever saw.

The Mexican style of building is peculiarly advantageous for
recluses; the great galleries and courts affording them a constant
supply of fresh air, while the fountains sound so cheerfully, and the
garden in this climate of perpetual spring affords them such a constant source of enjoyment all the year round, that one pities their
secluded state much less here than in any other country.

This convent is in fact a palace. The garden, into which they
led us first, is kept in good order, with its stone walks, stone benches,
and an ever-playing and sparkling fountain. The trees were bend-
ing with fruit, and they pulled quantities of the most beautiful flowers for us; sweet-peas and roses, with which all gardens here abound,

carnations, jasmine, and heliotrope. It was a pretty picture to see
them wandering about, or standing in groups in this high-walled
garden, while the sun was setting behind the hills, and the noise of
the city was completely excluded, everything breathing repose and
contentment. Most of the halls in the convent are noble rooms. We
visited the whole, from the refectory to the *botica,** and admired
the extreme cleanness of everything, especially of the immense
kitchen, which seems hallowed from the approach even of a par-
ticle of dust; this circumstance is partly accounted for by the fact
that each nun has a servant, and some have two; for this is not one
of the strictest orders. The convent is rich; each novice at her entrance pays five thousand dollars into the common stock. There are
about thirty nuns and ten novices.

The prevailing sin in a convent generally seems to be pride;

The pride that apes humility;

and it is perhaps nearly inseparable from the conventual state. Set
apart from the rest of the world, they, from their little world, are
too apt to look down with contempt which may be mingled with
envy, or modified by pity, but must be unsuited to a true Christian
spirit.   clothing demonstrated entrapment

The novices were presented to us—poor little entrapped things!
who really believe they will be let out at the end of the year if they
should grow tired, as if they would ever be permitted to grow tired!
The two eldest and most reverend ladies are sisters, thin, tall, and
stately, with high noses, and remains of beauty. They have been in
the convent since they were eight years old (which is remarkable,
as sisters are rarely allowed to profess in the same establishment),
and consider *La Encarnación* as a small piece of heaven upon earth.
There were some handsome faces amongst them, and one whose
expression and eyes were singularly lovely, but truth to say, these
were rather exceptions to the general rule.

Having visited the whole building, and admired one virgin's
blue satin and pearls, and another's black velvet and diamonds,
sleeping holy infants, saints, paintings, shrines, and confessionals,—
having even climbed up the Azotea, which commands a magnificent view, we came at length to a large hall, decorated with paintings
and furnished with antique high-backed arm-chairs, where a very
elegant supper, lighted up and ornamented, greeted our astonished

*Apothecary's store—Ed.

eyes; cakes, chocolate, ices, creams, custards, tarts, jellies, blanc-manges, orange and lemonade, and other profane dainties, orna-mented with gilt paper cut into little flags, etc. I was placed in a chair that might have served for a pope under a holy family; the Señora—and the Señorita—on either side. The elder nuns in stately array, occupied the other arm-chairs, and looked like statues carved in stone. A young girl, a sort of *pensionnaire*, brought in a little harp without pedals, and while we discussed cakes and ices, sung different ballads with a good deal of taste. The elder nuns helped us to everything, but tasted nothing themselves. The younger nuns and the novices were grouped upon a mat *à la Turque*, and a more picturesque scene altogether one could scarcely see.

The young novices in their white robes, white veils, and black eyes, the severe and dignified *madres* with their long dresses and mournful-looking black veils and rosaries, the veiled figures occa-sionally flitting along the corridor;—ourselves in contrast, with our *worldly* dresses and coloured ribbons; and the great hall lighted by one immense lamp that hung from the ceiling—I felt transported three centuries back, and half afraid that the whole would flit away, and prove a mere vision, a waking dream.

A gossiping old nun, who hospitably filled my plate with ev-erything, gave me the enclosed *flag* cut in gilt paper, which, to-gether with her custards and jellies, looked less unreal. They asked many questions in regard to Spanish affairs, and were not to be consoled for the defeat of Don Carlos,* which they feared would be an end of the true religion in Spain.

After supper we proceeded upstairs to the choir (where the nuns attend public worship, and which looks down upon the handsome convent church) to try the organ. I was set down to a Sonata of Mozart's, the servants blowing the bellows. It seems to me that I made more noise than music, for the organ is very old, perhaps as old as the convent, which dates three centuries back. However, the nuns were pleased, and after they had sung a hymn, we returned below. I was rather sorry to leave them, and I felt as if I could have passed some time there very contentedly; but it was near nine o'clock, and we were obliged to take our departure; so having been

---

*The defeat of the absolutist forces, known as Carlists, of Prince Carlos Isidro, the pious brother of Ferdinand VII of Spain, who had contested the suc-cession to the throne of a female, Ferdinand's young daughter Isabel II, in what had become a civil war—Ed.

embraced very cordially by the whole community, we left the hospitable walls of the Encarnación. . . .

June 4, 1840

Some days ago, having received a message from *my nun** that a girl was about to take the veil in her convent, I went there about six o'clock, and knowing that the church on these occasions is apt to be crowded to suffocation, I proceeded to the *reja*,[†] and speaking to an invisible within, requested to know in what part of the church I could have a place. Upon which a voice replied—

"Hermanita (my sister), I am rejoiced to see you. You shall have a place beside the godmother."

"Many thanks, Hermanita. Which way shall I go?"

Voice.—"You shall go through the sacristy. José Maria!"

José Maria, a thin, pale, lank individual, with hollow cheeks, who was standing near like a page in waiting, sprang forward—"*Madrecita*, I am here!"

Voice.—"José Maria—That lady is the Señora de C—n. You will conduct her excellency to the front of the grating, and give her a chair."

After I had thanked the *voice* for her kindness in attending to me on a day when she was so much occupied with other affairs, the obsequious José Maria led the way, and I followed him through the sacristy into the church, where there were already a few kneeling figures; and thence into the railed-off enclosure destined for the relatives of the future nun, where I was permitted to sit down in a comfortable velvet chair. I had been there but a little while when the aforesaid José Maria reappeared, picking his steps as if he were walking upon eggs in a sick-room. He brought me a message from the Madre—that the nun had arrived, and that the madrecita wished to know if I should like to give her an embrace before the ceremony began. I therefore followed my guide back into the sacristy, where the future nun was seated beside her godmother, and in the midst of her friends and relations, about thirty in all.

She was arrayed in pale blue satin, with diamonds, pearls, and a crown of flowers. She was literally smothered in blonde[‡] and jewels; and her face was flushed as well it might be, for she had

*Mother Adalid, an acquaintance in the convent of Santa Teresa—Ed.
†Iron gate—Ed.
‡A type of silk bobbin lace—Ed.

passed the day in taking leave of her friends at a fête they had given her, and had then, according to custom, been paraded through the town in all her finery. And now her last hour was at hand. When I came in she rose and embraced me with as much cordiality as if we had known each other for years. Beside her sat the Madrina,* also in white satin and jewels; all the relations being likewise decked out in their finest array. The nun kept laughing every now and then in the most unnatural and hysterical manner, as I thought, apparently to impress us with the conviction of her perfect happiness; for it is a great point of honour amongst girls similarly situated to look as cheerful and gay as possible; the same feeling, though in a different degree, which induces the gallant highwayman to jest in the presence of the multitude when the hangman's cord is within an inch of his neck, the same which makes the gallant general whose life is forfeited, command his men to fire on him; the same which makes the Hindoo widow mount the funeral pile without a tear in her eye, or a sigh on her lips. If the robber were to be strangled in a corner of his dungeon; if the general were to be put to death privately in his own apartment; if the widow were to be burnt quietly on her own hearth; if the nun were to be secretly smuggled in at the convent gate like a bale of contraband goods,—we might hear another tale. This girl was very young, but by no means pretty; on the contrary, rather *disgraciée par la nature*; and perhaps a knowledge of her own want of attraction may have caused the world to have few charms for her.

But José Maria cut short my train of reflections, by requesting me to return to my seat before the crowd arrived, which I did forthwith. Shortly after, the church doors were thrown open, and a crowd burst in, every one struggling to obtain the best seat. Musicians entered, carrying desks and music-books, and placed themselves in two rows, on either side of the enclosure where I was. Then the organ struck up its solemn psalmody, and was followed by the gay music of the band. Rockets were let off outside the church, and, at the same time, the Madrina and all the relations entered and knelt down in front of the grating which looks into the convent, but before which hung a dismal black curtain. I left my chair and knelt down beside the godmother.

Suddenly the curtain was withdrawn, and the picturesque beauty of the scene within baffles all description. Beside the altar, which

*That is, the godmother—Ed.

was in a blaze of light, was a perfect mass of crimson and gold drapery; the walls, the antique chairs, the table before which the priests sat, all hung with the same splendid material. The bishop wore his superb mitre and robes of crimson and gold; the attendant priests also glittering in crimson and gold embroidery.

In contrast to these, five-and-twenty figures, entirely robed in black from head to foot, were ranged on each side of the room prostrate, their faces touching the ground, and in their hands immense lighted tapers. On the foreground was spread a purple carpet bordered round with a garland of freshly gathered flowers, roses and carnations and heliotrope, the only thing that looked real and living in the whole scene; and in the middle of this knelt the novice, still arrayed in her blue satin, white lace veil and jewels, and also with a great lighted taper in her hand.

The black-robed nuns then rose and sang a hymn, every now and then falling on their faces and touching the floor with their foreheads. The whole looked like an incantation, or a scene in Robert le Diable. The novice was then raised from the ground and led to the feet of the bishop, who examined her as to her vocation, and gave her his blessing, and once more the black curtain fell between us and them.

In the *second act*, she was lying prostrate on the floor, disrobed of her profane dress, and covered over with a black cloth, while the black figures kneeling round her chanted a hymn. She was now dead to the world. The sunbeams had faded away, as if they would not look upon the scene, and all the light was concentrated in one great mass upon the convent group.

Again she was raised. All the blood had rushed into her face, and her attempt at a smile was truly painful. She then knelt before the bishop and received the benediction, with the sign of the cross, from a white hand with the pastoral ring. She then went round alone to embrace all the dark phantoms as they stood motionless, and as each dark shadow clasped her in its arms, it seemed like the dead welcoming a new arrival to the shades.

But I forget the sermon, which was delivered by a fat priest, who elbowed his way with some difficulty through the crowd to the grating, panting and in a prodigious heat, and ensconced himself in a great arm-chair close beside us. He assured her that she "had chosen the good part, which could not be taken away from her"; that she was now one of the elect, "chosen from amongst the wickedness and dangers of the world";—(picked out like a plum from a pie). He mentioned with pity and contempt those who were "yet struggling in the great Babylon"; and compared their miserable fate with hers, the Bride of Christ, who, after suffering a few privations here during a short term of years, should be received

Portrait of an eighteen-year-old Mexican nun on the occasion of joining her order in 1810. From Josefina Muriel, *Cultura feminina novohispana* (Mexico City: Universidad Nacional Autónoma de México, 1994), n.p.

at once into a kingdom of glory. The whole discourse was well calculated to rally her fainting spirits, if fainting they were, and to inspire us with a great disgust for ourselves.

When the sermon was concluded, the music again struck up— the heroine of the day came forward, and stood before the grating to take her last look of this wicked world. Down fell the black curtain. Up rose the relations, and I accompanied them into the sacristy. Here they coolly lighted their cigars, and very philosophically discoursed upon the exceeding good fortune of the new-made nun, and on her evident delight and satisfaction with her own situation. As we did not follow her behind the scenes, I could not give my opinion on this point. Shortly after, one of the gentlemen civilly led me to my carriage, and *so it was*.

As we were returning home, some soldiers rode up and stopped the carriage, desiring the coachman to take to the other side of the aqueduct, to avoid the body of a man who had just been murdered within a few doors of our house.

In the Convent of the Incarnation, I saw another girl sacrificed in a similar manner. She was received there without a dowry, on account of the exceeding fineness of her voice. She little thought what a fatal gift it would prove to her. The most cruel part of all was, that wishing to display her fine voice to the public, they made her sing a hymn alone, on her knees, her arms extended in the form of a cross, before all the immense crowd; "Ancilla Christi sum," "The Bride of Christ I am." She was a good-looking girl, fat and comely, who would probably have led a comfortable life in the world, for which she seemed well fitted; most likely without one touch of romance or enthusiasm in her composition; but having the unfortunate honour of being niece to two chanoines,* she was thus honourably provided for without expense in her nineteenth year. As might be expected, her voice faltered, and instead of singing, she seemed inclined to cry out. Each note came slowly, heavily, tremblingly; and at last she nearly fell forward exhausted, when two of the sisters caught and supported her.

I had almost made up my mind to see no more such scenes, which, unlike pulque† and bull-fights, I dislike more and more upon trial; when we received an invitation, which it was not easy to refuse, but was the more painful to accept, being acquainted, though slightly, with the victim. I send you the printed note of invitation.

*Church canons—Ed.
†Beverage made from the fermented juice of the manguey plant—Ed.

"On Wednesday, the — of this month, at six o'clock in the evening, my daughter, Doña Maria de la Concepción, P—e—, will assume the habit of a nun of the choir and the black veil in the Convent of Our Lady of the Incarnation. I have the honour to inform you of this, entreating you to cooperate with your presence in the solemnity of this act, a favour which will be highly esteemed by your affectionate servant, who kisses your hand.

"MARIA JOSEFA DE —.

"Mexico, June —, 1840."

Having gone out in the carriage to pay some visits, I suddenly recollected that it was the very morning of the day in which this young girl was to take the veil, and also that it was necessary to inquire where I was to be placed; for as to entering the church with the crowd on one of these occasions, it is out of the question; particularly when the girl being, as in the present case, of distinguished family, the ceremony is expected to be peculiarly magnificent. I accordingly called at the house, was shown upstairs, and to my horror, found myself in the midst of a "goodlie companie," in rich array, consisting of the relations of the family, to the number of about a hundred persons; the bishop himself in his purple robes and amethysts, a number of priests, the father of the young lady in his general's uniform; she herself in purple velvet, with diamonds and pearls, and a crown of flowers; the *corsage* of her gown entirely covered with little bows of ribbon of divers colours, which her friends had given her, each adding one, like stones thrown on a cairn in memory of the departed. She had also short sleeves and white satin shoes.

Being very handsome, with fine black eyes, good teeth, and fresh colour, and above all with the beauty of youth, for she is but eighteen, she was not disfigured even by this overloaded dress. Her mother, on the contrary, who was to act the part of Madrina, who wore a dress fac-simile, and who was pale and sad, her eyes almost extinguished with weeping, looked like a picture of misery in a ball-dress. In the adjoining room, long tables were laid out, on which servants were placing refreshments for the fête about to be given on this joyous occasion. I felt somewhat shocked, and inclined to say with Paul Pry, "Hope I don't intrude." But my apologies were instantly cut short, and I was welcomed with true Mexican hospitality; repeatedly thanked for my kindness in coming to see the nun, and hospitably pressed to join the family feast. I only got off upon a promise of returning at half-past five to accompany them to the ceremony, which, in fact, I greatly preferred to going there alone.

I arrived at the hour appointed, and being led upstairs by the Senator Don ——, found the morning party, with many additions, lingering over the dessert. There was some gaiety, but evidently forced. It reminded me of a marriage feast previous to the departure of the bride, who is about to be separated from her family for the first time. Yet how different in fact is this banquet, where the mother and daughter met together for the last time on earth!

At stated periods, indeed, the mother may hear her daughter's voice speaking to her as from the depths of the tomb; but she may never more fold her in her arms, never more share in her joys or in her sorrows, or nurse her in sickness; and when her own last hour arrives, though but a few streets divide them, she may not give her dying blessing to the child who has been for so many years the pride of her eyes and heart.

I have seen no country where families are so knit together as in Mexico, where the affections are so concentrated, or where such devoted respect and obedience are shown by the married sons and daughters to their parents. In that respect they always remain as little children. I know many families of which the married branches continue to live in their father's house, forming a sort of small colony, and living in the most perfect harmony. They cannot bear the idea of being separated, and nothing but dire necessity ever forces them to leave their *fatherland*. To all the accounts which travellers give them of the pleasures to be met with in the European capitals, they turn a deaf ear. Their families are in Mexico— their parents, and sisters, and relatives—and there is no happiness for them elsewhere. The greater therefore is the sacrifice which those parents make, who from religious motives devote their daughters to a conventual life.

——, however, was furious at the whole affair, which he said was entirely against the mother's consent, though that of the father had been obtained; and pointed out to me the confessor whose influence had brought it about. The girl herself was now very pale, but evidently resolved to conceal her agitation, and the mother seemed as if she could shed no more tears—quite exhausted with weeping. As the hour for the ceremony drew near, the whole party became more grave and sad, all but the priests, who were smiling and talking together in groups. The girl was not still a moment. She kept walking hastily through the house, taking leave of the servants, and naming probably her last wishes about everything. She was followed by her younger sisters, all in tears.

But it struck six, and the priests intimated that it was time to move. She and her mother went downstairs alone, and entered the carriage which was to drive them through all the principal streets, to show the nun to the public according to custom, and to let them take their last look, they of her, and she of them. As they got in, we all crowded to the balconies to see her take leave of her house, her aunts saying, "Yes, child, *despidete de tu casa*, take leave of your house, for you will never see it again!" Then came sobs from the sisters, and many of the gentlemen, ashamed of their emotion, hastily quitted the room. I hope, for the sake of humanity, I did not rightly interpret the look of constrained anguish which the poor girl threw from the window of the carriage at the home of her childhood.

They drove off, and the relations prepared to walk in procession to the church. I walked with the Count S—o, the others followed in pairs. The church was very brilliantly illuminated, and as we entered, the band was playing one of *Strauss's* waltzes! The crowd was so tremendous that we were nearly squeezed to a jelly in getting to our places. I was carried off my feet between two fat Señoras in mantillas and shaking diamond pendants, exactly as if I had been packed between two moveable feather-beds.

They gave me, however, an excellent place, quite close to the grating, beside the Countess de S—o, that is to say, a place to kneel on. A great bustle and much preparation seemed to be going on within the convent, and veiled figures were flitting about, whispering, arranging, etc. Sometimes a skinny old dame would come close to the grating, and lifting up her veil, bestow upon the pensive public a generous view of a very haughty and very wrinkled visage of some seventy years standing, and beckon into the church for the major-domo of the convent (an excellent and profitable situation by the way), or for padre this or that. Some of the holy ladies recognised and spoke to me through the grating.

But at the discharge of fireworks outside the church the curtain was dropped, for this was the signal that the nun and her mother had arrived. An opening was made in the crowd as they passed into the church, and the girl, kneeling down, was questioned by the bishop, but I could not make out the dialogue, which was carried on in a low voice. She then passed into the convent by a side door, and her mother, quite exhausted and nearly in hysterics, was supported through the crowd to a place beside us, in front of the grating. The music struck up; the curtain was again drawn aside. The scene was as striking here as in the convent of the Santa Teresa, but not so lugubrious. The nuns, all ranged around, and carrying lighted tapers in their hands, were dressed in mantles of bright blue, with a gold plate on the left shoulder. Their faces, however, were covered with deep black veils. The girl, kneeling in front, and also bearing a heavy lighted taper, looked beautiful, with her dark hair and rich dress, and the long black lashes resting on her glowing face. The churchmen near the illuminated and magnificently decked altar formed, as usual, a brilliant background to the picture. The ceremony was the same as on the former occasion, but there was no sermon.

The most terrible thing to witness was the last, straining, anxious look which the mother gave her daughter through the grating. She had seen her child pressed to the arms of strangers, and welcomed to her new home. She was no longer hers. All the sweet ties of nature had been rudely severed, and she had been forced to consign her, in the very bloom of youth and beauty, at the very age in which she most required a mother's care, and when she had but just fulfilled the promise of her childhood, to a living tomb. Still, as long as the curtain had not fallen, she could gaze upon her, as upon one on whom, though dead, the coffin-lid is not yet closed.

But while the new-made nun was in a blaze of light, and distinct on the foreground, so that we could mark each varying expression of her face, the crowd in the church, and the comparative faintness of the light, probably made it difficult for her to distinguish her mother; for, knowing that the end was at hand, she looked anxiously and hurriedly into the church, without seeming able to fix her eyes on any particular object; while her mother seemed as if her eyes were glazed, so intently were they fixed upon her daughter.

Suddenly, and without any preparation, down fell the black curtain like a pall, and the sobs and tears of the family broke forth. One beautiful little child was carried out almost in fits. Water was brought to the poor mother; and at last, making our way with difficulty through the dense crowd, we got into the sacristy. "I declare," said the Countess—to me, wiping her eyes, "it is worse than a marriage!" I expressed my horror at the sacrifice of a girl so young, that she could not possibly have known her own mind. Almost all the ladies agreed with me, especially all who had daughters, but many of the old gentlemen were of a different opinion. The young men were decidedly of my way of thinking; but many young girls, who were conversing together, seemed rather to envy their friend, who had looked so pretty and graceful, and "so happy," and whose dress "suited her so well," and to have no objection to "go, and do likewise."

I had the honour of a presentation to the bishop, a fat and portly prelate, with good manners, and well besuiting his priestly garments. I amused myself, while we waited for the carriages, by looking over a pamphlet which lay on the table, containing the ceremonial of the veil-taking. When we rose to go, all the ladies of the highest rank devoutly kissed the bishop's hand; and I went home, thinking by what law of God a child can thus be dragged from the mother who bore and bred her, and immured in a cloister for life, amongst strangers, to whom she has no tie, and towards whom she owes no duty. That a convent may be a blessed shelter from the calamities of life, a haven for the unprotected, a resting-place for the weary, a safe and holy asylum, where a new family and kind friends await those whose natural ties are broken and whose early friends are gone, I am willing to admit; but it is not in the flower of youth that the warm heart should be consigned to the cold cloister. Let the young take their chance of sunshine or of storm: the calm and shady retreat is for helpless and unprotected old age.

July 8, 1840

You ask me how Mexican women are educated. In answering you, I must put aside a few brilliant exceptions, and speak *en masse*, the most difficult thing in the world, for these exceptions are always rising up before me like accusing angels, and I begin to think of individuals, when I should keep to generalities. Generally speaking, then, the Mexican Señoras and Señoritas write, read, and play a little, sew, and take care of their houses and children. When I say they read, I mean they know how to read; when I say they write, I do not mean that they can always spell; and when I say they play, I do not assert that they have generally a knowledge of music. If we compare their education with that of girls in England, or in the United States, it is not a comparison, but a contrast. Compare it with that of Spanish women, and we shall be less severe upon their *far niente* descendants. In the first place, the climate inclines every one to indolence, both physically and morally. One cannot pore over a book when the blue sky is constantly smiling in at the open

geographic relativist

windows; then, out of doors after ten o'clock, the sun gives us due warning of our tropical latitude, and even though the breeze is so fresh and pleasant, one has no inclination to walk or ride far. Whatever be the cause, I am convinced that it is impossible to take the same exercise with the mind or with the body in this country, as in Europe or in the northern states. Then as to schools, there are none that can deserve the name, and no governesses. Young girls can have no emulation, for they never meet. They have no public diversion, and no private amusement. There are a few good foreign masters, most of whom have come to Mexico for the purpose of making their fortune, by teaching, or marriage, or both, and whose object, naturally, is to make the most money in the shortest possible time, that they may return home and enjoy it. The children generally appear to have an extraordinary disposition for music and drawing, yet there are few girls who are proficient in either.

When very young, they occasionally attend the schools, where boys and girls learn to read in common, or any other accomplishment that the old women can teach them; but at twelve they are already considered too old to attend these promiscuous assemblages, and masters are got for drawing and music to finish their education. I asked a lady the other day if her daughter went to school. "Good heavens!" said she, quite shocked, "she is past eleven years old!" It frequently happens that the least well-informed girls are the children of the cleverest men, who, keeping to the customs of their forefathers, are content if they confess regularly, attend church constantly, and can embroider and sing a little. Where there are more extended ideas, it is chiefly amongst families who have travelled in Europe, and have seen the different education of women in foreign countries. Of these the fathers occasionally devote a short portion of their time to the instruction of their daughters, perhaps during their leisure evening moments, but it may easily be supposed that this desultory system has little real influence on the minds of the children. I do not think there are above half-a-dozen married women, or as many girls above fourteen, who, with the exception of the mass-book, read any one book through in the whole course of the year. They thus greatly simplify the system of education in the United States, where parties are frequently divided between the advocates for solid learning and those for superficial accomplishments; and according to whom it is difficult to amalgamate the solid beef of science with the sweet sauce of *les beaux arts*.

But if a Mexican girl is ignorant, she rarely shows it. They have generally the greatest possible tact; never by any chance wandering out of their depth, or betraying by word or sign that they are not well informed of the subject under discussion. Though seldom graceful, they are never awkward, and always self-possessed. They have plenty of natural talent, and where it has been thoroughly cultivated, no women can surpass them. Of what is called literary society, there is of course none—

> *No bustling Botherbys have they to show 'em*
> *That charming passage in the last new poem.*

There is a little annual lying beside me called *"Calendario de las Señoritas Mejicanas,"* of which the preface, by Galvan, the editor, is very amusing.

"To none," he says, "better than to Mexican ladies, can I dedicate this mark of attention—(*obsequio*). Their graceful attractions well deserve any trouble that may have been taken to please them. Their bodies are graceful as the palms of the desert; their hair black as ebony, or golden as the rays of the sun, gracefully waves over their delicate shoulders; their glances are like the peaceful light of the moon. The Mexican ladies are not so white as the Europeans, but their whiteness is more agreeable to our eyes. Their words are soft, leading our hearts by gentleness, in the same manner as in their moments of just indignation they appall and confound us. Who can resist the magic of their song, always sweet, always gentle, and always natural? Let us leave to foreign ladies (*las ultramarinas*) these affected and scientific manners of singing; here nature surpasses art, as happens in everything, notwithstanding the cavillings of the learned.

"And what shall I say of their souls? I shall say that in Europe the minds are more cultivated, but in Mexico the hearts are more amiable. Here they are not only sentimental, but tender; not only soft, but virtuous; the body of a child is not more sensitive (*no es mas sensible el cuerpo de un niño*), nor a rose-bud softer. I have seen souls as beautiful as the borders of the rainbow, and purer than the drops of dew. Their passions are seldom tempestuous, and even then they are kindled and extinguished easily; but generally they emit a peaceful light, like the morning star, Venus. Modesty is painted in their eyes, and modesty is the greatest and most irresistible fascination of their souls. In short, the Mexican ladies, by their manifold virtues, are destined to serve as our support whilst we travel through the sad desert of life.

"Well do these attractions merit that we should try to please them; and in effect a new form, new lustre, and new graces have been given to the 'Almanac of the Mexican Ladies,' whom the editor submissively entreats to receive with benevolence this small tribute due to their enchantments and their virtues!"

There are in Mexico a few families of the old school, people of high rank, but who mingle very little in society; who are little known to the generality of foreigners, and who keep their daughters entirely at home, that they may not be contaminated by bad example. These select few, rich without ostentation, are certainly doing everything that is in their power to remedy the evils occasioned by the want of proper schools, or of competent instructresses for their daughters. Being nearly all allied by birth, or connected by marriage, they form a sort of *clan*; and it is sufficient to belong to one or other of these families, to be hospitably received by all. They meet together frequently, without ceremony, and whatever elements of good exist in Mexico, are to be found amongst them. The fathers are generally men of talent and learning, and the mothers, women of the highest respectability, to whose name no suspicion can be attached.

But, indeed, it is long before a stranger even suspects the state of morals in this country, for whatever be the private conduct of individuals, the most perfect decorum prevails in outward behaviour. But indolence is the mother of vice, and not only to little children might Doctor [Isaac] Watts have asserted that

> *Satan finds some mischief still,*
> *For idle hands to do.*

They are besides extremely *leal* [loyal] to each other, and with proper *esprit de corps*, rarely gossip to strangers concerning the errors of their neighbours' ways;—indeed, if such a thing is hinted at, deny all knowledge of the fact. So long as outward decency is preserved, habit has rendered them entirely indifferent as to the *liaisons* subsisting amongst their particular friends; and as long as a woman attends church regularly, is a patroness of charitable institutions, and gives no scandal by her outward behaviour, she may do pretty much as she pleases. As for flirtations in public, they are unknown.

I must, however, confess that this indulgence on the part of women of unimpeachable reputation is sometimes carried too far. We went lately to a breakfast, at which was a young and beautiful countess, lately married, and of very low birth. She looked very splendid, with all the—diamonds, and a dress of rose-coloured satin. After breakfast we adjourned to another room, where I admired the beauty of a little child who was playing about on the floor, when this lady said, "Yes, she is very pretty—very like my little girl, who is just the same age." I was rather surprised, but concluded she had been a widow, and made the inquiry of an old French lady who was sitting near me. "Oh, no!" said she—"she was never married before; she alludes to the children she had before the count became acquainted with her!" And yet the Señora de —, the strictest woman in Mexico, was loading her with attentions and caresses. I must say, however, that this was a singular instance.

There are no women more affectionate in their manners than those of Mexico. In fact, a foreigner, especially if he be an Englishman, and a shy man, and accustomed to the coolness of his fair countrywomen, need only live a few years here, and understand the language, and become accustomed to the peculiar style of beauty, to find the Mexican Señoritas perfectly irresistible.

And that this is so, may be judged of by the many instances of Englishmen married to the women of this country, who *invariably* make them excellent wives. But when an Englishman marries here, he ought to settle here, for it is very rare that a *Mexicaine* can live out of her own country. They miss the climate—they miss that warmth of manner, that universal cordiality by which they are surrounded here. They miss the *laissez-aller* and absence of all etiquette in habits, toilet, etc. They find themselves surrounded by women so differently educated, as to be doubly strangers to them, strangers in feeling as well as in country. A very few instances there are of girls, married very young, taken to Europe, and introduced into good society, who have acquired European ways of thinking, and even prefer other countries to their own; but this is so rare, as scarcely to form an exception. They are true patriots, and the visible horizon bounds their wishes. In England especially, they are completely out of their element. A language nearly impossible for them to acquire, a religion which they consider heretical, outward coldness covering inward warmth, a perpetual war between sun and fog, etiquette carried to excess, an insupportable stiffness and

[margin, handwritten:] Mexicans cannot adapt in Europe

[bottom, handwritten:] Critique of Europe is the artificiality of Europe anonymous?

order in the article of the toilet; rebosos* unknown, *cigaritos* considered barbarous. . . . They feel like exiles from paradise, and live but in hopes of a speedy return.

October 8, 1841

In the midst of the revolution [which returned Santa Anna to power], we were amused by a very peaceful sight—all the nurses belonging to the *Cuna*, or Foundling hospital, coming from the different villages to receive their monthly wages. Amongst the many charitable institutions of Mexico, there appears to me (in spite of the many prejudices existing against such institutions) none more useful than this. These otherwise unfortunate children, the offspring of abject poverty or guilt, are left at the gate of the establishment, where they are received without any questions being asked; and from that moment, they are protected and cared for, by the best and noblest families in the country. The members of the society consist of the first persons in Mexico, male and female. The men furnish the money; the women give their time and attention. There is no fixed number of members, and amongst them are the ladies in whose house we now live. The *President* is the Dowager Marquesa de Vivanco. When the child has been about a month in the *Cuna*, it is sent, with an Indian nurse, to one of the villages near Mexico. If sick or feeble it remains in the house, under the more immediate inspection of the society. These nurses have a *fiadora*, a responsible person, who lives in the village, and answers for their good conduct. Each nurse is paid four dollars per month, a sufficient sum to induce any poor Indian, with a family, to add one to her stock. Each lady of the society has a certain number under her peculiar care, and gives their clothes, which are poor enough, but according to the *village fashion*. The child thus put out to nurse, is brought back to the *Cuna* when weaned, and remains under the charge of the society for life; but of the hundreds and tens of hundreds that have passed through their hands, scarcely has one been left to grow up in the *Cuna*. They are constantly adopted by respectable persons, who, according to their inclination or abilities, bring them up either as favoured servants, or as their own children; and the condition of a *"huerfano,"* an orphan, as a child from the hospital is always called, is perfectly upon a level with that of the

*Rebozo, a type of shawl—Ed.

most petted child of the house. The nurses in the *Cuna* are paid eight dollars per month.

Upwards of a hundred nurses and babies arrived on Sunday, taking up their station on the grass, under the shade of a large ash-tree in the courtyard. The nurses are invariably bronze; the babies generally dark, though there was a sprinkling of fair English or German faces amongst them, with blue eyes and blonde hair, apparently not the growth of Mexican land. Great attention to cleanliness cannot be hoped for from this class, but the babies looked healthy and contented. Each nurse had to present a paper which had been given her for that purpose, containing her own name, the name of the child, and that of the lady under whose particular charge she was. Such as—"*Maria Josefa*—baby *Juanita de los Santos*—belonging to the *Señora Doña Matilde F——*, given on such a day to the charge of Maria Josefa." Constantly the nurse had lost this paper, and impossible for her to remember more than her own name; as to who gave her the baby, or when she got it, was entirely beyond her powers of calculation. However, then stept forward the *fiadora* Doña Tomaso, a sensible-looking village dame, grave and important as became her situation, and gave an account of the nurse and the baby, which being satisfactory, the copper was swept into the nurse's lap, and she and her baby went away contented. It was pleasant to see the kindness of the ladies to these poor women; how they praised the care that had been taken of the babies; admired the strong and healthy ones, which indeed nearly all were; took an interest in those who looked paler, or less robust; and how fond and proud the nurses were of their charges; and how little of a hired, mercenary, *hospital* feeling existed among them all.

November 10, 1841

We went in the evening to visit the *Cuna*, which is not a fine building, but a large, healthy, airy house. At the door, where there are a porter and his wife, the babies are now given in. Formerly they were put in at the *reja*, at the window of the porter's lodge; but this had to be given up, in consequence of the tricks played by boys or idle persons, who put in dogs, cats, or dead animals. As we were going upstairs, we heard an old woman singing a cheerful ditty in an awfully cracked voice, and as we got a full view of her before she could see us, we saw a clean, old body sitting, sewing and

singing, while a baby rolling on the floor in a state of perfect ec-
stasy, was keeping up a sort of crowing duet with her. She seemed
delighted to see these ladies, who belong to the *Junta* [society],
and led us into a large hall where a score of nurses and babies were
performing a symphony of singing, hushing, crying, lullabying, and
other nursery music. All along the room were little green painted
beds, and both nurses and babies looked clean and healthy. The —
knew every baby and nurse and directress by name. Some of the
babies were remarkably pretty, and when we had admired them
sufficiently, we were taken into the next hall, occupied by little
girls of two, three, and four years old. They were all seated on little
mats at the foot of their small green beds; a regiment of the finest
and healthiest children possible; a directress in the room sewing.
At our entrance, they all jumped up simultaneously, and surrounded
us with the noisiest expressions of delight. One told me in a confi-
dential whisper that "Manuelita had thumped her own head, and
had a pain in it"; but I could not see that Manuelita seemed to be
suffering any acute agonies, for she made more noise than any of
them. One little girl sidled up to me, and said in a most insinuating
voice, *"Me llevas tu?"* "Will you take me away with you?"—for
even at this early age they begin to have a glimmering idea that
those whom the ladies choose from amongst them are peculiarly
favoured. We staid some time with them, and admired their healthy,
happy, and well-fed appearance; and then proceeded to the apartment of the boys; all little things of the same age, sitting ranged in
a row like senators in congress, and, strange to say, much quieter
and graver than the female babies; but this must have been from
shyness, for before we came away, we saw them romping in great
style. The directresses seem good respectable women, and kind to
the children, who, as I mentioned before, are almost all taken away
and brought up by rich people, before they have time to know that
there is anything peculiar or unfortunate in their situation. After
this adoption, they are completely on a level with the other children of the family—an equal portion is left them, and although their
condition is never made a secret of, they frequently marry as well
as their adopted brothers and sisters.

Those who are opposed to this institution, are so on the plea
that it encourages and facilitates vice. That the number of children
in the hospital is a proof that much vice and much poverty do exist,
there is no doubt; that by enabling the vicious to conceal their guilt,
or by relieving the poor from their burden, it encourages either vice

or idleness, is scarcely probable. But even were it so, the certain benefits are so immense, when laid in the balance with the possible evils, that they cannot be put in competition. The mother who leaves her child at the *Cuna*, would she not abandon it to a worse fate, if this institution did not exist? if she does so to conceal her disgrace is it not seen that a woman will stop at no cruelty, to obtain this end? as exposure of her infant, even murder? and that, strong as maternal love is, the dread of the world's scorn has conquered it? if poverty be the cause, surely the misery must be great indeed, which induces the poorest beggar or the most destitute of the Indian women (whose love for their children amounts to a passion) to part with her child; and though it is suspected that the mother who has left her infant at the *Cuna*, has occasionally got herself hired as a nurse, that she may have the pleasure of bringing it up, it seems to me that no great evil can arise, even from that.

These orphans are thus rescued from the contamination of vice, from poverty, perhaps from the depths of depravity; perhaps their very lives are saved, and great sin prevented. Hundreds of innocent children are thus placed under the care of the first and best ladies in the country, and brought up to be worthy members of society.

Another day we devoted to visiting a different and more painful scene—the *Acordada*, or public jail; a great solid building, spacious, and well ventilated. For this also there is a *Junta*, or society of ladies of the first families, who devote themselves to teaching the female malefactors. It is painful and almost startling to see the first ladies of Mexico familiarly conversing with and embracing women who have been guilty of the most atrocious crimes; especially of murdering their husbands; which is the chief crime of the female prisoners. There are no bad faces amongst them; and probably not one who has committed a premeditated crime. A moment of jealousy during intoxication, violent passions without any curb, suddenly aroused and as suddenly extinguished, have led to these frightful results. We were first shown into a large and tolerably clean apartment, where were the female prisoners who are kept apart as being of a more *decent family* than the rest. Some were lying on the floor, others working—some were well dressed, others dirty and slovenly. Few looked sad; most appeared careless and happy, and *none* seemed ashamed. Amongst them were some of the handsomest faces I have seen in Mexico. One good-looking common woman, with a most joyous and benevolent countenance, and lame, came up to salute the ladies. I inquired what she had done.

"Murdered her husband, and buried him under the brick floor!"
Shade of Lavater!* It is some comfort to hear that their husbands
were generally such brutes, they deserved little better! Amongst
others confined here is the wife, or rather the widow, of a governor
of Mexico, who made away with her husband. We did not see her,
and they say she generally keeps out of the way when strangers
come. One very pretty and coquettish little woman, with a most
intellectual face, and very superior-looking, being in fact a relation
of Count —'s, is in jail on suspicion of having poisoned her lover.
A beautiful young creature, extremely like Mrs. —, of Boston, was
among the prisoners. I did not hear what her crime was. We were
attended by a woman who has the title of *Presidenta*, and who,
after some years of good conduct, has now the charge of her fellow
prisoners—but she also murdered her husband! We went upstairs,
accompanied by various of these distinguished criminals, to a room
looking down upon the chapel, in which room the ladies give them
instruction in reading, and in the Christian doctrine. With the time
which they devote to these charitable offices, together with their
numerous devotional exercises, and the care which their houses and
families require, it cannot be said that the life of a Mexican señora
is an idle one; nor, in such cases, can it be considered a useless one.

We then descended to the lower regions, where, in a great, damp,
vaulted gallery, hundreds of unfortunate women of the lowest class,
were occupied in *travaux forcés* [forced labor]—not indeed of a
very hard description. These were employed in baking tortillas for
the prisoners. Dirty, ragged, and miserable-looking creatures there
were in these dismal vaults, which looked like purgatory, and smelt
like—Heaven knows what! But, as I have frequently had occasion
to observe in Mexico, the sense of smell is a doubtful blessing.
Another large hall near this, which the prisoners were employed in
cleaning and sweeping, has at least fresh air, opening on one side
into a court, where poor little children, the saddest sight there, were
running about—the children of the prisoners.

---

*Johann Kaspar Lavater (1741–1801), proponent of the pseudoscience of
physiognomy that facial features determine character traits—Ed.

4

FREDRIKA BREMER

A Swedish Novelist in the New World

Fredrika Bremer (1801–1865), once internationally famous as a novelist, is now chiefly remembered as a Swedish pioneer for women's rights. Born on August 17, 1801, in Åbo, Finland, the daughter of a Swedish ironmonger, she grew up on a country estate outside Stockholm. In those comfortable provincial, Protestant surroundings, she passed an unhappy childhood with a father reputed to be melancholy and distant and a mother said to be severe and strict. But the plain, shy young girl displayed her literary inclinations at an early age, writing poems when only eight years old. In 1820–21 she and her family undertook an extensive tour of Europe, which deepened her knowledge of European literature. After returning to Sweden, Bremer busied herself with charity work and published her first book, *Sketches of Everyday Life*, in 1828 to raise funds for those endeavors.

The death of Bremer's father in 1830 provided her with the economic means to pursue a literary career, and undertake various trips abroad. Her fiction would play an influential role in the development of the modern Swedish novel. In her "family novels" of the 1830s, which were accounts of upper-middle-class domestic life, she presented the real Sweden in simple, direct prose. Those novels were translated into English and other languages during her lifetime.

From Fredrika Bremer, *The Homes of the New World. Impressions of America*, 2 vols., trans. Mary Howitt (New York: Harper and Brothers, 1853), ii, 311–13, 325–28, 331–38, 343–44.

Bremer set off on a two-year tour of the United States in September 1849. She was well received in New England, admired not only for her writings but also for her outspoken anti-slavery sentiments. Although she claimed that her letters home were not originally intended for publication, she did edit and publish them in 1853 as *The Homes of the New World*. This two-volume report, her first travel book, appeared in print in the United States only months after its publication in Sweden, winning her great popularity in both countries. Far more controversial was her novel *Hertha,* which appeared in 1856 and won her a reputation as Sweden's first feminist. In addition to her fiction, Bremer also published travel accounts of her stays in England (1851), Switzerland and Italy (1860), and Greece (1863). She spent her later years working for women's rights and other reforms and died at home in Årsta, Sweden, on December 31, 1865.

During the latter part of her extensive tour of the United States from 1849 to 1851, Bremer spent four months in Cuba. Suffering from ill health, she sought the benefits of a change of climate by sailing south, as did many Americans of the period. The Cuba that Bremer visited in 1851 was still a Spanish possession, the largest one left in the Western Hemisphere. Cuba, like Puerto Rico, had not undergone the independence struggles of mainland Spanish colonies such as Mexico, which had secured independence by the early 1820s. But distance from Spain combined with proximity to the United States would help change Cuba's orientation in the nineteenth century. Cuba rested uneasily under the gaze of various interests in the United States, including the covetous eyes of pro-slavery expansionists from the southern states seeking new slave territories in the early 1850s. By the midnineteenth century, sugar production had become Cuba's dominant economic activity, and the United States its principal market. Sugar, the island's main export, depended on slave labor. Although England pressured Spain to end the slave trade with Africa, a vast clandestine trade supplied large numbers of new slaves for Cuban plantations until the 1860s. Cuba, and Brazil, would remain the major strongholds of slavery in the hemisphere, for slavery would not officially end in Cuba until 1886, two years before complete abolition came to Brazil.

While in Cuba, Bremer pursued her serious mission of investigating servitude, rather than just attending to her health. As a Swede, she stood outside the imperialistic framework enveloping many other foreign travelers. She never confined her observations to urban activities or pleasures, as did many other visitors. Nor did she dwell on pleasant rides in horse-drawn carriages through city streets. In fact, she persisted in walking rather than riding in those carriages, even though, as she noted, ladies did not do so. Bremer spent most of her time in Cuba on sugar plantations worked by slave labor and noted details of slaves' activities, housing, and diet, including their varied treatment on different plantations. In contrast to some other foreign visitors who expressed unflattering opinions about slave dances, a very visible aspect of black culture, Bremer viewed them as athletic and rhythmical, not lewd. However, Bremer, like other Northern European travelers to Latin America (who far outnumbered those from the Iberian Peninsula), came from a country where church-sanctioned unions predominated and where the illegitimacy rate was low, certainly as compared to Spain and Portugal or to the free populations of Latin America. She repeated generalizations concerning crowded slave living arrangements and temporary unions. But Bremer also sought out and found slaves living in stable, long-term, and loving unions. Her letters, with positive comments on slaves' behavior and appearances, provide much information on their activities and gender relations.

March 7, 1851

Ariadne Inhegno [in Limomar, near Matanzas], March 7th.

I have now been here for more than a week in the very lap of slavery, and during the first few days of my visit I was so depressed that I was not able to do much. Close before my window—the residence of the planter is a large one-storied house—I could not avoid seeing the whole day a group of negro women working under the whip, the cracking of which (in the air, however) above their heads, and the driver's (a negro) impatiently-repeated cry of *"Arrea! Arrea!"* be quick! get on! kept them working on without any intermission. And through the night—the whole night—I heard their

weary footsteps, as they spread out to dry upon the flagged pavement, outside my window, the crushed sugar-cane which they carried from the sugar-mill. In the daytime it is their work to rake up
together the sun-dried canes, *la bagaza*, and carry them in baskets
again to the sugar-mill, where they serve as fuel to heat the furnaces in which the sugar is boiled. The work on a sugar-plantation
must go on incessantly, night and day, during the whole time of the
sugar-harvest, which is, in Cuba, during the whole season called *la
Secca*, which is probably half the year. It is true that I frequently
heard the women chattering and laughing during their incessant
labor, untroubled by the cracking of the whip, and that during the
night I often heard African songs and merry shouts, but which—
sounding from the sugar-mill—lacked all melody and music. I know
also that the laborers on this plantation were changed every seven
hours, so that they always have six hours in every four-and-twenty
for rest and refreshment; and that during two nights in the week the
sugar-mill rests, and they are able to sleep; but still I could not
reconcile myself to it. Neither can I now, but I can bear it better,
since I have seen the cheerfulness of the slaves at their work, and
their good, pleasant, and even joyous appearance, as a general rule,
on this plantation.

   I have several times visited the Negro-Slaves' Bohea, which is
a kind of low fortress-like wall, built on the four sides of a large,
square court-yard, with a large gateway on one side, which is locked
at night. The slaves' dwellings are within the wall—one room for
each family—and open into the court. Nothing is to be seen on the
outside of the wall but a row of small openings, secured with iron
bars, one to each room, and so high in the wall that the slaves can
not look out from within. In the middle of the large court-yard is a
building which serves as a cooking-kitchen, wash-house, &c. I have
been present in this bohea more than once at the slaves' meal-times,
and seen them fetch their calabash bowls full of snow-white rice,
which had been boiled for them in an immense kettle, and which
the black cook dealt out with a ladle, and with what seemed to me
unreserved liberality. I have seen the slaves' white teeth shine out,
and heard them chattering and laughing as they devoured the white
rice grains, of which they are very fond (many times helping themselves to them with their fingers). They have, besides, salt fish and
smoked meat; I saw also, in some of their rooms, bunches of bananas and tomatoes. According to law, a planter must furnish each
slave with a certain measure of dried fish or salted meat per week,

together with a certain number of bananas. But the slave-master, of course, does just as he pleases, for what law will call him to account? The appearance, however, of the slaves on this plantation testifies evidently of their being well fed and well contented.

I often made the inquiry as I pointed to their food, *E buono?* And always received in reply the words *Si, e buono!* with a contended and ready smile. . . .

After the dance. There stands in the grass, at the back of the house, a large Otaheitan almond-tree, the leafy head of which casts a broad shadow. In the shade of this tree were assembled between forty and fifty negroes, men and women, all in clean attire, the men mostly in shirts or blouses, the women in long, plain dresses. I here saw representatives of the various African nations*—Congoes, Mandingoes, Luccomées, Caraballis, and others dancing in the African fashion. Each nation has some variations of its own, but the principal features of the dance are in all essentially the same. The dance always requires a man and a woman, and always represents a series of courtship and coquetry; during which the lover expresses his feelings, partly by tremor in all his joints, so that he seems ready to fall to pieces as he turns round and round his fair one, like the planet around its sun, and partly by wonderful leaps and evolutions, often enfolding the lady with both his arms, but without touching her; yet still, as I said, this mode varied with the various nations. One negro, a Caraballis, threw one arm tenderly round the neck of his little lady during the dance, while with the other he placed a small silver coin in her mouth. And the black driver, an ugly little fellow (he under whose whip I saw the women at work), availed himself frequently of his rank, sometimes by kissing, during the dance, the prettiest of the girls that he danced with, and sometimes by interrupting the dancing of another man with a handsome young negro girl, or with one of the best dancers, and then taking his place; for it is the custom that if any one of the bystanders can thrust a stick or a hat between two dancers, they are parted, and he can take the man's place. In this manner a woman will sometimes have to dance with three or four partners without leaving her place. Women, also, may exclude each other from the dance, generally by throwing a handkerchief between the dancers, when they take the place

---

*The term "nation" had long been used by the Spanish and Portuguese for autonomous peoples and was applied to African communities in nineteenth-century Latin America—Ed.

of the other who retires, such interruptions being generally taken in very good part, the one who retires smiling and seeming well pleased to rest a little, only again to come forward, and the man laughing still more heartily to see himself the object of choice with so many. The dancing of the women always expresses a kind of bashfulness, mingled with a desire to charm, while, with downcast eyes, she turns herself round upon one spot with an air and grace very much resembling a turkey-hen, and with a neckerchief or colored handkerchief in her hand, sometimes one in each hand, she half drives away from her the advancing lover and half entices him to her—a mode of dancing which, in its symbolic intention, would suit all nations and all classes of people, though—Heaven be praised—not all the beloved. The spectators stood in a ring around the dancers, one or two couples accompanying the dance with singing, which consisted of the lively but monotonous repetition of a few words which were given out by one person in the circle, who seemed to be a sort of *improvisatore*, and who had been chosen as leader of the song. Each time that a fresh couple entered the dance they were greeted by shrill cries, and the words and tune of the song were changed; but both tune and voices were devoid of melody. It is difficult to imagine that these voices would develop that beauty, that incomparable, melodious purity, and this people that musical talent which they have attained to in the slave states of America. The wild African apple-tree has, when transplanted into American soil, ennobled both its nature and its fruit. The words of the singer were, I was told, insignificant, nor could I get any clew to their purport. . . .

If either man or woman wish to choose a partner, they go out of the circle and place their handkerchief on the shoulder of the desired partner, or put a hat upon his or her head, or an ornament of some kind upon them; and I saw, on this occasion, one young negro woman whirling round with a man's hat on her head, and hung all over with handkerchiefs. It is also a common custom, but not of the most refined kind, to place a small silver coin in the mouth of the dancing lady at the close of the dance. The music consisted, besides the singing, of drums. Three drummers stood beside the tree-trunk beating with their hands, their fists, their thumbs, and drumsticks upon skin stretched over hollowed tree-stems. They made as much noise as possible, but always keeping time and tune most correctly.

It was a very warm day, and I saw that the linen of the quivering and grimacing gentlemen was in a state as if it had just been taken out of the sea. Yet not the less danced they, evidently from the pleasure of their hearts, and seemed as if they would continue to dance to eternity; but a loud crack of the whip was heard not far from the dancing-ground, and immediately the dancing ceased, and the dancers hastened away obediently to labor. Sugar-grinding and boiling must again begin.

The slaves of Cuba have no holiday during *la Secca*, although on Mr. C's plantation labor has a pause for two hours on Sunday morning.

How much more lively and full of intelligence was this dance under the almond-tree than the greater number of our dances in society, at least if we except the waltz. Our dances have not enough of natural life; this dance has perhaps too much; but it is full of animation and straightforwardness, and has this good quality belonging to it, that every one in company may take part in it, either singing, or dancing, or applauding. Nobody is excluded; there is no need for any body to stand against the walls, for any body to be dull or have *ennui*. Long live the African dance! . . .

Santa Amelia Ingenho, March 15, 1851

This plantation is much larger than the one I visited in Limonar, and a considerable portion of the slaves—two hundred in number—have lately been brought hither from Africa, and have a much wilder appearance than those I saw at Ariadne. They are worked also with much more severity, because here they are allowed only four and a half hours out of the four-and-twenty for rest; that is to say, for their meals and sleep, and that during six or seven months of the year! Through the remaining portion of the twelve months, the "dead season," as it is called, the slaves are allowed to sleep the whole night. It is true, nevertheless, that even now, upon this plantation, they have *one night* a week for sleep, and a few hours in the forenoon of each alternate Sunday for rest. It is extraordinary how any human beings can sustain existence under such circumstances; and yet I see here powerful negroes who have been on the plantations for twenty or thirty years. When the negroes have once become accustomed to the labor and the life of the plantation, it seems to agree with them; but during the first years, when they are brought here free and wild from Africa, it is very hard to them, and many seek to free themselves from slavery by suicide. This is frequently the case among the Luccomées, who appear to be among the noblest tribes of Africa, and it is not long since eleven Luccomées were found hanging from the branches of a guasima-tree—a tree which has long, horizontal branches. They had each one bound his breakfast in a girdle around him; for the African believes that such as die here immediately arise again to new life in their native land. Many female slaves, therefore, will lay upon the corpse of the self-murdered the kerchief, or the head-gear, which she most admires, in the belief that it will thus be conveyed to those who are dear to her in the mother-country, and will bear to them a salutation from her. The corpse of a suicide-slave has been seen covered with hundreds of such tokens.

I am told here that nothing but severity will answer in the treatment of slaves; that they always must know that the whip is over them; that they are an ungrateful people; that in the disturbances of 1846 it was the kindest masters who were first massacred with their whole families, while, on the other hand, the severe masters were carried off by their slaves into the woods, there to be concealed during the disturbances. I am told that, in order for a man to be loved by his slaves, he must be feared. I do not believe it; such is not human nature; but there is a difference between fear and fear. There is one fear which does not exclude love, and one which produces hatred and revolution.

The slaves have here, in a general way, a dark and brooding appearance. They go to their work in the sugar fields sleepy and weary. As they drive the oxen to and fro, I frequently see them sucking sugar-cane, which they are very fond of, and of which they seem allowed here to have as much as they like. This is, at all events, a refreshment. They are not fed here on rice, but principally upon a species of root called malanga [manioc], which, it is said, they like, but which seemed to me insipid. It is yellow, and something like the potato, but has a poor and somewhat bitter taste; each slave receives a portion of such root boiled for dinner, and eats it with his salt meat. They have for breakfast boiled maize, which they bruise and mix with wild tomatoes, the fruit of the plantain, or vegetables; for they are allowed a little land on the plantation where they may sow and reap for themselves, and besides this, each family has a pig, which they kill yearly and sell.

Sunday, March 17. It is the Sabbath, and forenoon; but the sugar-mill is still grinding, and the whip-lash sounds commanding labor. The slaves will continue to work the whole day as if it were a week-day. Next Sunday, they say, is the one on which the slaves will rest for some hours, and dance if they are inclined; but—they look so worn out!

There are in Cuba plantations where the slaves work twenty-one out of the four-and-twenty hours; plantations where there are only men who are driven like oxen to work, but with less mercy than oxen. The planter calculates that he is a gainer by so driving his slaves, that they may die within seven years, within which time he again supplies his plantation with fresh slaves, which are brought hither from Africa, and which he can purchase for two hundred dollars a head. The continuance of the slave-trade in Cuba keeps down the price of slaves. I have heard of "gangs" of male slaves, six hundred in each gang, who are treated as prisoners, and at night locked up in a jail; but this is on the plantation in the southern part of the island.

It is amid circumstances such as these that one may become enamored of the ideal communities of socialism, and when men such as Alcott* seem like the saviors and high-priests of the earth. How beautiful appear to me associated brotherhoods on the earth, with all their extravagance of love, when compared with a social state in which human powers are so awfully abused, and human rights trampled under foot! Here I feel myself more ardent than ever for those social doctrines which are laboring to advance themselves in the free states of America; and when I return thither, I shall endeavor to become better acquainted with them and their leaders, and to do more justice to both.

Yet even here I have derived some little comfort with regard to the condition of the slaves on this plantation, at least from the visit which I have paid to their bohea. This is a large, square, but low fortress-like wall, in which the slaves live as at Ariadne plantation, and in which they are secured by bolts and bars during the night. I have often visited them here during meal-times, and have always felt it a refreshment to witness their vigorous life and their cheerfulness; nevertheless, I have seen countenances here steeped in such

*Amos Bronson Alcott, U.S. educator and philospher, the father of Louisa May Alcott.

gloom, that not all the tropical sunshine would illumine, so hopeless, so bitter, so speechless were they—it was dreadful! The countenance of one young woman, in particular, I shall never forget!

I can not but often admire the Herculean frames among the men, the energetic countenances in which a savage power seems united to a manly good-heartedness, which last shows itself especially in their treatment of the children, and by the very manner in which they look at them. The little ones are not here familiar and merry as they are on the plantations in America; they do not stretch out their little hands for a friendly salutation; they look at the white man with suspicious glances—they are shy; but the very little Bambinos, which are quite naked, fat, and plump, as shiny as black, or black-brown silk, dance upon their mother's knees, generally with a blue or red string of beads around the loins, and another round the neck; they are the very prettiest little things one ever saw; and the mothers, with their strings of beads round their necks, their showy kerchiefs fastened, turban-wise, around the head, look very well too, especially when, with delighted glances, and shining, pearly teeth, they are laughing and dancing with their fat little ones. Such a young mother, with her child beneath a banana-tree, is a picture worthy of the pencil of a good painter.

I saw in those dark little rooms—very like those at Ariadne plantation—more than one slave occupied during the short time allowed him for rest in weaving little baskets and hats of palm-leaves, and one of them had constructed a fine head-dress of showy patches and cock's feathers!

In other respects the slaves live in the bohea very much like cattle. Men and women live together, and part again according to fancy or whim. If a couple, after having lived together for some time, grow weary of each other, the one will give the other some cause of displeasure, and then they separate. In case of any noisy quarrel, the majoral is at hand with his whip to establish peace.

"Are there here no couples who live constantly together as in proper marriage; no men and women who love one another sufficiently well to be faithful to each other as husband and wife?" inquired I from my young, candid conductor.

"Yes," replied he, "there are really such couples who have always remained together since they have been upon this plantation."

"Lead me to one of these couples," said I.

It was just dinner-time. My companion led me to one of the rooms in the wall. The door stood open, as is commonly the case, to admit light and air. The man was out; the woman sat alone in the room; she might be about fifty, and was busy at some work. She had a round face, without beauty, but with a good and peaceful expression.

I asked her, through my interpreter, whether she was fond of her husband?

She replied cheerfully and without hesitation, "Yes; he is a good husband."

I inquired whether she had been attached to him in Africa?

"Yes, in Africa," she replied.

I asked how long she had been united to her husband—how many years?

This question seemed to trouble or perplex her; she smiled, and replied at length that she had had him *always!*

Always! She did not know how vast and profound that word was on her lips. It went to my heart. Weeks, months, seasons, years, youth, strength, many changes had passed by unnoted, unobserved; hemisphere had been changed for hemisphere, freedom for slavery, the palm-tree hut for the bohea, a life of liberty for a life of labor— every thing had changed; but one thing had remained steadfast, one thing had remained the same—her love—her fidelity! She had *always* had him, the husband whom she loved—he had always had her. Of that which was variable and evanescent she knew not, made no account—she knew merely of time as regarded that which was eternal. She had had her husband *always;* she should have him always. That was evidently written in her calm countenance and in her calm voice. It could not be otherwise.

"Love requires to be sustained by duty!" said Geijer to me, on one occasion when he spoke of marriage. So it does; but it is beautiful to see that the natural marriage between two kindred souls can remain firm and strong merely through the law of love, amid the wild license of the bohea, and that in the case of two black people, two of the wild offspring of the desert!

Poets and philosophers have spoken of souls predestined for each other. Here I found two such. They had *always* belonged to each other. In the profound consciousness of God they had belonged to each other, and would belong to each other through all time— that is, in—eternity.

The man entered while I was still in the room. He seemed to be about the same age as the woman, and had the same good-hearted expression; but there was in his smile a sort of imprisoned sunshine, a cheerful beam of light, which, lit up from the heart itself, seemed as if it would gladly have free diffusion. I have often observed this imprisoned beam of light in the countenances of these children of bondage. They have brought it with them as an inheritance from their mother-country.

I went from this married pair to the prison cell, in which the slaves are placed after they have suffered punishment—women as well as men—and while the mind is still in a state of fermentation, after having endured bodily suffering. They are placed here in irons, made fast to a wooden frame, and here they sit, bound hands and feet—women as well as men—till their minds are again calm and their wounds healed, so that they can again go to their work. They are said to get fat while they remain here! The room was now empty, and inhabited merely by swarms of fleas.

I only wonder that suicide is not of more frequent occurrence among this people. How strong and tenacious the instinct of life must be!

[handwritten annotation: females writing makes them unique, unlike the men's words among paragraphs]

5

ADÈLE TOUSSAINT-SAMSON

A Parisian in a Slavocrat Society

In the middle of the nineteenth century, when Brazil was still an over-whelmingly rural, slave-holding nation, a high-spirited and enter-prising young Parisian and her husband (he born in Brazil of French parents) traveled from France to Brazil, where they would spend over ten years seeking to improve their family fortunes. Unlike some other foreign visitors, Adèle Toussaint-Samson (1826–c.1886), au-thor of *A Parisian in Brazil*, never became a well-known writer or personage.

The daughter of Joseph-Isidore Samson, renowned actor, teacher, and playwright, and the doyen of the Comédie Française for some two decades, Toussaint-Samson was raised in "the artistic centre of Paris." As she wrote, she was "accustomed to listen to the debating of all social, political, literary, and artistic questions in my father's drawing-room."* In the early 1850s, Adèle, her husband, and their baby boy sailed from France, drawn to Brazil by the pres-ence of an uncle living in Rio de Janeiro who had made his fortune there. The family not only experienced life in the capital but also spent time on plantations worked by slave labor. A second son was born in Brazil. After a dozen years they returned to Paris, where a daughter was born who would later produce the English-language translation of her mother's account of her Brazilian

From Adèle Toussaint-Samson, *A Parisian in Brazil*, trans. Emma Toussaint (Boston: James H. Earle, 1891), 26–29, 44–45, 59–61, 80–89, 104–8, 115–24.

*Adèle Toussaint-Samson, *A Parisian in Brazil*, trans. Emma Toussaint (Boston: James H. Earle, 1891), 134.

sojourn, *Une Parisienne au Brésil avec photographies originales*, published in Paris as well as in Rio de Janeiro in 1883. Earlier attempts by Toussaint-Samson to publish her sketches had met with rejection from Parisian printers who preferred foreign tales of tigers, serpents, and savages. But, when Brazil's Emperor Pedro II visited Paris in 1872, *Le Figaro*, which had previously purchased various articles by her, printed excerpts from her "souvenirs." Although the Brazilian colony in Paris found them unflattering, she maintained that her aim was to present Brazil and its people "correctly," not as "redskins with jewels on all fingers," as was commonly done, and to "have praised as well as blamed a nation congenial" to her, wielding "an impartial but friendly pen."*

The dozen years that Toussaint-Samson and her family spent in Brazil included much time in the countryside as well as in the cities, in contrast to the experience of the far better-known writer Maria Graham some three decades earlier. Yet travel still was unsafe and life far from easy. Toussaint-Samson endured not only the discomforts and dangers—particularly of shipwreck—of several voyages across the Atlantic but also attacks of yellow fever and encounters with poisonous snakes in Brazil.

A highly stratified society with an economy dependent on slave labor, Brazil appeared backward in the eyes of visiting Europeans. As in other parts of the New World, slavery in Brazil tended to flourish in those areas where plantations produced export crops. Some of the densest slave concentrations were found on the historic sugar coast of the northeast, in the province of Rio de Janeiro, and, later, in the coffee-producing province of São Paulo. Foreign visitors to Rio de Janeiro in the midnineteenth century compared the Brazilian capital to an African city, with over one-third of its population enslaved. After 1850 and the end of the slave trade from Africa, and then the steady increase in European immigration, the number and percentage of the enslaved among Rio's population would decline steadily until the final abolition of slavery in 1888.

Although all slaves remained "private property," individuals' specific situations and experiences differed greatly. Not just gender but race, occupation, and location also helped to determine

*Toussant-Samson, *A Parisian in Brazil*, 13–14.

many aspects of their lives. However, while some scholars stress slaves' resistance and adaptation, others emphasize their privations. Certainly, female slaves, unlike free women, might be forcibly separated from their children and even obliged to serve as wet nurses to their owners' offspring. Slave women remained subject to sexual violence and the advances of their masters. Yet some, particularly in the cities, still succeeded in constructing limited family or personal lives, even though ultimate control remained in their masters' hands. As we can see in the accounts of foreigners such as Toussaint-Samson, slave women in the cities sometimes enjoyed considerable personal freedom, going about (with their masters' permission) selling food they prepared or fruits and vegetables they raised. Their mistresses generally remained cloistered at home, shielded from the perceived vulgarities or dangers of the street. However, as in other countries, most Brazilian slaves worked in the fields, not as street sellers or domestic servants, and both men and women engaged in hard physical labor on the plantations.

Conscious of herself as a Parisian, not just a cultured Frenchwoman, Toussaint-Samson commented pointedly on gender relations among Brazilians as well as on the behavior of Brazilian males toward foreign females. However, she made no mention of the received opinion of the period in Brazil concerning the sexual availability of most Frenchwomen or the fact that many high-class prostitutes claimed to be French. Toussaint-Samson detailed her own dealings with Brazilians, from sequestered upper-class women to maltreated slaves. She even began her book with advice to foreign women facing the social snares of crossing the Atlantic alone at a time when few respectable women traveled without a male escort. Like some male foreign travelers, Toussaint-Samson portrayed upper-class Brazilian women as being treated like dolls by their husbands, but she also noted their ability to run large households. She appreciated the Brazilians' hospitality and openness and their country's sunshine and abundance of fruit. As a European woman of the midnineteenth century, Toussaint-Samson abhorred slavery and described its cruelties while also displaying her strong distaste for aspects of the slaves' appearance, behavior, and imputed morality. But her descriptions of slave life, especially her account of a visit to a plantation owned by a friend of her husband's

in the province of Rio de Janeiro, included detailed information rarely
provided either by Brazilians or foreign travelers on slaves' diet and
treatment.

Now, I think I must give you some advice, ladies: if ever you travel
alone, [across the ocean] be on [ship]board the most reserved possible; for there is no little provincial town, no janitor's closet even,
where there is as much gossip as there. If you have, for travelling
companions, English people, do not bow to them, above all, and do
not even notice them the first eight days. The Englishman wishes
to know whom he bows to, and gives himself the trouble of studying a little his people before risking the least politeness. Do you
think he is very much in the wrong? But from the moment he has
judged you worthy of his society, the Englishman becomes the most
amiable travelling companion, obliging without being gallant, pol-
ished without flattery, and always a perfect gentleman in his relations with women.

Unfortunately, it is not always so with our own [French] compatriots while travelling, who, in the majority, do not always show
themselves very proper, presently showing gallantry, bordering upon
silliness, to young and pretty women; by and by, rudeness, wellnigh
vulgarity, towards old or ugly women; they do not know whether
to compromise a woman, or turn her into ridicule. Mistrust, above
all things, ladies, the officers on deck. Nothing equals the conceit-
edness of these gentlemen; they must at each passage inscribe a
fresh conquest on their list. As the attentions, the welfare, the thousand details of material existence, depend upon them in some way
or other, there are no end of provocations and flirtations which the
lady passengers permit in their favor.

When, during one of these long voyages, there are on board
one or two ladies,—how shall we say?—frivolous? yes,—well, then,
it is a race between them which one shall carry it off, by captivat-
ing the captain, the first officer, the purser. In reality, to be in the
captain's good graces means to have the best place, the best cut, to
have the tent spread on the after-deck on calm and sunny days, to
have a comfortable easy-chair, to be authorized to keep light in
one's state-room; it is to obtain permission to have one's trunks
carried up at any time from between-decks, so as to be able to ex-
hibit each day a fresh toilet; it is, in short and above all, to surpass
all the other women. Judge of the efforts! the many killing glances
to get there!

[marginalia: in pretentious; vain, isolated → anonymiting → in hiding, in; undressed many times a day; anonymous as well]

There are generally on board three or four kinds of lady travellers, whom I have met with in all my travels. The first one is she whom I would call the *poseuse*. That one, on account of her rank or ① fortune, thinks herself *so* much above her fellow-travellers that she but rarely deigns to appear at table. Ordinarily, she is served in her state-room, occupies alone the best room, does not deign to exchange a few words but with the captain, has an air of not even seeing the other people, passes two or three hours at her toilet, and does not put in an appearance until nearly two o'clock, always accompanied by her lady's-maid, carrying her cloak or her vinaigrette.

The second one belongs to a certain class called—well, never mind. That one dresses two or three times a day, laughs and speaks ② very loud, is generally on the best of terms with the first officer and the purser, takes one day the airs of an *ingénue,* and the next day says things which would make a dragoon blush; passes her days stretched at full length on the settees on deck, with her hair to the wind, without losing an occasion of showing foot and limb; makes it uncomfortable for other women; sings operatic airs when night approaches; dances and waltzes Thursdays and Sundays; remains on deck until one o'clock in the morning with the officers and gentlemen of her choice; and defrays the voyage by a lot of episodes more or less piquant.

The third one of these lady travellers is the "earnest" one, or ③ the "*artiste,*" speaking with all, without becoming intimate with any; going on deck, when every one leaves it, to enjoy a beautiful sunrise or a fine moonlight; arranging her day so as to keep a few hours for study or solitude, attending to her correspondence, reading, embroidering; dressed simply, but gloved with care, and having well-fitting boots; never joining in gossip, neither seeking nor escaping the society of her fellow-travellers; not desiring to carry off any one's heart, remaining calm amidst all these littlenesses and all these vanities, incurring the respect of all, and frequently more surrounded at the end of the voyage than those who have tried to be so. It is in this class, ladies, that we advise you to place yourself if you ever happen to travel alone, which, we trust, you may not. . . .

The whole length of the street [Rua Direita, Rio de Janeiro's principal artery], on the steps of the churches, or at the doors of the shops, are squatted the large Minas negresses (the Minas originally came from the province of Mina, in occidental Africa), adorned in their most beautiful things: a fine chemise, and a skirt of white muslin with ruffles, worn over another skirt of some bright color, form all their costume; they have their feet bare in a sort of slipper with high heel, called *tamancas*, where only the point of the foot can enter; their neck and their arms are loaded with gold chains, strings of pearl, and all sorts of pieces of ivory and of teeth, short of manitous, which, according to them, must conjure evil fortune; a large piece of muslin is rolled three or four times around their head, turban shape, and another piece of striped cloth is thrown over their shoulders, to cover themselves with when they are cold, or to encircle their hips when they carry a child.

Many men find these negresses handsome; as for me, I acknowledge that the curled wool, which does duty for hair, their low and debased forehead, their blood-shot eyes, their enormous mouth with bestial lips, their disjointed teeth, like those of deer, as well as their flattened nose, had never appeared to me to constitute but a very ugly type. What is the least vulgar is their carriage. They walk with head held high, chest prominent, hips raised, arms akimbo, holding their load of fruits always placed on the head. Their feet and their hands are small, their waists are firm and curving, and their walk, of easy gait, is always accompanied by a movement of the hips quite suggestive, and yet filled with a certain dignity, like that of the Spanish woman. Their bosom is hardly veiled by their fine chemise, and sometimes even one breast is seen; but few among them have fine necks. It is only in the very young mulattresses that this beauty is sometimes found.

As regards the negresses, nothing has been exaggerated in saying that they easily nursed their children placed on their backs. I have seen it done by some of my servants, only that it is really not from the middle of the back that the child nurses, but from under the arm. There is nothing more debauched than these Minas negresses; they are the ones who deprave and corrupt the young people of Rio Janeiro; it is not rare to see foreigners, especially Englishmen, maintain them and ruin themselves for them. . . .

We had as a neighbor in Rosario Street [in Rio] in the upper story, a Spanish señora, who had at her service three or four slaves. Every day the most terrible scenes took place over our head. For the least omission, for the least fault of either of them, the señora would beat them or give them blows with the *palmatoria* (a sort of little palette pierced with holes), and we would hear these poor

Laundresses in Brazil, circa 1850. From James C. Fletcher and Daniel Parish Kidder, *Brazil and the Brazilians Portrayed in Historical and Descriptive Sketches*, 7th ed. (Boston: Little, Brown and Co., 1867), 102.

A Brazilian street vendor (*quitandeira*), circa 1850. From James C. Fletcher and Daniel
Parish Kidder, *Brazil and the Brazilians Portrayed in Historical and Descriptive Sketches*,
7th ed. (Boston: Little, Brown and Co., 1867), 167.

negresses throw themselves on their knees, in crying, "Mercy! señora!" But the pitiless mistress would never be touched, and gave without pity the number of blows she would consider necessary to be given. These scenes would give me great pain.

One day, when the blows of the *chicote* (whip) rained harder than ever, and when the screams were heard more heart-rending than usual, I arose all at once, and addressing myself to my husband, who, born in Brazil, of French parents, spoke Portuguese as his native language,—

"How do you say executioner?" I asked him.

"*Carasco*," he replied, without understanding why I set him this question. Immediately I rush to the stairs, which I mount in running. I open the door of the señora, flinging this one word at her, "*Carasco!*" This was my first word of Portuguese. That woman remained stupefied. Afterwards, hearing no noise whatever, I thought I had saved these unfortunate ones. Nothing of the kind: simply since that time she gagged them, so that their screams should no longer reach me. This was all that they had gained. This sight of slavery was, during the first years of my sojourn in Brazil, one of the torments of my life, and did not in a little contribute to give me homesickness, of which I expected to die. At every instant my heart revolted or bled when I passed before one of those *leitaös* [*leilões*] (auctions), where the poor negroes, standing upon a table, were put up at auction, and examined by their teeth and their legs, like horses or mules; when I saw the auction over, and that a young negress was being handed over to the *fazendeiro*,* who would reserve her for his "intimate" service, while her little child was sometimes sold to another master. Before all these scenes of barbarism my heart would rise up and generous anger would boil in me, and I was obliged to do me violence in not screaming to all these men who were making a traffic in human flesh, "*Carascos!*" as I had flung it at my Spanish neighbor. Scarcely had I succeeded in pacifying myself, than I would meet a few steps farther a poor negro wearing a mask of iron. This was still the fashion in which drunkenness was punished on the slave some twelve or fifteen years ago. Those who drank were condemned to wear a mask of iron, which was on the back of the head by means of a chain, and which was only removed during meals. One cannot imagine the impression caused by these men with iron heads. It was frightful; and think what a torment

*Plantation owner—Ed.

under this heat of the tropics! Those who had run away were fastened by one leg to a post; others carried around their neck a large iron collar, a kind of yoke, like that which is put upon oxen; others, in short, were sent to the *correccâo* (penitentiary), where, after they had been bound to a post, they would be lashed forty, fifty, or even sixty times. When the blood would flow they would stop, their wounds would be dressed with vinegar and the day following it would begin again. . . .

[On a Saturday evening on a plantation in the Province of Rio de Janeiro the plantation owner told his foreman,] "Call the negroes now for prayer."

We then all proceeded to the parlor, [a] room ordinarily placed in the middle of the house, lighted only by three large doors leading on to the veranda, which is in some way the real drawing-room of the hot countries.

The master rang a heavy bell, then called, in a formidable voice, "*Salta para a resa!*" (Hurry up for prayer.)

Night had almost come. Oxen and horses were sleeping in the meadows. Before the house, and all around it, ranged in a circle, were the *sauzales* (negro cabins), to the number of seventy about.

At the master's call, one saw rising up out of the dusk these sort of phantoms; each one came out of their cabin, a sort of hut made of clay and mud, with dried banana leaves for roofing, gloomy abode, where the water penetrates when it rains, where the wind blows from everywhere, and from where a most dreadful smoke arises at the hour when the negro gets his supper, for the cabin has neither chimney nor window, so that the fire is made with a fagot, oftentimes green, which is lighted in the centre of the cabin.

The negroes cross the meadow and ascend one by one the two flights of stairs to the veranda, where a sort of cupboard had been opened, forming an altar in one of the corners. Here it was that the miseries of slavery appeared to me in all their horror and hideousness. Negresses covered in rags, others half naked, having as covering only a handkerchief fastened behind their back and over their bosoms, which scarcely veiled their throats, and a calico skirt, through whose rents could be seen their poor, scraggy bodies; some negroes, with tawny or besotted looks, came and kneeled down on the marble slabs of the veranda. The majority carried on their shoulders the marks of scars which the lash had inflicted; several were affected with horrible maladies, such as elephantiasis, or leprosy.

All this was dirty, repulsive, hideous. Fear or hate, that is what could be read on all these faces, which I never have seen smile.

Four candles were lighted, and the two subordinate overseers placed themselves on the steps of the altar, where the Christ appeared, in the centre of four vases. These two negroes officiated after their own fashion; they had retained a smattering of Latin, which a chaplain, formerly at the plantation, had taught them, and then added their own most picturesquely, which served as a beginning to the litany of saints. After the *Kyrie eleison* they begin to sing in unison, *Santa Maria, mai de Deos, ora pro nobis!* Then all the saints in paradise followed, to whom they thought fit to add this, *Santa Pè de cana, ora pro nobis!* (Holy Foot, made of sugarcane, pray for us!) Finally their singing ended with this heart-rending cry, which they all gave, prostrating themselves, their faces on the ground, *Miserere nobis!* This cry touched me to the inmost recesses of my heart, and tears streamed silently from my eyes, while, after the devotions, the negroes filed past us one by one in asking our benediction, to which each white person must reply, "I bless thee." . . .

The following day scenes not less sad awaited me. Having been awakened at four o'clock in the morning by the great bell in the veranda, which the *feitor** was ringing for the rising up of the negroes, I wished to witness these proceedings, and jumped out of my bed.

Day was scarcely dawning in the horizon, a soft and melancholy color was enveloping the landscape. From the summit of the mountain, in the rear of the *fazenda,†* a beautiful cascade was unrolling its sheets of silvery water, and this mountain was covered with wild woods, where fruits and flowers interlaced each other in charming confusion.

From the other side, in front of the house, immense pastures could be seen, where more than a hundred head of cattle were collected. The oxen were still sleeping.

Some of the negroes began to come out of their cabins. If one of them was late in appearing, old Ventura‡ would shake his big whip in crying out, *"O Patife! puxa para fora!"* (O good-for-nothing, get out!)

---

*Negro foreman—Ed.
†Estate or plantation—Ed.
‡Ventura was the Negro foreman on this plantation—Ed.

Slaves picking coffee in Brazil, circa 1870. From Herbert E. Smith, *Brazil. The Amazons and the Coast* (New York: Charles Scribner's Sons, 1879), 517.

Then three gangs, each of about twenty-five negroes and negresses, were formed: one was under the direction of Ventura, and took the way to the *matto* (woods); the second proceeded to the plantations with one of the subordinate superintendents; and the third drove immense wagons with wheels of solid wood, yoked by four oxen, and was getting ready to cut the sugar-cane, which the wagons were to carry back. One of the little shepherds in his turn collected all the oxen, the second followed him with a flock of sheep; the field gates were opened, and all this human live stock started with the rest for work. . . .

At nine o'clock the bell would ring again; it was rung for the negroes' breakfast, and I had the curiosity to be present at the distribution of the rations. There are always two cooks at a plantation,—one for the whites and one for the blacks,—and there are even two kitchens. I repaired to the large smoky room which served for the darkies' kitchen, and there I saw two negresses having be-

fore them two immense caldrons, one of them containing *feijoes**
and the other *angú* (a dough made of manioca flour and boiling
water). Each slave soon arrived, gourd in hand. The cook would
pour in a large ladleful of *feijoes*, adding a little piece of *carne
secca*† of the poorest quality, as also a little manioca flour sprinkled
over all; the other one distributed the *augú* to the old men and children. The poor slaves would leave with this, murmuring in a low
tone that the meat was rotten, and that there was not enough.

Our dogs would certainly not have eaten such food. The little
darkies of three or four years, entirely naked, were returning with
their rations of *feijoes*, which their delicate stomachs could hardly
digest; also did they nearly all have large stomachs, enormous heads,
and lank arms and legs,—in short, all the signs of the rickets. It
caused pity to see them; and I never understood, from a speculative
stand-point even, that these merchants of human flesh did not take
better care of their merchandise. Happily I was assured that it was
not thus everywhere, and that in several plantations the slaves were
very well treated. I wish to believe it; for myself, I tell what I have
seen.

One day while I was out walking a little far out in the plantations, I was accosted by a very young negress who came to ask me
to intercede for her to her master, so that she might be freed of the
chain she was carrying. In saying this, she lifted up her coarse linen
skirt, and showed me a ring riveted around her ankle, to which was
attached a heavy chain carried from her waist. Here is the conversation I had with her, I immediately wrote down textually:—

"I am very willing," said I to the poor slave, "to ask your pardon, but what bad action have you committed to have deserved this
punishment? Did you steal?"

"No, senhora, I fled."

"And why did you flee?"

"Because the slave must flee from slavery always."

"And if your chain is taken from you, then you will flee again?"

"No; because I see that the white man is always stronger than
we are, and that I would again be caught and martyrized. This chain
breaks me down."

"Then you promise me that if I obtain your pardon, you will
never attempt to fly?"

*Beans (*feijões*)—Ed.
†Dried or salted meat—Ed.

"I promise it," replied the poor African woman, in a low tone.

"How old are you?"

"I do not know."

"What! more or less, you do not know how old you are?"

"No."

"Is it long since you were brought to Brazil?"

"Sugar-cane has been cut five times since then."

"Do you remember your country?"

"Always!" she replied, with a wild and passionate accent.

"You did not work in your native land?"

"No; when I had pounded the rice for the repasts, I danced and sang the rest of the day."

"Do you remember the dances of your country?"

"Do I remember them? Every night, after the superintendents sleep, we get up and dance our dances till morning."

"And if some one bought you, to give you your liberty, you would return to Africa?"

"Yes, if I can find the way, for one must cross much water to get there."

"Have hope, my child: you will have better days."

I came home that day feeling sad, and did not have much trouble in obtaining the pardon of the young negress; for a Brazilian never refuses a pardon asked for a slave, especially if it is asked by a woman, and that woman happens to be the *madrinha* (godmother) of one of his children; the title of godfather and godmother being nearly a tie of relationship in Brazil. Also, when I took leave to make a year's travel in France, Senhor P—, who accompanied us to the steamer, asked me what he could do to make himself agreeable to his *comadre*.*

"Not to beat your slaves any more," I answered him.

He promised it to me, and during a year religiously kept his promise; only he begged me, upon my return, never to ask him such a thing again, because his slaves would be lost forevermore. . . .

[On another plantation] I had noticed, the evening before, a young woman, white, or rather yellow, with large eyes darkly circled, badly combed hair, who walked barefooted, dressed in a miserable skirt, and a child at one hand; another in arms, and I had

---

*Co-mother, or godmother as viewed by the godchild's parents—Ed.

suspected that it might well be the wife of the [white] *administrador*, who, however, had himself fine linen, a proper suit of clothes, and a certain varnish of books and science.

I had communicated my suspicions to my husband, who, like all the husbands in the world, did not give it credence, and had even plagued me of that mania all women have, of seeing romances and dramas in everything.

Well, before leaving I wished to have a clear conscience about it. I asked for some bowls of milk, and it was this woman, accompanied by the two children, who served them to us. I resolved thereupon to satisfy my curiosity; and while my children were eating and our horses were being saddled, noticing on her face the traces of great suffering, "You seem sad, madam," I said to her.

"I am very unhappy, senhora," she replied.

"Are you not the wife of the *administrador?*"

"To my sorrow."

"How?"

"He treats me badly. Those are his mulattresses," she continued, in pointing towards one, "who are the real senhoras of the plantation; for them my husband overwhelms me with outrages."

"How can you live with him? Leave him."

She looked at me in utter astonishment.

"Leave my husband?" she uttered. "And by what should I live?"

"You will work."

"I do not know how to earn money; and my children?"

"The father will be obliged to bring them up; but you can leave them no longer with such a sight under their eyes: a mother cannot allow herself to be outraged before her children. If they are to respect you, make yourself respected."

The poor woman listened to me with all ears, trying to understand, and opening wide her large eyes.

"That's all very well for you Frenchwomen, who know how to earn your bread," she finally said; "but we, to whom nothing has been taught, we are obliged to be the servants of our husbands."

"Well, do what you like; but when you will have suffered enough, and find yourself at the end of your strength, remember the Frenchwoman who passed a night at the plantation, and come to her: she will give you the means of living by your work. Here is my address."

Thereupon I jumped into the saddle. The wife of the superintendent thanked me by look, and accompanied me to the gate of the plantation; she remained there, looking after me fixedly as long as she could see something of me.

I could well see that I had enlightened this soul, and opened new longings before her.

Daybreak was appearing and began to lighten a little the dark foliage of the woods; nature awakened, still enveloped in the mist, and the dew was sprinkled over the ground. The *senhor administrador* came to give us his adieus, in wishing us God-speed. I involuntarily looked back. After what I knew, he gave me the horrors.

When we arrived on the borders of the *fazenda*, we found the mulattresses of the day before looking haughty and cynical, who wished to see in broad daylight the French lady and her husband.

They gave me, for a last adieu, a look full of hate, yet bowing all the same when I passed; and I, from my side, acknowledged it by an easy bow, into which I put all the disdain and disgust which they inspired.

Then, taking a little gallop, we started towards the São Jozé plantation, at which we arrived two hours later.

Three months later, my door-bell rang. It was the Senhora Maria, the wife of the *administrador*, who came, with one of her children on her arm, asking me to fulfil the promise I had made her; so I took her into my home as house-keeper, to overlook the negro servants, and to take charge of the household linen.

To say that in the end she repaid me with the most profound ingratitude teaches nothing new to my readers. What matters it? My end had been gained: I had developed in her soul the sentiment of human dignity, and had taught her how to earn her daily bread; I had raised her up morally, and cured her physically. The Senhora Maria has never been able to forget me, this I am sure of. . . .

Don't want to be forgetable

As the Brazilian ladies [in Rio de Janeiro] never went out alone in the streets at this epoch, one would meet only in the city the French ladies or English ladies, who, by the very fact of going out alone, would see themselves exposed to many adventures. Therefore the French ladies, were they married or not, could not step outside without seeing themselves assailed with compliments, ogled, and with *billets-doux*, in a style as cavalierly about as this: "Madam, I love you. Can you receive me at your house this evening?" Not more ceremony than this.

These gentlemen thought they had only to present themselves, and that, as the French ladies smiled pleasantly and conversed as

How does this relate to a society w/o memory?

easily with men as with women, their conquest was of the easiest. Happily more than one received of our fair compatriots some good lessons.

Some wagers were taken in the city in regard to a French lady, and it was the doctor with the skeleton . . . who, sceptic in the highest degree, wagered for the ruin of our fair compatriot.

Immediately a handsome officer, very much smitten with the lady, began the campaign, showering upon her bouquets and *billets-doux*, through the intermediary of the blacks, whom he bribed, while another one, a not less charming cavalier, followed our "Parisienne" everywhere, and passed whole nights under her window. Lost labors! The lady mercilessly shut doors and windows in their faces, and returned their love-letters without answers. They, all abashed, returned each day to the doctor, telling their ill-success, who would tell them, "Do not lose courage, it is only a question of time."

However, at the end of two years, seeing their walks and labors at their own loss, they summoned the doctor to pay the wager he had lost; which did not prevent our Brazilian from repeating that he did not believe in the virtue of any woman in general, and the French ladies in particular.

It was not until long afterwards that our fair compatriot learned that she had been the subject of a wager, and doubly congratulated herself in having put these fops in their places.

I admit, as for me, that nothing has ever amused me so much as to see these Brazilians, so sure of their conquest, laughed at by our French ladies, who, as you know, in point of mockery or coquetry, can teach lessons to all the nations of the earth.

By means of little lessons of this kind the Americans of the South have at last understood that there are women who, because they go alone on foot, under a scorching sun, earning their living in teaching, are but the more honorable, and they begin by no longer saying, with that air of profound disdain, "It is a madame!" because more than one madame has taught them how to behave.

As for the Brazilian ladies, penned up as they are by their husbands in the enclosure of their houses, in the midst of their children and their slaves; never going out unaccompanied to either mass or processions, one must not imagine, on that account, that they are more virtuous than others, only they have the art of appearing so.

Everything is done mysteriously in these impenetrable abodes, where the lash has made the slave as silent as the tomb. Under the

[handwritten margin notes: "Defined by family?" / "go out alone" / "Brazilians never go out alone"]

Wealthy urban family in Brazil going to Mass, circa 1850. From James C. Fletcher and
Daniel Parish Kidder, *Brazil and the Brazilians Portrayed in Historical and Descriptive
Sketches*, 7th ed. (Boston: Little, Brown and Co., 1867), 165.

cloak of the family even, many things are hidden. All this *is*, or at
least *was* (for since several years the Brazilian ladies go out alone),
—all this is the fruit of the sequestration imposed upon women.
Besides, the appearances are so well guarded that one must live
years in the land to begin to know the inner life of these homes, of
such patriarchal customs and habits, at first sight, where frequently
three generations live together under the same roof in the most perfect concord; for one must say, in this regard, that the Brazilians
are much our superiors. They have found the secret of uniting in
the same house son-in-law, mother-in-law, daughter-in-law, without there ever being conflict. That ferocious hatred for the mother-
in-law, which is at present professed in France, is unknown over
there. One does not believe that, by the simple fact of marrying her
daughter or her son, a mother who has been good and devoted all
her life can suddenly become a monster. One has the greatest respect for the father and the mother.

When the Brazilian comes home he finds in his house a dutiful
wife, whom he treats as a spoilt child, bringing her desserts, jewels, and ornaments of all kinds; but this woman is not associated to

him, neither in his business, his preoccupations, nor his thoughts. It is a doll whom he dresses for an occasion, and who, in reality, is but the first slave of the house; although the Brazilian of Rio Janeiro is never brutal, and exercises his despotism in a manner almost gentle. All this besides, as I have already said, is undergoing complete changes.

The Brazilian ladies of to-day, educated in French or English boarding schools, have little by little taken our habits and our manners of seeing; so that very gradually they acquire their liberty. Then, as their intelligence is very quick, I think that in a short time they will have surpassed their teachers.

It is in the interior of the country, whose roads are impassable but on donkey-back, and which render communication with the capital very difficult, that one can still study all these customs of Portuguese or Spanish origin. Likewise, when you arrive in a *fazenda*, do you never perceive the senhora, while she always has the means of seeing the stranger without their ever being aware of it. The *mascatoes* [mascates] (pedlers) have alone the privilege of being introduced near the lady of the house, and it is one of the grand events at the *fazenda* when the *mascato* comes. One must see him open his boxes and spread out before the *dona da casa* (lady of the house) and her slaves the pieces of *chita* (printed calico), of *cassa* (muslin), of *cambraia* (cambric), the *fitas* (ribbons) of all colors, the *joias* (jewelry) of all makes. Mulattresses and negresses stand there with staring eyes and open mouth, wishing to buy all, with a *pataca* (sixteen cents) as their sole fortune, and always ending with the purchase of a simple kerchief.

The *mascato* is petted in secret by the negresses of the *fazenda*, who do not treat him cruelly, for little, if he wishes; but he is badly treated enough by the master of the house, who knows him to be a thief generally, and takes care to have the silver guarded when he sees him appear. However, he is given, like everybody, the hospitality of the night in the guest chamber, room opening on the veranda of the house and not differently connected with any other apartments.

When you come to ask for hospitality, this room is always open to you, and a negress comes and brings you your bath, which every Brazilian is accustomed to take before going to bed, the same as the *feijoada** or the rice for your supper. When the traveller is of a

*A dish made of black beans cooked with pieces of various meats—Ed.

certain class, the *fazendeiro* even has the kindness of sending his bath to him by the handsomest slave of the house.

The Brazilian is very hospitable; his table is open to all. I know of one who has his office in town, where he receives all who wish to come and dine with him, which makes that his man cook prepares a dinner for twenty or thirty persons daily. In our countries this seems princely. At Rio Janeiro it is not even noticed. Likewise, the stinginess of our habits and our boards greatly surprise the South Americans when they come to France.

One of the opinions most generally accredited to the Brazilian lady is that she is lazy and remains unoccupied all day. One is mistaken: the Brazilian lady does nothing herself, but has others do it; she takes great pride in never being seen in any occupation whatever. However, when one is admitted into her intimacy, one finds her in the morning, her bare feet in *tamancas*, a dressing-gown of muslin for dress, presiding at the making of *doces* (preserves of all sorts), of the *cocada* (cocoa jelly), and arranging them on the *taboleiro* (large wooden platter) of her negresses or negroes, who soon leave to sell in the city the *doces*, the fruits, the vegetables of the plantation.

They gone, the senhoras prepare the sewing for the mulattresses; for nearly all the clothes of the children, of the master and mistress are cut and sewn at home. Then there are also napkins and handkerchiefs made in *crivo* point, which are sent to be sold, like the rest. Each one of the slaves, called *ganho*, must bring back to his mistress a certain designated sum at the end of each day, and many are beaten when they return without this sum. This is what constitutes the pocket money of the Brazilian ladies, and allows them to satisfy their whims.

They receive from France fashion plates, which they try to copy; but the majority have their dresses made by the great French dressmakers, where the least expensive ball dress costs from fifteen to eighteen hundred francs.

As I was saying a little while ago, a Brazilian lady would blush to be caught in any occupation whatever, for they profess the greatest disdain for all who work. The pride of the South American is extreme. Everybody wants to be a master, no one wishes to serve. One admits, in Brazil, of no other profession but that of physician, lawyer, or wholesale merchant.

A Brazilian or Brazilian lady must never be surprised at anything whatever. When I would return from France with toilets of the latest fashion, I noticed the ladies looked at me secretly, by stealth, so as to study without appearing to do so the cut of my clothes, which not one of them would have acknowledged seeing for the first time. Should one have spoken to them about it, they would all have replied, unquestionably, "It is quite a long time since we wear that here."

One cannot say that the Brazilian ladies are beautiful, although, in general, they have beautiful eyes and splendid hair. There are certainly some very pretty ones; but the majority are either too thin or too stout, and what they lack above all is charm. They dress badly, generally ignoring elegant undress, and those thousand little nothings which make the Parisienne so bewitching. The expression of their faces is haughty and disdainful. They think by this that they give themselves the correct air, ignoring that, on the contrary, the true great ladies are simple, affable, and of the most exquisite politeness. They are willingly insolent enough, if one does not take the master hand over them. Money is the only superiority which they acknowledge; likewise, the most eminent artist is little thought of if he has not a cent. One should see the manner in which the natives say, in speaking of some one who is not rich, "*Coitadinho dèellel Coitado!*" It is untranslatable. It means, poor unfortunate! But it is full of a compassion mixed with disdain, which we cannot render in French.

6

ELIZABETH AGASSIZ BOSTON

A Naturalist's Wife and Educator in Brazil

Elizabeth Cabot Cary Agassiz (1822–1907), the first president of Radcliffe College, was born in Boston on December 5, 1822. Both her parents, Thomas Graves Cary and Mary Ann Cushing Perkins Cary, came from old, distinguished Massachusetts families. A bright, enthusiastic girl, educated at home due to her delicate health, Lizzie, as she was called, easily entered upper-class Boston society. Through her older sister's marriage to a Harvard professor, she joined a circle of intellectuals in Cambridge. There she met Louis Agassiz, a renowned Swiss naturalist and widower, who had done his early scientific work as an ichthyologist on Brazilian materials. The two were married in 1850. Elizabeth Agassiz handled family finances, mothered the three children of his first marriage, and, through the notes she took of her husband's public lectures, provided much of the material for his publications. Theirs was a close marriage, and she generally accompanied him on trips, including the 1865–66 scientific expedition that gave rise to *A Journey in Brazil*.

In April 1865, Louis and Elizabeth Agassiz set sail for Brazil, accompanied by a staff of some dozen men, including several unpaid student assistants. One of these was William James, later to become one of America's leading psychologists and philosophers and the major exponent of pragmatism. On shipboard, Professor Agassiz lectured the students on scientific matters while Elizabeth Agassiz

From Louis and Elizabeth Agassiz, *A Journey in Brazil* (Boston: Ticknor and Fields, 1867), 82–85, 173–78, 268–70, 478–82, 502–3.

studied Portuguese. Since this was a collecting expedition to be spent gathering zoological specimens for the museum in Cambridge, the Agassizes spent much of their time in the Amazon, as well as visiting the capital city of Rio de Janeiro at the start and end of the voyage. In Rio, where they were well received by the imperial family, Elizabeth Agassiz's determination to attend public lectures delivered by her husband led to the opening of the lectures to women by the Emperor Pedro II, who sanctioned the growing female presence by bringing his wife and daughter. During the Agassizes' Brazilian travels, Elizabeth demonstrated abundant good humor, curiosity, and resourcefulness, sleeping in hammocks in Indian homes in the Amazon (although not identifying the Indians by tribe), battling mosquitos, and even performing a waltz with a companion when the Indians whom they had persuaded to demonstrate their dances asked to see her country's dance. She served as the expedition's scribe, recording her husband's lectures and observations and keeping the journal that served as the basis for *A Journey in Brazil* by "Professor and Mrs. Louis Agassiz." The book, which dealt more with people and places than with fish and animals, was published in 1867 and sold well in the United States, going through a number of editions.

Louis Agassiz's fame continued to grow, and Elizabeth accompanied him on other expeditions, aiding him in his work. After his death in 1873, she prepared *Louis Agassiz: His Life and Correspondence*, published in 1885 to contemporary acclaim. She also became involved in a new program of higher education for women taught by Harvard faculty, the "Harvard Annex," which began classes in 1879. In 1882 it became a corporation, with Elizabeth as president. Her duties included fund-raising and delicate negotiations with Harvard officials. In 1893 the Harvard Corporation agreed to an institutional link, and she remained president of what is now called Radcliffe College until her retirement in 1903. Elizabeth suffered a cerebral hemorrhage in 1904 and died three years later.

Elizabeth Agassiz's lifelong concern for women's education together with her interest in intellectual life are reflected in *A Journey in Brazil*. At the time of the Agassizes' visit, formal education in that country was largely limited to those entitled to its benefits by birth or position. But far fewer women than men, no matter what their class, received any schooling. According to the census of 1872, only 19.8 percent of Brazil's men and 11.5 percent of its women could read and write.* In 1873 the country contained only 5,077 schools, public and private. These schools had a total of 114,014 male and 46,246 female pupils, while Brazil's population exceeded ten million people.† By then, the idea of schooling for girls had been added to the older idea of domestic education, but it was not identical to that given to boys. Rich girls could study French, piano, and dancing so as to provide more charming and agreeable company on social occasions, just as they had learned to prepare cakes and sweets and to sew, embroider, and make lace. Women were still taught only what they were expected to need for functioning in society. Those relatively few schools found in nineteenth-century Brazil emphasized activities that would complement women's roles as wives and mothers. Although several male foreign visitors also noted the restrictions placed on female education, unlike Elizabeth Agassiz they never experienced those restrictions personally. She not only described the limitations of Brazilian women's education but also recounted the condescending treatment she herself endured when a plantation owner tried to restrict her own reading material. When she contrasted the lives of Indian women in the Amazon with the lives of town dwellers, those of the Indians appeared more free.

As Elizabeth noted in a letter to her mother written from the Amazon city of Manaus, "A woman is exposed to every sort of scrutiny and scandal who goes out unattended, and her only safety is to stay at home. I believe I am loooked upon as a very extraordinary specimen; but everything is forgiven to a stranger, so I go on my way unmolested." She found the Indian women's life "a thousand times pleasanter than the ladies' life," placing the blame for upper-class women's constricted existence on Brazilian men. However, she also recounted receiving a parting gift from half a dozen

*Brazil, Directoria Geral de Estatística, *Recenseamento da população do Império do Brasil o que se procedeu no dia 1 de agosto de 1872.* Município Neutro, 21:102.

†Rui Barbosa, *Reforma do ensino primario e varias instituições complimentares da instrução pública,* vol. 10, book 1 of *Obras completas de Rui Barbosa* (Rio de Janeiro: Ministério da Educãcao e Saude, 1947), 9–11.

women in Manaus whom she did not know particularly well. Their accompanying letter demonstrated that "there are some women here who are conscious of the injustice done them and that their feeling for me is rather because I am, as it were, an exponent to them of a freer kind of life than any they have ever known."*

Rio de Janeiro

May 25th, [1865].—The fish-market is, in all seaport towns, a favorite haunt with Mr. Agassiz, and here it has an especial interest for him on account of the variety and beauty of the fishes brought in every morning. I sometimes accompany him in these rambles for the pleasure of seeing the fresh loads of oranges, flowers, and vegetables, and of watching the picturesque negro groups selling their wares or sitting about in knots to gossip. We have already learned that the fine-looking athletic negroes of a nobler type, at least physically, than any we see in the States, are the so-called Mina negroes, from the province of Mina, in Western Africa. They are a very powerful-looking race, and the women especially are finely made and have quite a dignified presence. I am never tired of watching them in the street and market, where they are to be seen in numbers, being more commonly employed as venders of fruit and vegetables than as house-servants. It is said that a certain wild and independent element in their character makes them unfit for domestic service. The women always wear a high muslin turban, and a long, bright-colored shawl, either crossed on the breast and thrown carelessly over the shoulder, or, if the day be chilly, drawn closely around them, their arms hidden in its folds. The amount of expression they throw into the use of this shawl is quite amazing. I watched a tall, superbly made woman in the street to-day who was in a great passion. Gesticulating violently, she flung her shawl wide, throwing out both arms, then, drawing it suddenly in, folded it about her, and stretched herself to her full height; presently opening it once more, she shook her fist in the face of her opponent, and then, casting one end of her long drapery over her shoulder, stalked away with the air of a tragedy queen. It serves as a cradle also, for, tying it loosely round their hips, they slip the

---

*Elizabeth Agassiz to Mrs. Thomas G. Cary, Manaus, November 18 and December 11, 1865, in Lucy Allen Paton, *Elizabeth Cary Agassiz. A Biography* (Boston: Houghton Mifflin, 1919), 90–91.

baby into the folds behind, and there it hangs, rocked to sleep by the mother's movement as she walks on with her long, swinging tread. The Mina negress is almost invariably remarkable for her beautiful hand and arm. She seems to be conscious of this, and usually wears close-fitting bracelets at the wrist, made of some bright-colored beads, which set off the form of the hand and are exceedingly becoming on her dark, shining skin. The negroes are

Mina African woman, circa 1865. From Elizabeth and Louis Agassiz, *A Journey in Brazil* (Boston: Ticknor and Fields, 1867), 83.

Mohammedans, and are said to remain faithful to their prophet, though surrounded by the observances of the Catholic Church. They do not seem to me so affable and responsive as the Congo negroes, but are, on the contrary, rather haughty. One morning I came upon a cluster of them in the market breakfasting after their work was done, and I stopped to talk with them, asking what they had for breakfast, and trying various subjects on which to open an acquaintance. But they looked at me coldly and suspiciously, barely answering my questions, and were evidently relieved when I walked away.

[At an Indian village beyond Manaus]

August 29th.—Finding yesterday that our shelter grew more uncomfortable as the day wore on, and being obliged to wait for the night fishing, we determined to cross the lake to a "Sitio" (as the inhabitants call their plantations) on the other side of the lake. Here we found one of the better specimens of Indian houses. On one side of the house is the open porch, quite gay at this moment with our brightly colored hammocks; adjoining this is a large chamber, opening into the porch by a wide straw, or rather palm-leaf door; which does not swing on hinges, however, but is taken down and put up like a mat. On the other side of the room is an unglazed window, closed at will in the same way by a palm-leaf mat. For the present this chamber is given up to my use. On the other side of the porch is another veranda-like room, also open at the sides, and apparently the working-room of the family; for here is the great round oven, built of mud, where the farinha* is dried, and the baskets of mandioca-root are standing ready to be picked and grated, and here also is the rough log table where we take our meals. Everything has an air of decency and cleanliness; the mud-floors are swept, the ground about the house is tidy and free from rubbish, the little plantation around it of cacáo and mandioca, with here and there a coffee-shrub, is in nice order. The house stands on a slightly rising ground, sloping gently upward from the lake, and just below, under some trees on the shore, are moored the Indians' "Montaria"† and our two canoes. We were received with the most cordial friendliness, the Indian women gathering about me and examining, though

*Manioc meal—Ed.
†An Indian boat—Ed.

not in a rough or rude way, my dress, the net on my hair, touching my rings and watch-chain, and evidently discussing the "branca"* between themselves. In the evening, after dinner, I walked up and down outside the house, enjoying the picturesqueness of the scene. The husband had just come in from the lake, and the fire on the ground, over which the fresh fish was broiling for the supper of the family, shone on the figures of the women and children as they moved about, and shed its glow under the thatched roof of the working-room, making its interior warm and ruddy; a lantern in the corner of the porch threw a dim, uncertain light over hammocks and half-recumbent figures, and without, the moon shone over lake and forest. The mosquitoes, however, presently began to disturb the romance of the scene, and, as we were all rather tired from our broken rest the night before, we retired early. My own sleep, under an excellent mosquito-net, was very quiet and refreshing, but there were some of the party who had not provided themselves with this indispensable accompaniment of a hammock, and they passed the night in misery, affording a repast to the voracious hordes buzzing about them. I was awakened shortly after daylight by the Indian women, bringing me a bouquet of roses and jessamine from the vines which grew about the cottage, and wishing me good morning. After such a kindly greeting, I could not refuse them the pleasure of assisting at my toilet, of watching the opening of my valise, and handling every article as it came out.

The night fishing was unfavorable, but this morning the fishermen have brought in new species enough to keep Mr. Agassiz and his artist busy for many hours, so that we are likely to pass another night among these hospitable people. I must say that the primitive life of the better class of Indians on the Amazons is much more attractive than the so-called civilized life in the white settlements. Anything more bald, dreary, and uninviting than life in the Amazonian towns, with an attempt at the conventionalisms of civilization, but without one of its graces, I can hardly conceive. This morning my Indian friends have been showing me the various processes to which the Mandioca is subjected. This plant is invaluable to these people. It gives them their farinha,—a coarse kind of flour, their only substitute for bread,—their tapioca, and also a kind of fermented juice called tucupí,—a more questionable blessing, perhaps, since it affords them the means of getting intoxicated. After

*Literally, "white"—Ed.

being peeled, the roots of the mandioca are scraped on a very coarse grater; in this condition they make a moist kind of paste, which is then packed in elastic straw tubes, made of the fibres of the Jacitará Palm (Desmonchus). When her tube, which has always a loop at either end, is full, the Indian woman hangs it on the branch of a tree; she then passes a pole through the lower loop and into a hole in the trunk of the tree, and, sitting down on the other end of the pole, she thus transforms it into a primitive kind of lever, drawing on the tube to its utmost length by the pressure of her own weight. The juice is thus expressed, flowing into a bowl placed under the tube. This juice is poisonous at first, but after being fermented becomes quite harmless, and is then used for the tucupí. The tapioca is made by mixing the grated mandioca with water. It is then pressed on a sieve, and the fluid which flows out is left to stand. It soon makes a deposit like starch, and when hardened they make it into a kind of porridge. It is a favorite article of food with them.

August 30th.—As time goes on, we grow more at home with our rustic friends here, and begin to understand their relations to each other. The name of our host is Laudigári (I spell the name as it sounds), and that of his wife Esperança. He, like all the Indians living upon the Amazons, is a fisherman, and, with the exception of such little care as his small plantation requires, this is his only occupation. An Indian is never seen to do any of the work of the house, not even to bring wood or water or lift the heavy burdens, and as the fishing is done chiefly at certain seasons, he is a very idle fellow for a great part of the time. The women are said, on the contrary, to be very industrious; and certainly those whom we have an opportunity of seeing here justify this reputation. Esperança is always busy at some household work or other,—grating mandioca, drying farinha, packing tobacco, cooking or sweeping. Her children are active and obedient, the older ones making themselves useful in bringing water from the lake, in washing the mandioca, or in taking care of the younger ones. Esperança can hardly be called pretty, but she has a pleasant smile and a remarkably sweet voice, with a kind of child-like intonation, which is very winning; and when sometimes, after her work is over, she puts on her white chemise, falling loose from her brown shoulders, her dark skirt, and a rose or a sprig of white jessamine in her jetty hair, she is by no means unattractive in her personal appearance, though I must confess that the pipe which she is apt to smoke in the evening injures the general effect. Her husband looks somewhat sombre; but his

hearty laugh occasionally, and his enjoyment of the glass of cachaça*
which rewards him when he brings in a new lot of specimens, shows
that he has his bright side. He is greatly amused at the value
Mr. Agassiz attaches to the fishes, especially the little ones, which
appear to him only fit to throw away. It seems that the other family
who have been about here since our arrival are neighbors, who have
come in to help in the making of mandioca. They come in the morning with all their children and remain through the day. The names
of the father and mother are Pedro Manuel and Michelina. He is a
tall, handsome fellow, whose chief occupation seems to be that of
standing about in picturesque attitudes, and watching his rather
pretty wife, as she bustles round in her various work of grating or
pressing or straining the mandioca, generally with her baby astride
her hip,—the Indian woman's favorite way of carrying her child.
Occasionally, however, Pedro Manuel is aroused to bear some part
in the collecting; and the other day, when he brought in some specimens which seemed to him quite valueless, Mr. Agassiz rewarded
him with a chicken. His surprise and delight were great, perhaps a
little mingled with contempt for the man who would barter a chicken
for a few worthless fishes, fit only to throw into the river. . . .

   October 29th.—Yesterday, after breakfast, I retreated to the
room where we had passed the night, hoping to find time and quiet
for writing letters and completing my journal. But I found it already occupied by the old Senhora† and her guests, who were loung-
ing in the hammocks or squatting on the floor and smoking their
pipes. The house is indeed full to overflowing, as the whole party
assembled for the ball are to stay during the President's‡ visit. But
in this way of living it is an easy matter to accommodate any number of people, for if they cannot all be received under the roof, they
can hang their hammocks under the trees outside. As I went to my
room last evening, I stopped to look at a pretty picture of an Indian
mother with her two little children asleep on either arm, all in one
hammock, in the open air. My Indian friends were too much interested in my occupations to allow of my continuing them uninter-
ruptedly. They were delighted with my books (I happened to have
"The Naturalist on the Amazons" with me, in which I showed them
some pictures of Amazonian scenery and insects), and asked me

*A rough sugarcane distillate—Ed.
†The lady of the house, their hostess, an Indian woman—Ed.
‡The provincial governor—Ed.

many questions about my country, my voyage, and my travels here. In return they gave me much information about their own way of life. They said the present gathering of neighbors and friends was no unusual occurrence, for they have a great many festas,* which, though partly religious in character, are also occasions of great festivity. These festas are celebrated at different sitios in turn, the saint of the day being carried, with all his ornaments, candles, bouquets, &c., to the house where the ceremony is to take place, and where all the people of the village congregate. Sometimes the festa lasts for several days, and is accompanied with processions, music, and dances in the evening. But the women said the forest was very sad now, because their men had all been taken as [army] recruits, or were seeking safety in the woods. The old Senhora told me a sad story of the brutality exercised in recruiting the Indians. She assured me that they were taken wherever found, without regard to age or circumstances, women and children often being dependent upon them; and if they made resistance, were carried off by force, and frequently handcuffed or had heavy weights attached to their feet. Such proceedings are entirely illegal; but these forest villages are so remote, that the men employed to recruit may practice any cruelty without being called to account for it. If the recruits are brought in in good condition, no questions are asked. These women said that all the work of the sitios—the making of farinha, the fishing, the turtle-hunting—was stopped for want of hands. The appearance of things certainly confirms this, for we scarcely see any men in the villages, and the canoes we meet are mostly rowed by women.

Yet I must say that the life of the Indian woman, so far as we have seen it, seems enviable, in comparison with that of the Brazilian lady in the Amazonian towns. The former has a healthful out-of-door life; she has her canoe on the lake or river and her paths through the forest, with perfect liberty to come and go; she has her appointed daily occupations, being busy not only with the care of her house and children, but in making farinha or tapioca, or in drying and rolling tobacco, while the men are fishing and turtle-hunting; and she has her frequent festa-days to enliven her working life. It is, on the contrary, impossible to imagine anything more dreary and monotonous than the life of the Brazilian Senhora in the smaller towns. In the northern provinces especially the old Portu-

*Festive celebrations—Ed.

everything monotonous loses identity

guese notions about shutting women up and making their home life as colorless as that of a cloistered nun, without even the element of religious enthusiasm to give it zest, still prevail. Many a Brazilian

Wealthy woman at the window of her home in a Brazilian town in the Amazon, circa 1870. From Herbert E. Smith, *Brazil. The Amazons and the Coast* (New York: Charles Scribner's Sons, 1879), 123.

lady passes day after day without stirring beyond her four walls, scarcely ever showing herself at the door or window; for she is always in a slovenly dishabille, unless she expects company. It is sad to see these stifled existences; without any contact with the world outside, without any charm of domestic life, without books or culture of any kind, the Brazilian Senhora in this part of the country either sinks contentedly into a vapid, empty, aimless life, or frets against her chains, and is as discontented as she is useless.

Rio de Janeiro, June 7, 1866

Of the public school for girls not much can be said. The education of women is little regarded in Brazil, and the standard of instruction for girls in the public schools is low. Even in the private schools, where the children of the better class are sent, it is the complaint of all teachers that they are taken away from school just at the time when their minds begin to develop. The majority of girls in Brazil who go to school at all are sent at about seven or eight years of age, and are considered to have finished their education at thirteen or fourteen. The next step in their life is marriage. Of course there are exceptions; some parents wisely leave their children at school, or direct their instruction at home, till they are seventeen or eighteen years of age, and others send their girls abroad. But usually, with the exception of one or two accomplishments, such as French or music, the education of women is neglected, and this neglect affects the whole tone of society. It does not change the general truth of this statement, that there are Brazilian ladies who would be recognized in the best society as women of the highest intelligence and culture. But they are the exceptions, as they inevitably must be under the present system of instruction, and they feel its influence upon their social position only the more bitterly.

Indeed, many of the women I have known most intimately here have spoken to me with deep regret of their limited, imprisoned existence. There is not a Brazilian senhora, who has ever thought about the subject at all, who is not aware that her life is one of repression and constraint. She cannot go out of her house, except under certain conditions, without awakening scandal. Her education leaves her wholly ignorant of the most comon topics of a wider interest, though perhaps with a tolerable knowledge of French and music. The world of books is closed to her; for there is little Portuguese literature into which she is allowed to look, and that of other languages is still less at her command. She knows little of the history of her own country, almost nothing of that of others, and she is hardly aware that there is any religious faith except the uniform one of Brazil; she has probably never heard of the Reformation, nor does she dream that there is a sea of thought surging in the world outside, constantly developing new phases of national and individual life; indeed, of all but her own narrow domestic existence she is profoundly ignorant.

On one occasion, when staying at a fazenda, I took up a volume which was lying on the piano. A book is such a rare sight, in the rooms occupied by the family, that I was curious to see its contents. As I stood turning over the leaves (it proved to be a romance), the master of the house came up, and remarked that the book was not suitable reading for ladies, but that here (putting into my hand a small volume) was a work adapted to the use of women and children, which he had provided for the senhoras of his family. I opened it, and found it to be a sort of textbook of morals, filled with commonplace sentiments, copybook phrases, written in a tone of condescending indulgence for the feminine intellect, women being, after all, the mothers of men, and understood to have some little influence on their education. I could hardly wonder, after seeing this specimen of their intellectual food, that the wife and daughters of our host were not greatly addicted to reading. Nothing strikes a stranger more than the absence of books in Brazilian houses. If the father is a professional man, he had his small library of medicine or law, but books are never seen scattered about as if in common use; they make no part of the daily life. I repeat, that there are exceptions. I well remember finding in the sitting-room of a young girl, by whose family we had been most cordially received, a well-selected library of the best literary and historical works in German and French; but this is the only instance of the kind we met with during our year in Brazil. Even when the Brazilian women have received the ordinary advantages of education, there is something in their home life so restricted, so shut out from natural contact with external influences, that this in itself tends to cripple their development. Their amusements are as meagre and scanty as their means of instruction.

In writing these things I but echo the thought of many intelligent Brazilians, who lament a social evil which they do not well know how to reform. If among our Brazilian friends there are some who, familiar with the more progressive aspect of life in Rio de

Janeiro, question the accuracy of my statements, I can only say that they do not know the condition of society in the northern cities and provinces. Among my own sex, I have never seen such sad lives as became known to me there,—lives deprived of healthy, invigorating happiness, and intolerably monotonous,—a negative suffering, having its source, it is true, in the absence of enjoyment rather than in the presence of positive evils, but all the more to be deplored because so stagnant and inactive.

Behind all defects in methods of instruction, there lies a fault of domestic education, to be lamented throughout Brazil. This is the constant association with black servants, and, worse still, with negro children, of whom there are usually a number in every house. Whether the low and vicious habits of the negroes are the result of slavery or not, they cannot be denied; and it is singular to see persons, otherwise careful and conscientious about their children, allowing them to live in the constant companionship of their blacks, waited upon by the older ones, playing all day with the younger ones. It shows how blind we may become, by custom, to the most palpable dangers. A stranger observes at once the evil results of this contact with vulgarity and vice, though often unnoticed by the parents. In the capital, some of these evils are fast disappearing; indeed, those who remember Rio de Janeiro forty years ago have witnessed, during that short period, a remarkable change for the better in the state of society. Nor should it be forgotten that the highest authority in the community is exerted in the cause of a liberal culture for women. It is well known that the education of the Imperial princesses has been not only superintended, but in a great measure personally conducted, by their father.

Rio de Janeiro

I cannot close what I have to say of instruction in Brazil without adding that, in a country where only half the nation is educated, there can be no complete intellectual progress. Where the difference of education makes an intelligent sympathy between men and women almost impossible, so that their relation is necessarily limited to that of the domestic affections, never raised except in some very exceptional cases to that of cultivated companionship, the development of the people as a whole must remain imperfect and partial. I believe, however, that, especially in this direction, a rapid reform may be expected. I have heard so many intelligent Brazil-

ians lament the want of suitable instruction for wc
schools, that I think the standard of education for girl
be raised. Remembering the antecedents of the Brazilians, ...
inherited notions as to what is becoming in the privacy and restraint
of a woman's life, we are not justified, however false these ideas
may seem to us, in considering the present generation as responsible for them; they are also too deeply rooted to be changed in a
day.

7

INA VON BINZER

A German Schoolteacher in Brazil

In 1881, Ina Sofie Amalie von Binzer (1856–1916?), a young German schoolteacher, sailed to Brazil. There she remained until 1884, working as a governess for prosperous coffee planter families in the provinces of Rio de Janeiro and São Paulo with a brief interval spent in Rio de Janeiro teaching at a private girls' school for the less wealthy. Adventurous, observant, and occasionally homesick, this young educator wrote a series of letters describing life among the planter elite as well as in the nation's capital. Although her letters, perhaps slightly fictionalized, appeared in book form in Germany in 1887, a Brazilian translation would not be published until 1956.

Born in Schleswig-Holstein on December 3, 1856, Ina von Binzer received her education in Westphalia and later moved to Prussia with her family. She trained as a teacher, passed her examinations, and taught in German schools before traveling to Brazil. Three years after her return home, she published her first book—her letters from Brazil—as *Leid und Freud' einer Erzieherin in Brasilien* (Joys and Sorrows of a School Teacher in Brazil), under the pseudonym of Ulla von Eck. With the help of an uncle, she was able to dedicate herself to writing, publishing *Gypsies of the Big City* (1894) and *Aunt Cordula's Nieces* (1897). After moving from Berlin back to her

From Ina von Binzer (Ulla von Eck, pseud.), *Alegrias e tristezas de uma educadora alemã no Brasil*, trans. Alice Rossi and Luisita da Gama Cerqueira from the original 1887 edition of *Leid und Freud' einer Erzieherin in Brasilien* (São Paulo: Editora Anhembi, 1956), 23–24, 48–49, 65–69. English translation by June E. Hahner.

native province of Schleswig-Holstein, she married Adolf von Bentivegni, a local judge. Her death seems to have occurred in 1916.

Only a few years before the final abolition of slavery in 1888, Von Binzer began her Brazilian teaching career in the province of Rio de Janeiro on a coffee plantation worked by over two hundred slaves. As did many Brazilians she realized that the long history of this institution was drawing to a close. To the chagrin of many foreign-oriented members of the elite, the gradual elimination of slavery elsewhere in the Western Hemisphere had left Brazil as the institution's largest and last bastion. Slavery had declined in importance in impoverished northeast Brazil and was concentrated within the prosperous southern coffee provinces. In 1887 the city of Rio de Janeiro, an abolitionist stronghold with a total population of 500,000, contained fewer than 7,500 slaves, while the province of São Paulo (with well over one million inhabitants) had over 100,000 slaves.

Von Binzer's letters focus on life among the masters, not the slaves, although she does describe relations between slave owners and house servants. Unlike those foreigners whose social interactions with members of the Brazilian elite were limited to paying calls at their homes or attending their parties and formal functions, von Binzer lived in their households—on far more intimate terms. As a governess, she occupied a dependent position, one that in theory gave her independence but in fact deprived her of virtually all autonomy. Schoolteaching, as she later learned in Rio de Janeiro, would not prove much different. Neither a servant nor an equal in the eyes of her Brazilian employers, she viewed elite family life from a distinctive angle. This well-educated German woman did not appreciate the superior airs assumed by some of her pupils, who were unaccustomed to obeying others; she expressed her exasperation with her rambunctious, undisciplined, and high-spirited charges. In her letters home, von Binzer could also puncture the pretensions of some older Brazilians, citing cases of leading members of the Republican Party who knew little of their country's constitution and history, or positivists who lacked basic knowledge of Auguste Comte's philosophy. Nor could she cease being critical of certain customs, such as frequent spitting, while she gratefully acknowledged the kindnesses shown her and the beauties of Brazil. She also criticized her German compatriots in Brazil as conceited and arrogant. Conscious of the cultural differences separating her from her pupils and their society, she wished to modify her Teutonic pedagogy and attitudes and adapt them to Brazilian conditions and culture.

The private boarding school for girls in Rio de Janeiro where von Binzer spent several months between her plantation stays presented similar educational challenges and gave her very little more freedom or independence. In the cities as in the countryside, Brazil's "first families" employed private tutors or governesses. Some also sent their daughters to convent schools. Children from less wealthy families attended other private schools, such as the one where von Binzer taught, while poorer children frequented public primary schools or had no schools at all. Even in 1890 only half the capital's population was literate. Schoolteaching was one of the few "respectable" jobs open to women, and wages were meager. Despite the low pay, difficult working conditions, and poor housing described by von Binzer, schoolteaching gave some women more economic independence than they otherwise would have had. In the following selections from von Binzer's letters we witness life with her pupils both on plantations and in city schoolrooms.

São Francisco [Plantation (Rio de Janeiro Province)]
June 9, 1881
Dear Grete,

Do you know who I dropped into the very deepest recesses of my trunk today? Our Bormann, that is, his 40 pedagogical letters, which are not of the slightest use here. And I had placed such trust in them!

During the voyage, when I was attacked by the fear that I would never arrive at any kind of understanding with my Brazilian students, I always thought about that most worthy book, nestled there among my baggage and I immediately felt calmer, telling myself, "do things this way!" And now, Grete, I believe that Bormann himself very often would not know what to do here.

I feel bewildered in the midst of so many evident and palpable but unattainable things.

This blessed family has 12 children and 7 of them are under my educational supervision. At 7 o'clock in the morning, we begin: first the "grown-ups" arrive and have a German lesson. Dona

Gabriela, Dona Olimpia and Dona Emilia are 19, 21, and 22 years old, and, therefore, to Brazilians are practically old maids.

With my 22 years, this greatly astonished me. And I am obliged to always address them with the title of "Dona."

The first mornings they generally arrived late to class, so that I was compelled to request them to be punctual, since I was still following Bormann's advice.

Since then, every morning when I enter the classroom, I find them sitting around the table, with their listless Brazilian faces, and not even lettting an apathetic or indifferent "Bon jour, Mademoiselle" escape them. No natural cheerfulness, no pleasure in study, no personal warmth. Ah! Grete, this trio has such a terribly numbing effect.

The appearance of these three always makes me think of the Holy Inquisition, with judges sitting around a table who could not look any grimmer or colder. I feel such a villain and regret that I asked them to be punctual.

We proceed painfully through German class always with the assistance of French, which still is the greatest source of assistance, since I do not understand a single thing when they begin to speak German.

I feel saved, but nearly exhausted, when the little ones arrive at 8 o'clock. Even though ill-behaved, they at least are just children, and only the eldest somewhat resembles the Holy Inquisition.

Ah! Grete! They are so "provoking" [original word in English]. They do everything I tell them to do, they solve the problems I give them, but they are still inexplicably irritating. I am sure that they wish me no harm, and at times I find the smallest ones very amusing.

One Sunday, I was sitting on a bench in a paradise-like garden, under an imposing mango tree and dreaming—ah! Grete!—about German horses, when suddenly I looked up and saw a horrible little black creature who frightened me, bringing me right back to the tropics. Imagine him: more or less 12 years old, looking more like a monkey than a person, with a smile extending to his ears, repugnant kinky hair, a narrow forehead, a terribly fat stomach, and sticklike black legs that were almost purple from so much dust.

Imagine this personage, who wore just a very short shirt of indeterminate color, and you will understand that I did not feel enraptured by this noble fellow citizen. On the contrary, I seem to have jumped up in fright, because little Leonila immediately came out from behind a bush, and, trying to calm me, said, in French, in an almost protective manner: "Do not be afraid, Mademoiselle, it is Jacob." But when she then saw that my face still did not display great enthusiasm for the honor of becoming acquainted with this "holy church father," she added in a half indignant, half explanatory fashion: "He is mine. Grandmother gave him to me as a birthday present." I assure you that this was comical, a young slave mistress gazing with pride on her living present, and her horrible small piece of property smiling in satisfaction upon hearing this statement of ownership, one he must have intuited rather than understood, so that it made me laugh.

Incidentally, this attitude of superiority which is assumed even by children, due to the institution of slavery here, generally displays a humorous side. In recompense, it is quite moving to see how fond they are of their good and loyal blacks.

Little five-year-old Maria da Glória, for example, routinely saves a little bit of her dessert for her nurse, a lovely young mulatta, and always asks as well for something for the slave child that was reared with her.

Alfonsina, who really likes finery, gave a multi-colored ribbon to her old nursemaid, who she thought would be pleased by it.

They all like to be generous and to satisfy your wishes, but even so, even so!...

Your Ulla . . .

São Francisco [Plantation]
September 17, 1881

Ah! dear Grete, if you only knew how bitter are my days here! How the time drags, how everything is a burden! The children are naughty, the "Holy Inquisition" [the three eldest sisters] is apathetic, the entire house is noisy, and I feel so alone, so incredibly lonely!

Then all this starts making me more nervous. The neuralgic pains continue, but are less severe, thank God. However, I have many migraines, which I attribute to the noise and discomfort of the household arrangements.

These peoples' nerves must be made of steel, unfortunately! Otherwise, they would show some consideration for other peoples'!

Picture the following scene, and ask if your own nerves would stand it.

I generally give piano lessons in D. Alfonsina's so-called work room because the children do not practice on the grand piano in the parlor but on an old upright piano.

This work room is located in the center of the house and various rooms connect with it: a dispensary, the bathroom, the children's bedroom, the Holy Inquisition's bedroom, a cloakroom, and the sewing room. Hence you can guess how much noise one hears in this agreeable sanctuary under normal conditions. Today, however, it was as if the "Old Gentleman" [the devil; original phrase in English] was amusing himself there.

Mice had turned up in the dispensary, so D. Alfonsina immediately called two Negro women and a Negro man and ordered them to completely empty out the room in order to find the holes.

At the same time as I was seated at the out-of-tune piano, resignedly counting one, two, three, and that Leonila, ever persistent, was making the same mistakes, a barricade of crates, barrels, sacks, etc. was being built in front of us under D. Alfonsina's loud command. The noise and occasional scoldings administered by the lady of the house was overwhelming by itself! But on top of this, right next to the piano was the open door to the sewing room with two noisy sewing machines going. From the next room came the cries and squawks of the parrots and other birds. To top off everything, because of the barricade of boxes piled up in the corner where she was studying, a little mulatta girl who D. Gabriela was teaching to read all of a sudden stationed herself behind my chair and intoned her monotonous aa, bb, cc! It was just too much!

I got up, furious, grabbed my music, called Leonila, and finished the lesson in the parlor.

They took offense, and the party at fault in this entire incident was me!

Yes! Yes! It is very objectionable for people to seem extremely nervous. But when one is not even a little bit, so much the worse for others.

That is how I regard the Brazilians. I doubt that my health can hold out much longer.

Write me frequently. I feel abandoned and cut off from the world. If I could at least see one German!

Your poor Ulla

I finally changed my bedroom. I could not stand the other one due to the humidity, and the lack of sunshine, and the fact that one day I saw a snake right under my window. Oh, these loathsome creatures. We have seen several of them. . . .

Rio, February 12, 1882
    Dearest Grete!
    I have to write you again: just think, yesterday I was hired by a "colégio" here.
    A "colégio" is a girls' secondary school, a boarding school. I have to teach four classes, initiating the daughters of this country into the mysteries of the German and English languages. In addition, I give countless piano lessons.
    Ah! Grete! Both languages are like a closed book to my pupils, and they learn so little with me, especially the German. I still can't figure out if it is my fault or theirs. Perhaps all this is explained by the difference between the Germanic and Latin peoples, since the girls learn French almost in their sleep, and the French teachers get much better results in their classrooms than I do.
    Several times I was tempted to revive old Bormann. However, I left the book permanently where it is because I know that it would only level endless accusations at me.
    As few classrooms are available, I generally give my lessons in the same room as another teacher. On one side of the room students recite Portuguese poems while on the other I explain to my bored "young ladies" the complicated inflected forms of German nouns. The three articles with their four inflected forms and their 12 obscure parts (not counting the plural) seem so repellent to this band of sullen girls in front of me that they clearly consider them a cunning and treacherous trap set for students. . . .
    The best families never, never send their daughters to "colégios," so that those here are, generally, the rudest and least educated people imaginable. They get angry, they shout, and their faces often became as red as cherries.
    On those occasions, our youngest French teacher, Mlle. Serôt, locks them up inside an empty wardrobe until they calm down. We rarely see the school's directress before meal time. She is the only person who exercises any authority over this band of savages, perhaps because she is rarely present.
    She is always well dressed, sitting in her office where she receives the students' parents. And she just gives one recitation lesson in each class.

She does not like to be asked about school matters so that I have no option but to manage things by myself, like Mlle. Serôt.

Up to now I could not figure out a lesson plan, let alone a schedule. For the time being, all this makes me feel like I am lost in a wilderness.

Even with the best of intentions I could not even calculate the number of students in my music classes.

When I sit down at the piano at 6:30 A.M. more of them show up every half hour until 10:00 A.M., almost like clockwork.

Now, having noted each one, and through much effort and cunning, I think I have established an exact count.

However, they like me very much, perhaps because I dress well, as Mlle. Serôt says (how she has won the children's hearts!), and I do not resemble the other Germans.

While this latter comment should be taken as a compliment, it still makes me feel indignant! How can I command the girls' respect if the very adults are not ashamed of being so rude?

Today the directress passed by the music room with a Brazilian lady, mother of one of the students, who remarked in a loud voice, speaking Portuguese: "She is German? She does not look the Germanic type, and furthermore she is very well dressed."

To deny me a German appearance, a person like me, so inflexibly German, is as you know quite painful, and at the same time incomprehensible, since I am blonde. What kind of clothes did my predecessors and other German colleagues wear that would so displease the Brazilians?

Furthermore, the scorn for German clothing is widespread. What happened the other day at a hairdresser's salon when I came to have my hair curled and cut short was not uncommon nor unrelated to this.

I did not know that I was calling attention to myself, as no Brazilian lady goes out alone on the street, or even has her hair done outside her home.

The hairdresser first took me for a Frenchwoman, as I spoke with him in French. Later he asked me if I were Russian, and, finally, having run out of countries, he ended up querying me, to my simultaneous amusement and indignation,

—"Then can you be German?"

—"And why not?"—I inquired, already trembling with anger.

—"Ah! Bah!"—he uttered, with contempt—"That cannot be. German women are always poorly dressed, and not at all chic."

"German women" thank you, I thought. And I left there swearing eternal enmity towards this shop.

However, the bell for tea has just rung. Oh! This school's tea! Right now, I will use the tremendous heat as a pretext for refusing it. Cajú fruit juice is a thousand times preferable. A lot of it is drunk here, and it is very refreshing. The second bell—I must rush.

Your Ulla

Rio, February 21, 1882

Oh! Grete,

How this colégio is weighing me down!

I honestly believe I am the worst teacher! They do not learn anything with me, and if there were any school inspectors here, I would be very disheartened! I can't manage to adapt to this superficial way of teaching. But when I try to do things more thoroughly, it is even worse! I become completely discouraged.

When it comes to discipline! The word alone makes the blood rush to my head!

Picture this: the other day when I entered the classroom I found the students so restless and noisy that in my confusion I turned to Bormann. When I got them quiet enough so that I could be heard, I ordered them to "Get up and sit down" five times in a row, which in our country a class always considers a shameful punishment. But here—oh! heaven help us—when I finally made them understand what they were expected to do, the children could not imagine it was a punishment, but instead treated it as a new game and hopped up and down, up and down, like mechanical toys, having a royal good time.

I recognize the fact that pedagogy is absolutely necessary here, but it should be a Brazilian not a German pedagogy, tailored to Brazilian conditions and adapted to this people's character and life style. Brazilian children should absolutely not be educated by Germans. It is wasted work, for alien views cannot be imposed on them.

The same thing happens with me and this nation's children as with St. Francis and the plants—We do not understand one another—we speak an unwavering, psychologically foreign language, which makes my life here very unpleasant. My material situation also leaves a great deal to be desired.

"My room" is a windowless alcove off one of the classrooms with light coming just from the door!

The furniture consists of only a bed (a cheap version of that on the São Francisco plantation), a washstand and a chair. I have no wardrobe or chest of drawers. My trunk substitutes for a clothes closet, and for my best dresses I hope to be able to enter into the good graces of Mlle. Serôt in order to get the wardrobe used to punish students, which will also win me their gratitude.

I am actually writing this letter in that Frenchwoman's room, for despite traditional enmities, she is the one I like most here.

Her room is not much better than mine, but it has a desk and a tiny window high up near the ceiling, whereas in my dark hole, which resembles those found in all Brazilian homes, I feel almost asphyxiated. I must add that in this building we suffer terribly from cockroaches, dark, repugnant insects, full of disease, that look like our May bugs.

Cockroaches are a common scourge here. But even so, I have never seen anything like the hundreds of thousands in this building.

At night, when the children and I go to their bedrooms, the floor is crawling with these disgusting insects. We immediately start to chase them with shoes or any other solid object close at hand.

Hundreds escape us, but other hundreds of corpses remain on the battlefield and are later swept up.

Don't think that I exaggerate, Grete. It is the same way in all the old houses, and any other foreign visitor traveling around Brazil would certainly encounter exactly the same thing.

I'm not mentioning mosquitos, flies, ants, lizards, or the rest of the vermin, because they do not compare with the cockroaches, which on top of everything else, eat and spoil everything they can get to.

These last nights they devoured the cover of my Goethe! Besides, my enthusiasm for Rio has cooled down a great deal. Life in a colégio holds no real charms, and to stroll on the streets of Rio is torture, due to the men's excessive courtesy.

They are not accustomed to seeing their female compatriots on the streets, and even though they know that foreigners enjoy this liberty, they consider it their right to direct streams of exaggerated pleasantries to unaccompanied European women.

—"How are you, Mademoiselle?"

—"Where are you rushing to, my child?"

These and other comments I endure without getting upset simply by ignoring them. But what do you say about this? When I was leaving a glove store recently, a tall dried-out looking Brazilian planted himself directly in front of me, and, with the world's most cynical expression, murmured: "Extremely pretty, so nice, so very nice."

I left in a huff, which seemed to amuse him immensely.

Ah! Grete! If I could at least find a kindred spirit!

Mlle. Serôt and Miss Dahlman are unquestionably very kind and agreeable, but I want to have a real friend, my Grete! Ah! If you were only here!

So things go here. But (let me whisper into your ear) I will return when I collect sufficient funds for the voyage home.

Currently my fortunes are at low tide and my wages at the colégio will not make them rise.

Hence I must continue to stay still and quiet because ship's passage alone to Hamburg costs 30 pounds.

On the 22nd of last month, I went to see the Pastor of the German community here as well as the German Consul. Both were very considerate and the Consul, who is a smart man and someone who knows how to deal with Brazilians, advised me that it was best to go to the Province of São Paulo, if I could obtain a position there, since the one I hold here is not the right one for me. In São Paulo I would also find other compatriots.

After he told me this, I looked for something suitable in the *Jornal do Comércio*, among the advertisements for fugitive slaves and notices of slaves for sale, which is where they also place advertisements for teachers, who must be extremely capable and accomplished.

At the colégio, I also learned that they confer the title of "professora" on us only when they esteem us highly. Otherwise, they downgrade us to the lesser type of teacher, "mestra."

We are fortunate that they do not sign contracts here, or penalize anyone who breaks an agreement. Even though we are threatened day after day with dismissal, we can at least pack our bags when we have had enough.

Adieu, my precious. Commend me into the care of the 9 Muses so that they can help me get to São Paulo!

Your Ulla

8

FANNY CHAMBERS GOOCH   *Southern*

USA

Keeping House in Northern Mexico

Frances Chambers Gooch Iglehart (1851?–1913?) was born in Hills-boro, Mississippi, the eighth of thirteen children of William and Feriba Mage Chambers. She obtained her formal schooling in Texas, where she lived with her brother Lem. A sociable and talkative person who was enamored of travel, Fanny Chambers married G. W. Gooch, a Virginian, and undertook her first trip to Mexico with him. They settled in Saltillo, capital of the northern state of Coahuila, where she spent most of her first long stay in Mexico. Following a return to Texas, perhaps in 1883 (the dates of many key events in her life are uncertain), Fanny Chambers Gooch again ventured into Mexico in preparation for writing a volume intended for a large audience. She visited other parts of the country for the first time, and enjoyed contacts with Mexican intellectuals, political figures, members of the emerging middle sectors, and some of the poorer strata of society.

At the time that her account, *Face to Face with the Mexicans*, was published in December 1887, Gooch's marriage had ended, leaving her in an uncertain financial position. She therefore invested much time and energy in the dissemination of her book, and it won favorable reviews in the United States and England. In 1889 she was again living in Austin, Texas, the wife of cotton factor D. T.

From Fanny Chambers Gooch, *Face to Face with the Mexicans. The Domestic Life, Educational, Social, and Business Ways, Statesmanship and Literature, Legendary and General History of the Mexican People, as Seen and Studied by an American Woman During Seven Years of Intercourse with Them* (New York: Fords, Howard, and Hulbert, 1887), 84–101, 277–82, 408–13.

Iglehart and carrying on an active social life. In 1900 she briefly returned to Mexico and then published *Tradition of Guadalupe and Christmas in Old Mexico.* Her last book, *The Boy Captain of the Texas-Mier Expedition,* a novel for teenagers about the Texas secession, appeared in 1909. On the death of her second husband, she married Dr. Richard H. L. Bibb, whom she later divorced.

The Mexico in which Fanny Chambers Gooch lived during the 1880s was that of President Porfirio Díaz. The Porfiriato, as the period of his long dictatorship (1876–1911) is termed, made Mexico safer for foreign travelers and tourists, not just investors. Unlike Annie Sampson Poole,* the wife of a British mining engineer who kept house in Guanajuato in the late 1860s when the liberals under Benito Juárez were in power, Gooch would not have to fear robberies and murders in town or brigands and kidnappers on rough country roads. Díaz brought order and stability and the trappings of material progress to Mexico. He consolidated authority and welcomed foreign capital, granting concessions to foreign railroad promoters and exploiters of Mexico's mineral wealth. His conservative, centralized, long-lived government rested on a powerful alliance of the army, large landowners, foreign capitalists, and the Roman Catholic Church, who reaped the material rewards of supporting the Díaz regime while the mass of the population was brutally suppressed. Land concentration and the number of landless in this overwhelmingly rural nation increased, and average food consumption and real wages fell. But the price that the poor would pay for Mexico's modernization was not obvious to sympathetic observers such as Gooch at the beginning of the Porfiriato.

The apparent stability imposed by Porfirio Díaz together with the construction of railroad lines running southward from the United States to Mexico City attracted a wave of foreign travelers, travel writers, and investors to Mexico in the 1880s. Among the dozens of authors of travel accounts were several women whose narratives derived from far shorter stays in that country than Gooch's. Rather than live among Mexicans, they generally remained with their compatriots, insulated by tour parties and isolated by language. After spending some six weeks in a special passenger car as members

*Annie Sampson Poole, *Mexicans at Home in the Interior. By a Resident* (London: Chapman and Hall, 1884).

of the first Raymond and Whitcomb excursion aboard the Mexican Central Railroad (newly completed in February 1885), Mary Elizabeth Blake and Margaret F. Sullivan chose to write a book describing the "fascinations" of this "picturesque" country inhabited by a "strange people" speaking a "strange tongue."* Also ignorant of Spanish, Cora Hayward Crawford based her travel account on a similar short trip with a tour group.† However, Alice Le Plongeon did spend several years with her husband in Yucatán before writing journal articles that were collected and published in book form.‡ And, as the title of her book declares, reporter Nellie Bly spent *Six Months in Mexico*, traveling with her mother as chaperone. Bly contended that at crowded stations where Mexican women all had escorts, she "defied [the Mexicans'] gaze and showed them that a free American girl can accommodate herself to circumstances without the aid of a man."§

Fanny Chambers Gooch claimed that she wrote *Face to Face with the Mexicans*, based on her experiences during several stays in Mexico between 1800 and 1887, to acquaint her countrymen with the Mexican people, who were "not properly understood by their Anglo-Saxon neighbors," and to "secure a fairer appreciation" of them and their achievements.# Yet she could also pen apparently contradictory statements, for a desire to facilitate business and trade relations between the United States and Mexico accompanied her goal of promoting greater awareness of and sensitivity to Mexican culture. She noted that the United States needed more markets for manufactured goods and gave advice to U.S. businessmen while also expressing the wish that Mexicans not be disturbed by

---

*Mary Elizabeth Blake and Margaret F. Sullivan, *Mexico, Picturesque, Political, Progressive* (Boston: Lee and Shepard, 1888), 8.

†Cora Hayward Crawford, *The Land of the Montezumas* (Troy, NY: Nims and Knight, 1890).

‡Alice D. Le Plongeon, *Here and There in Yucatán* (New York: J. W. Bouton, 1886).

§Nellie Bly, *Six Months in Mexico* (New York: American Publishing Corp., 1888), 113.

#Fanny Chambers Gooch, *Face to Face with the Mexicans. The Domestic Life, Educational, Social, and Business Ways, Statesmanship and Literature, Legendary and General History of the Mexican People, as Seen and Studied by an American Woman During Seven Years of Intercourse with Them* (New York: Fords, Howard, and Hulbert, 1887), 13.

contaminating or progressive foreign influences; at the end of the book she proclaimed that "a new era" was dawning in Mexico. Rather than just spending her time in the nation's capital or taking cross-country train trips, Gooch also experienced provincial life and ran a household in Saltillo, her first place of residence. Conscious of cultural variation, she concentrated her account on Mexican social life, describing not just literature and history but also housing and religious holidays, food and clothing, and songs and dances. Yet her discussion of mistress-servant relationships, which follows, demonstrates how she violated local customs, which often caused her servants to leave her. The gender divisions of labor in Mexico were very strong and could not easily be challenged.

"No Es Costumbre"*

We were overshadowed by the dome of a magnificent cathedral, the exterior of which was embellished with life-sized statues of saints. The interior presented a costly display of tinted walls, jeweled and bedecked images, and gilded altars. Its mammoth tower had loomed grimly under the suns and stars of a hundred years, and the solidity of its perfect masonry has so far defied the encroachments of time.

The city of our adoption boasted an Alameda, where the air was redolent of the odor of the rose and violet, and made musical with the tinkling of fountains; and where could be seen the "beauty and chivalry" of a civilization three centuries old, taking the evening air.

Plazas beautified with flowers, shrubs, and trees, upon which neither money nor pains had been spared, lent a further charm. Stores were at hand wherein could be purchased fabrics of costly texture, as well as rare jewels—in fact, a fair share of the elegant superfluities of life; and yet in the midst of so much civilization, so much art, so much luxury of a certain kind, so much wealth, I found to my dismay, upon investigation, that I was at least fifty miles from an available broom!

Imagine the dilemma, you famously neat housekeepers of the United States! A house with floors of pounded dirt, tile, brick, and

---

*The higher classes use the term "Eso no se acostumbra;" while the idiom of the common people abbreviates the expression into "No es costumbre."

cement, and no broom to be had for money, though, I am pleased to add, one was finally obtained for love. My generous little Mexican neighbor and friend, Pomposita, taking pity on my despair, gave me one—which enabled me to return the half-worn borrowed broom of another friend.

Owing to the exorbitant demands of the custom-house, such humble though necessary articles were not then imported; and the untutored sons of La República manufactured them on haciendas, from materials crude beyond imagination.

Once or twice a year long strings of *burros* may be seen, wending their way solemnly through the streets; girt about with a burden of the most wonderful brooms.

These brooms were of two varieties: one had handles as knotty and unwieldy as the thorny *mesquite*, while the other was still more primitive in design, and looked like old field Virginia sedge grass tied up in bundles. They were retailed by men who carried them through the streets on their backs.

For the rude character of their brooms, however, the manufacturers are not to blame, but the sterility of the country, and the failure of nature to provide suitable vegetable growths.

Every housekeeper takes advantage o the advent of the *escobero* (broom-maker), to lay in a stock of brooms sufficient to last until his next visit. It was two months before an opportunity of buying a broom, even from a "wandering Bavarian," was afforded me, and during that time I came to regard Doña Pomposita's gift as the apple of my eye.

"*Mer-ca-ran las es-co-bas!*" One morning a new sound assailed my ears, as it came up the street, gathering force and volume the nearer it approached. I heard it over and over without divining its meaning. But at last a man entered our portal and in a tone that made my hair stand on end and with a vim that almost shook the house, he screamed—"*Es-co-bas, Señ-o-ra!*"—drawling each word out as long as a broom-handle, then rolling it into a low hum, which finally died into a whispered—"Will you buy some brooms?" Had he known my disposition and special fondness for broom-handles— without reference to my household need—he would have brought them to me directly, dispensing with his ear-splitting medley—to a woman for three months without a broom!

On ascertaining that the *escobero* would not visit the city again for some time, I bought his entire stock, and laid them up with prudent foresight, against the possibility of another broom famine.

With a genuine American spirit, I concluded to have a general house-cleaning, and, equipped with these wonderful brooms, with Pancho's* assistance the work began. The first place demanding attention was the immense parlor, with its floor of solid cement. Pancho began to sweep, but the more he swept, the worse it looked—ringed, streaked, and striped with dust. I thought he was not using his best efforts, so with a will, I took the broom and made several vigorous strokes, but to my amazement, it looked worse than ever. In my despair a friend came in, who comprehended the situation at a glance, and explained that floors of that kind could not be cleaned with a broom; that *amoli*—the root of the *ixtli* (eastly)—soap-root—applied with a wet cloth, was the medium of renovation.

The *amoli* was first macerated and soaked for some time in water. A portion of the liquid was taken in one vessel and clear water in another. The cleansing was done in small squares, the rubbing all in one direction. The effect was magical—my dingy floor being restored to its original rich Indian red.

Now and then, while on his knees, rubbing away with might and main, Pancho would throw his eyes up at me with a peculiar expression of despair, while he muttered in undertone: "*No es costumbre de los mozos lavar los suelos*" ("It is not customary for mozos† to wash floors").

Insatiable curiosity is the birthright of the poor of Mexico, and on this remarkable day they gathered about the windows until not another one could find room—talking to Pancho, who looked as if already under sentence for an infraction of the criminal code. They made strange motions with their fingers, exclaiming at the same time: "*Es una verguenza el mozo hacer tales cosas!*" ("It is a shame for a mozo to do such things!") Others replied by saying: "*Es un insulto!*" ("It is an insult!"), while others took up the argument of the case by saying: "*Por supuesto que si*" ("Why, of course it is"). But all this did not cause Pancho to give me a rude look or an impertinent word.

The floor now looked red and shiny, the windows were clear and glistening, and the six hair-cloth chairs stood grimly along the wall, in deference to the custom. My little friend took her departure, and Pancho moved lamely about, as if stiffened by his arduous labor.

---

*Pancho was the author's manservant or *mozo*—Ed.
†Menservants—Ed.

[handwritten margin note: She still continued despite it's clear insulting manner]

In all my housekeeping experiences nothing ever occurred which for novelty was comparable to the events of that morning. I felt sure that when Mother Noah descended from Mount Ararat, and assumed the responsibilities of housekeeping—or more properly tent-keeping—on the damp plain, however embarrassing the limitation of her equipments may have been, she was at least spared the provocation of a scornful and wondering audience, greeting her efforts on every side with that now unendurable remark, *"No es costumbre."*

I afterward learned the cause of the commotion, when it transpired that such services as floor-cleaning are performed, not by the *mozo*, but by a servant hired for the occasion, outside the household.

In a few moments my *lavandera*—washerwoman—entered, accompanied by her two pretty, shy little girls. Having complimented the fresh appearance of the house,—Pancho now and then explaining what he had done,—she informed me that the following day would be the *dia de santo*—saint's day—of one of her bright-eyed *chiquitas*, and *"hay costumbre"* ("there is a custom") of receiving tokens on these days from interested friends. Acting upon this hint, I went to my bedroom, followed by Juana and the *niñas*, who displayed great surprise at every step. My red and yellow covered beds they tapped and talked to as if they had been animate things, calling them, *"camas bonitas, coloradas y amarillas!"* ("pretty beds, red and yellow!")

I turned the bright blankets over, that they might see the springs, and the sight utterly overcame them. Their astonishment at the revelation of such mysterious and luxurious appendages made them regard me with mingled awe, astonishment, and suspicion. The mother struck the springs with her fists, and as the sound rang out and vibrated, the children retreated hastily, shaking with alarm.

Wishing to conform to the customs, and remembering Juana's hint, I unlocked my "Saratoga." The *chiquitas* stood aside, fearing, I suppose, that from the trunk some frightful apparition might spring forth. When the lid went back they exclaimed: *"Valgame Dios!"* ("Help me, God"), and crossed themselves hastily, as if to be prepared for the worst. I invited them to come near, at the same time opening a compartment filled with bright flowers and ribbons.

This was a magnet they could not resist, and overcoming their fears, they came and stood close to the trunk, now and then touching the pretty things I exhibited to their wondering eyes. I gave each of them a gay ribbon, and while they were talking delightedly and caressing the pretty trifles, by some mischance the fastening of the upper tray lost its hold. Down it came with a crash—being still heavily packed—and away went the children, screaming and crying, one taking one direction, the other another.

We went in pursuit of them, and when found, one was crouching down in the court-yard under a rose-bush, while the other stood in terror behind the heavy parlor door. Both were shaking, their teeth chattering, while they muttered something about "*el diablo! el diablo!*" the devil

By this time I understood the line which people of this class in Mexico unflinchingly draw between their own humble station and mine, yet I felt moved to treat the frightened children with the same hospitality which in my own land would have proved soothing under similar circumstances. Acting upon this inspiration, I went quickly and brought a basin of water to wash their tear-stained faces. To my utter surprise, they exclaimed in the same breath: "*No lo permito!*" ("We cannot permit it!") "*No es costumbre.*"

The mother approached me with an expression of deep concern and seriousness in her eyes, and with her forefinger raised in gentle admonition. Looking me earnestly in the face, she began moving her finger slowly from side to side directly before my eyes, saying: "*Oiga, Señorita, sepa V. que en esta tierra, cuando nosotros los Mexicanos*" (referring of course to her own class) "*tenemos el catarro*" (emphasizing the last word on G sharp), "*nunca nos lavamos las caras*" ("Listen to me, my good lady, in this country, when we have the catarrh (meaning a bad cold), we never put water on our faces").

"Why not?" I asked.

"*Porque no estamos acostumbradas, y por el clima, sale más mala la enfermedad*" ("Because we are not accustomed to it, and on account of the climate, the sickness is made worse").

Thus ended the dialogue. But the children did not hold me responsible for their fright, and bade me a kindly *adios*, promising to return again, a promise fulfilled every week, but on no account would they ever venture near *that* trunk again.

Pancho was determined to give to us and our belongings, as far as possible, the exterior appearance of the "*costumbres.*" On entering my room after a little absence, one day, I found him straining every nerve and panting for breath. He had made a low bench, and was trying to place my Saratoga on it, but his strength was not

"NO ES COSTUMBRE."

Servant in northern Mexico telling her foreign mistress, "It is not customary," circa 1885. From Fanny Chambers Gooch, *Face to Face with the Mexicans: The Domestic Life, Educational, Social, and Business Ways, Statesmanship and Literature, Legendary and General History of the Mexican People, as Seen and Studied by an American Woman During Seven Years of Intercourse with Them* (New York: Fords, Howard, and Hulbert, 1887), 89.

equal to the task. The explanation came voluntarily that, on account of the *animalitos*, it was customary for families to keep trunks on benches or tables. I soon found the *animalitos* had reference to the various bugs and scorpions which infest the houses, and all trunks were really kept as Pancho said.

As time passed, Pancho constituted himself our instructor and guide in every manner possible, including both diet and health. He warned us against the evil effects of walking out in the sun after ten o'clock in the morning, and especially enjoined upon us not to drink water or wash our faces on returning, as catarrh and headache would be sure to follow. Supposing this only the superstition of an ignorant servant, I took a special delight in taking just such walks, and violating these rules, but every time I paid the forfeit in a cold and headache, according to prediction. I was now satisfied that Pancho was not only wise as a serpent and harmless as a dove, blest with a keen eye of discrimination, but also a first-class health officer, and in the movement of his forefinger lay tomes of reason and good sense. But I had soon to discover that he would have no infringement of his privileges; and, come what would, he was determined to have his *pilon* in the market.

The servants who came and went often warned me that under no consideration must I go to market, but this was one of my home customs, and I could see no reason for its discontinuance. The system of giving the *pilon* (fee) to the servants, by merchants and market-people, as I already knew, would be a stumbling-block in my way. I had discussed in Pancho's presence my determination to go regularly, when I fancied I saw a strange light come into his eyes, which soon explained itself. He came humbly before me, in a short time, hat in hand, his face bearing the sorrowful, woe-begone look of one in the depths of an overwhelming calamity, saying, that a cart had run over his grandmother, and he would have to leave. He had been so kind and considerate in every way—never tiring of any task he had to perform—and so faithful, that I would prove my sympathy and good will to him by an extra sum—outside his wages—which might be a blessing, and aid in restoring his aged grandmother. He walked off, as if distressed beyond measure, at the same time assuring me that he would send his *comadrita* (little godmother of his children) and her husband, who would serve me well.

They came, but it was unfortunate for Pancho. The woman was an inveterate talker, and soon informed me that she was not the *comadrita* of his children; nor had a cart run over his grandmother; in fact, he had none, as she had died before Pancho was born. This was a new phase of the subject, but I was not long in solving the enigma. He had been goaded long enough by my American methods; he had become the butt of ridicule from his friends, and now he would assert himself.

However well he was treated in our house, to be called upon to surrender the most precious boon of all his *"costumbres"*—the market fees—never! But to wound my feelings in leaving was far from his wishes, so he shrewdly planned and carried out the tragic story of the mishap to his grandmother.

The *comadrita* introduced herself with chastened dignity as Jesusita Lopez; but with head loftily erect, and an air of much consequence, informed me that the name of her *marido*—(husband)—was Don Juan Bautista (John the Baptist), *servidores de V.*—("your obedient servants").

She smiled at every word, a way she had of assuring me of her delight in being allowed to serve me, but at the same time, glanced ominously at the cooking-stove. The smile lengthened into a broad grin when Don Juan Bautista came in sight; in her eyes he was "kingdoms, principalities, and powers." Together they examined the stove—talking in undertone—stooping low and scrutinizing every compartment. At last Don Juan Bautista arose, and turning to me said, "Jesusita cannot cook on this *máquina Americana*" (American machine).

"Why?" I asked. He straightened himself up to the highest point, half on tip toe, at the same time nodding his head, and pointing his forefinger at Jesusita, emphatically replied:

"Because it will give her disease of the liver—*como siempre*—as always, with the servants here."

On going to the kitchen a little later, I was surprised to see the gentle Jesusita seated in the middle of the floor, by a charcoal fire, with all my pottery vessels in a heap beside her. Meats, vegetables, and water were all at hand, and she was busily engaged in preparations for dinner. I told her to come and see how well she could cook on that American machine, but she only answered, *"No es costumbre"*; besides, "Don Juan Bautista said it would give her the *enfermedad*, or sickness, before mentioned—and no man knew more than he"—which meant I should use my own machine.

I called upon Don Juan Bautista to go with me to market, when he at once entered into a lengthy discourse about ladies going to

Young Mexican girl grinding corn for tortillas, circa 1905. Nevin O. Winter, *Mexico and Her People Today* (Boston: Page Co., 1918), n.p.

such places; that the *jente decente* (people of pedigree) never did such things; that "the people in the streets and markets would talk much and say many things." But of this I had already had a foretaste.

I was about to lead the way through the big door, when Jesusita came forward and laid her soft hand upon me, saying: "Señora, *do not go*; Juan knows better than you about such business. In this country ladies like you send the *mozo*." But I was proof against her persuasive eloquence. To surrender my entire nationality and individuality was not possible for a good American. *rigid foreigner*

The pair talked aside in a low undertone, which I watched with feigned indifference and half-closed eyes. Jesusita glanced commiseratively at me, as if she had used her best efforts to no purpose; but Don Juan Bautista threw his most determined and unrelenting expression upon me, as if to say: "Well, she has had enough warning; now the responsibility rests on her own shoulders!"

He looked back at Jesusita as he stepped from the door, nodding his head—"Well,—I will go; but she will wish she had not gone!"

In the market Juan Bautista never left me for a moment, inspecting closely everything I bought—now and then throwing in a word when he thought I was paying too much. He counted every cent as fast as I paid it out, and noted every article placed in the basket. I had nearly completed my purchases, and was talking to a woman about the prospect for butter—regretting the difficulty of getting it,—when she leaned across the table, waggling that tireless forefinger at me, saying, *"En este tiempo ya no hay, no es costumbre"* ("At this time of the year there is none"), Juan Bautista chiming in (with the interminable waggle of his forefinger also), *"No! no hay!"* ("No, indeed, there is none").

The last purchase was made, and I was about closing my purse, when glancing up, I saw Juan Bautista's great merciless eyes fixed upon me, while he said in a firm voice: "But, *mi pilon*, Señora!" This is the custom of the country. If you stay at home, I get my *pilon* from the merchants and market people; if you come—I must have it anyhow. A wrangle was impossible, and handing him *dos reales* (twenty-five cents), I went home a far wiser woman.

Jesusita looked proudly upon the towering form of Juan Bautista as he entered the portal—basket in one hand, *dos reales* in the other. Not a word was spoken between them, but looks told volumes. *She* knew what Juan could do, and *he* had proved to her his ability to

cope with the stranger from any part of the world. To myself I con-
fessed that in Don Juan Bautista I had found a foeman worthy of
my steel.

I asked him to light the fire in the stove and I would make another effort to instruct Jesusita in its management. He went about
it, while I withdrew for a few moments to my room. Very soon I
noticed that the house was full of smoke. Supposing it to be on fire,
I ran to the kitchen, which was in a dense fog, but no fire visible.
Nor was Jesusita or Don Juan Bautista to be found. The cause of
the smoke was soon discovered. He had built the fire in the oven,
and closed the doors!

I clapped my hands for them, according to custom; but they
came not. I then found them sitting in the shady court; Jesusita's
right arm lay confidingly on Juan Bautista's big left shoulder, as
she looked up entreatingly at the harsh countenance of the arbiter
of her fate.

I gleaned from their conversation that she wished to remain,
but her *marido* was evidently bent on going. On my approach they
rose politely, and Juan Bautista delivered the valedictory, assuring
me in pleasant terms of their good-will; and it was not the *pilon*
business—*that* had been settled—but the certainty that Jesusita's
health would be injured by using the cooking-stove decided him.

He said they would go to their *"pobre casa"*—I knew they had
none; then gathering up their goods and chattels, with the unvary-
ing politeness of the country, *"Hasta otro vista"* ("Until I see you
again"), *"Vaya V. con Dios!"* ("May God be with you!"), they
stepped lightly over the threshold—looked up and down the street,
uncertain which way to go—then out they went into the great busy
world. Thus disappeared forever from my sight Pancho's *comadrita*.

In every new servant we employed new characteristics were
developed. All agreed in their leading *costumbres*, yet differed in
the manner of carrying them into effect, while their quaintness and
individuality afforded me constant entertainment. Some came humbly, giving only one name, while others used much formality, never
failing to give the prefix Don or Doña.

Their names were as puzzling as their hereditary customs. I
found that while the Southern negro had been shrewd in appropri-
ating the names of such great men as George Washington, Henry
Clay, and Thomas Jefferson, the Mexican servants had likewise
availed themselves of the names of their own great men. I hired
Miguel Hidalgo twice, Porfirio Díaz once, Manuel Gonzales three

times, as also numerous others. But when a little, old, weazened, solemn-looking man, with a face as sanctimonious as an Aztec deity, wanted employment, and gave his name as "Pio Quinto" ([Pope] Pius V), assuring me he would guard well my front door, he quite took my breath away.

Among the many who came immediately under my observation was a newly married pair who had walked a hundred miles, seeking employment. They had neither beds nor bedding; nor, in fact, anything save the soiled, tattered clothing they wore.

The wife's name was Juanita, and knowing that Juan meant John, I then supposed that the addition of the *ita*, signifying little, made it Little John; but a further knowledge of names and idioms revealed the fact that Juana was Jane, and Juanita little Jane. But I began by calling her Little John, and so continued as long as she was in my employ. The diminutive was peculiarly appropriate. I see her now—this patient, docile, helpful child-woman. Her wealth of shining black hair hung in a long plait; her eyes, soft, yet glowing with a strange peculiar, half-human, half-animal fire.

When the *rebozo* fell from her shoulders, a dainty figure was revealed—the contour exquisitely rounded. Her hand and arm would have delighted an artist for a model. Her step on the stone floor was light and free—noiseless as that of a kitten. Her voice was plaintive, sweet, and low, accompanied by a manner so gentle, so humble—expressing without saying, "May I do something for you?" If I were sick, Little John would take her place on the floor by the bedside, hold my hands, stroking them tenderly, bathe my brow and feet, murmuring in pathetic tones, "*Mi pobre Señora!*" ("My poor lady or madame"), which finally died away on half-parted lips, with "*Pobrecita!*" ("Poor little thing!")

I was curious about her family ties, and asked her of her people, a hundred miles away. "Have you a father and mother?" said I one day. The little form swayed back and forth. She made a low wail—the most pitiful heart-cry—a smothered pent-up sob, laden with all the griefs of Little John's orphaned life. With tearful eyes and bowed head, clasping my hands, she wailed out again and again, "*Muertos!*" ("Dead!") "*No tengo mas que mi marido!*" ("I have only my husband"). The poor little creature's story was told.

In consideration of my many difficulties in this line, I was glad to give them employment, when, according to custom, they solicited a portion of their wages in advance. Having received it, the wife, ignoring her own great needs, bought material for clothing for her husband. She borrowed my scissors; and I, curious to see how she would manage the cutting, went to her room to note the process.

As thought Pancho about "fingers having been made before knives and forks," so thought this young *pobre* about seats, as she sat, tailor fashion, on the dirt floor.

Such measuring and calculating as she had, in order to get two shirts out of three yards and a half! I laughed until I cried over her dilemma, as well as over the solicitude of her spouse about the result. He was evidently deeply interested.

She was only fourteen years of age, which gave an additional interest and a touching pathos to her anxious devotion. I thought to myself: "Woman-like, you will give your last farthing, take sleep from your eyes, even die, for the man you love!"

She finally cut out the shirts, the material being heavy brown domestic, and with the same untiring earnestness drew threads, made tiny tucks in the bosom, and when they were completed, brought them to me for inspection. More exquisite stitching or more perfectly made garments I never saw; but, as might be imagined, they would have been a close fit on a mere boy. This, however, was no impediment to the enthusiastic zeal of this interesting pair, and the shirts were duly worn by his lordship.

All the money which they earned jointly, with commendable unselfishness on her part went for his adornment, she continuing, with the aid of a calico dress which I gave her, the possessor of one suit and a half. With the same ever predominating feminine instinct, shoes were purchased for the husband; and very soon he was strutting about the premises as if monarch of all he surveyed.

In every possible way he made pretexts for errands that he might show off his clothes. His peacock strut was inimitably funny, and caused me unending amusement, though the smile was often checked by the thought of the poor little wife's unselfishness. The heart of woman is, after all, everywhere the same, and too frequently her devotion must be its own and sole reward.

One of his edicts was, that his wife should not dress fowls. The custom of skinning instead of plucking fowls exists in Mexico. But I was leaving nothing untried to have everything done according to my notions. One day, when he was detained away for several hours, I ordered a pair of chickens for dinner, and directed poor Little Johnny how to prepare them. Without remonstrance she went willingly at the task; but before the chickens were ready for cooking, *señor*, the husband, returned.

I was watching with bated breath, feeling sure there would be a tempest. He did not intend I should witness the *dénouement*, but I was determined to see the fun.

Without speaking audibly, he passed by where she was standing, wrenched from her hands the partly dressed fowls, and in a moment more disappeared in the *corral*.

I took another route to find my chickens, and instinct led me to the spot. On going to the carriage-house, I found them with strong cords tied around their necks, suspended from the old vehicle. By hanging the poor dead chickens, he retaliated for my presumption in directing his wife to prepare them without his consent and in his absence.

My curiosity next led me to see whether he had hanged his wife, or was erecting a gallows for me. Searching about the garden and out-houses, I found the couple in an unfrequented walk. She was wringing her hands and crying, while he stood bolt upright, bestowing upon her every severe expression and word of chastisement at his command. His jetty, straight hair stood up all over his head, his eyes glittered with rage, his brown lips were white, and his teeth champed viciously! All this was accompanied by the popping of his fists together, in the most effective manner. Every time this tragic part of the performance was executed, she would jump, and give a fresh howl of agony over the disobedience she had so innocently practiced, saying: "*Perdóname, no lo vuelvo á hacer*" ("Oh, forgive me, I won't do it again.").

The end of all this was that they took up their pallets of maguey and walked, leaving me to a pious meditation on the frailties and foibles of human nature in general, and on the peculiarities of Mexican servants in particular; and also to the disagreeable necessity of cutting the chickens down, and preparing my dinner single-handed.

The meek little wife, guarded by her grim liege, looked back at me askant, slyly kissed her hand, and smiled. This was the last I saw of Juanita.

The *mozo*, of all the various servants, was daily becoming more and more a vexatious problem. Indispensable, but to the last degree puzzling, I was anxious to know at what point in my experience the tolerated or "customary" labors of this individual would be introduced. The time had now come when, as I feared, his entire vocabulary would narrow down to this one familiar sentence, "*No es costumbre*," and he would assume the immovable and useless position of a mere figurehead. My imagination was wrought to an exalted state of anticipation, and I knew not what a day would bring forth. Every day carried me nearer to the time of Mother Noah, and to a world of chance. Wood, when not in small pieces and sold from the backs of burrows, brought root, branch, and top, on ancient carts with wooden wheels, larger than the Aztec calendar; dogs called "Sal" regardless of sex; the yellow of the egg white; corn husks sold by the hundred; vinegar from France; and the tomato, our delicious vegetable, here assuming the masculine prefix he-tomato (spelled *jitomati*); all these things formed a grotesque panorama of curious contradictions all safely fortified behind the cast-iron "*Costumbres.*"

Courtship and Marriage

Courtship is something of a serious matter as undertaken under Mexican auspices. The probation may extend from five to ten years, or may even exceed that of Jacob, and at the end of this period the devoted Romeo has perhaps never entered the house—possibly not even spoken to his Juliet. Patience is a virtue all possess; and as time is of no consequence, they content themselves with waiting for something in the future. The lover walks slowly back and forth before her house for hours at a time, days and nights alike. Perhaps it is from this fact that he assumes the unromantic appellation of *haciendo el oso* (playing the bear). He may also play the bear on horseback, and his "ladye faire" knows by intuition when he will pass, and, securely screened from public gaze remains behind the curtain on the balcony and merely shows her head or salutes him with her finger-tips. She goes to church or on the plaza, sure that he is not far away, and though they do not speak, a glance or smile each day is worth a lifetime. But frequently tiny *billets doux* find their way to the angel upstairs, by means of strings, and the family is none the wiser.

I remember to have seen one young man "playing the bear" until my deepest sympathies were enlisted in his behalf. Day by day he repaired to the same spot, on the corner of the street opposite my window, at No. 6 la Primera de la Providencia. For months the trying business had gone on, until he was reduced to a mere skeleton, and his hollow eyes had that expectant expression which marks the victim of love in Mexico. So interested was I that I determined to know something of the fair creature to whom the luckless swain was yielding up his mental, moral and physical strength.

The father of the girl was so much opposed to the match, the young man being only a medical student, he forbade his going nearer than two squares of the house.

Having seen the effect of "playing the bear" on this lover, I was curious to see how the girl sustained the ordeal. Directed by his fixed and steady gaze upon the house, I found her standing on the balcony with only her head visible. Her eyes were fixed on him, and now and then the dainty little hand made motions towards him. After a few months thus spent, the poor fellow disappeared from the corner, which was perhaps the end of their love-making.

I was told by several English-speaking Mexicans that the larger proportion of the young men of the country greatly prefer "playing the bear" from the sidewalk, to entering the homes of the señoritas, even if permitted by custom.

I witnessed the opposite of this in the case of a young Mexican girl who had been reared by an American sister-in-law. Lupe was pretty and attractive, and naturally at an early age was the recipient, from the young men who had come within sight of her, of numerous bearish favors; but two of them, Fernando — and Julio —; became more deeply enamored than the rest; but the sister was determined there should be no "playing the bear," so she invited the young men to call at the house. I have seen as many as ten or twelve in her parlor in one evening, all animated and interested—each one being only too pleased to take his turn at a few moments' conversation with the señorita.

But a *dénouement*, quite unexpected, came. One of the young men who had become desperately enamored of the girl, found he had a rival in one of his friends. A dispute arose, some of the boys espousing one side and the remainder the other, until bloodshed seemed inevitable. No case in chancery ever required more skillful diplomacy than this, calling for the good offices of at least half a dozen outside friends to adjust the matter and prevent a catastrophe. The rupture between the boys was never healed, but neither of them won the señorita. So, after all, perhaps it is better that they should have "bear playing" in order to win their wives. I confess that after witnessing these love affairs I was for once, as our latter-day politicians say, "on the fence," and quite as ready to fall on the "bear side" as on that of our less conventional, more modern lovemaking.

A Mexican lady related to me a method of courtship somewhat different. A señorita is sometimes made aware of the interest a young man takes in her, by being continually followed when walking along the street. In the course of time he writes a letter which he leaves with the *portero*,* and it is always necessary to enlist the interest of these men by the bestowal of a little cash. She pays no attention to his first letters, but after a while she may perhaps notice his advances. He goes to the house each day and finds out her movements from the *portero*, governing himself accordingly. At last, accompanied by a responsible friend, he makes bold to call on the father and asks her hand in marriage. Then the father asks the girl if she is willing to marry the young man. She replies she cannot say until she has met him. When at length he calls, every member of the family, and even the servants, have the privilege of being present. After this, he is the *novio oficial* (accepted lover) [suitor], but even if the marriage be postponed six months or as many years, he is never left alone for a moment with his *fiancée*.

Once admitted as *novio oficial*, it may be imagined that the fervor of his devotion will find vent in many lover-like expressions. As indicative of their warm, poetic imagination and passionate Southern nature, I append a few of the most characteristic of these phrases as used by both sexes:

Niña de mi alma!	Child of my soul!
¿Me quieres?	Dost thou love me?
Te adoro, te idolatro!	I adore thee, I idolize thee!
Me muero por ti!	I die for thee!
Eres mi dicha!	Thou art my happiness!
Te amo mas que á mi vida!	I love thee more than my life!
Eres mi único pensamiento!	Thou art my only thought!
Me mato por ti!	I kill myself for thee!
No te olvides de mi!	Do not forget me!
Siempre serás mi!	Thou wilt always be mine!
Tú serás mi solo amor!	Thou wilt be my only love!
No me engañes!	Do not deceive me!
No sabes cuanto te amo!	Thou dost not know how much I love thee!
Oye, hijito, ¿me quieres de veras?	Say, my boy, dost really love me!
Que feliz soy á tu lado!	How happy I am by thy side!

*Gatekeeper—Ed.

No dejes de escribirme!	Don't fail to write me!
¿Vienes mañana?	Will you come to-morrow?
Ingrato, Ya lo sé todo!	Ingrate, I know all!
Pero hija, eso no es cierto!	But daughter, it is not true!
¿No me crees?	Dost thou not believe me?
Perdoname corazon!	Pardon me, heart!
Adios chula, hasta mañana!	Good-bye, precious, until to-morrow!
Sueño contigo!	I dream of thee!

The señorita is not intentionally, or by nature, a flirt. She would scorn to inveigle in her meshes the affections of her admirer. But, in addition to her irresistible eyes, there are certain little social and toilet graces which she unconsciously employs in a most expressive manner that never fail to bring him to her feet.

The most effectual and indispensable toilet accessory is the fan. Of every size, style, and color, it is often an expensive item in a fashionable lady's outfit. When manipulated by the fair owner—opened wide and waved in graceful challenge, raised to eyes or lips in witching coquetry, or even when peacefully folded in jeweled fingers—its language is varied and expressive.

Great care and attention is bestowed upon the *pañuelo* (handkerchief), which plays, too, an important part, second only to that of the fan.

For a young man of moderate means, matrimony is a serious undertaking. He not only furnishes the house and home, but the bridal outfit as well. But in some of the wealthier families parents furnish the greater part of the latter themselves, restricting the purchases of the groom elect to perhaps the bridal dresses, the jewels, and other accessories. An ivory-covered prayer-book is an indispensable offering from the groom. The bridal tour is one expense from which he is now exempt, but as facilities for travel increase, perhaps in the near future, this item may be added to his already long list of expenditures. I believe the event of matrimony is no less troublesome than the long and tedious courtship. The war of reform made three marriage ceremonies necessary. Two months before, the young people must register at the cathedral, giving date of birth, in what city or country, vocation, etc., whether widow or widower. After this, the priest registers the same at the civil office, and their intentions must be placed on a bulletin board outside the office for twenty days. For five Sundays the priest publishes the banns. After this, accompanied by the notary public, he goes to the house of the bride, where she is asked if she acts of her "own free will and accord," and other necessary questions are put with as much freedom as though the subject were a transfer of real estate. A few days prior to the church wedding, the judge of the court, accompanied by six witnesses, the priest being one, performs the civil marriage. The dress worn on this occasion is presented by the groom. . . .

Courtship and Love among the Lower Classes

They [the mixed-race lower classes] are possessed of a certain amount of piquancy, as expressed in their peculiar dialect and idioms. With this there is united also a strong vein of humor, and they usually see a point as quickly as any people.

In consideration of the fact that they have but little education, their native shrewdness and intelligence are surprising. The most highly educated and enlightened cannot cope with them in the matter of barter and sale and the counting of money. By instinct they know just how, when, and where to strike the weak point of a stranger in any business transaction. . . .

Their social life is of a free nature, and consequently but few marriages take place among them. The women are vulgarly called *gatas* (cats), or *garbanceras* (bastards); the former are those who usually perform the offices of chambermaids, nurses and cooks, the latter generally do the marketing.

As the shops where the marketing is done are kept by the common people, when a *marchanta* (customer) appears, the shopkeeper begins to pay her compliments, and say things with double meanings. She usually answers in the same manner, which causes the shopkeeper to laugh. If the servant is at all attractive, and the clerk understands that she is a match for him, and sees that she receives his compliments with pleasure, he takes her basket, keeps on talking to her, and tries to keep her as long as possible. They carry on something like the following dialogue by the clerk saying to her:

"Que cosa se le ofrece, mi vida?" ("What do you want, my life?")

"No se enoje porque hasta eso sale perdiendo" ("Don't get mad, for you will only be the loser").

"No le importa, anda dispacheme," she replies ("Mind your own business, come wait on me").

"Pues deme la mano y digame como se llama" ("Well, give me your hand and tell me your name"), he rejoins.

Her reply to this is full of stinging sarcasm, which finds vent in the following way:

"Ora si! que encamisado, tan igualado! Parece que soy su jugete. Anda dispacheme y no esté moliendo que se me hace tarde y la niña me regaña porque me tardo con el mandado" ("Well, I should say you were a naked upstart. One would think I was your plaything. Come, wait on me, and don't bother me, for it is getting late, and the mistress will scold me for being so long doing the errands").

When he sees she is a little angry, he gives her back the basket with the things she has bought. She then throws the money to him on the counter, in an angry manner, for him to take out the cost of what she has bought. When he gives her back the change, he takes her hand, which she pulls away, after he has given it a squeeze. The next day she returns to the same shop or stand, but this time she presents herself a little less reluctantly than before, and without minding at all what is said to her. On the contrary, she leads him on, by throwing little stones at him or giving him a sly pinch.

At the end of a month or two they make an appointment to meet where they may take advantage of the opportunity to treat of their love affair more freely. The day, hour and place being appointed, by means of which they can see each other alone (which is the first object of all lovers), they get permission from their employers, and dressing themselves the best they can, hasten to the trysting place.

The first time they look at each other they are somewhat disconcerted, and try to pretend indifference. But she is not so severe in her manner but that he feels authorized in venturing on a caress. From that time he thinks it proper that she should not serve any longer where she has been, although she has been giving him a part of all her wages. In reply she says she "does not want to lose her peace of mind, because men always say the same thing to women, and she does not want him to repent by and by and put her out into the street." But at last she adds, "If you will not forsake me and will treat me kindly, I am disposed to love you; only you must tell my parents, and, if they consent, and your intentions are good, you can rely upon my being your sweetheart."

After this, the man takes the woman by the hand or puts his arm around her; and covering her with his own *serape*, which is the general custom, they go to some stand where things, if not of very good quality, are excessively cheap, and eat *enchiladas* and *tamales* and drink *pulque*.

Often the honeymoon does not last long; dissension and strife are apt to ensue, and the old story of domestic infelicity is repeated. Still, though the woman concludes her husband does not love her, if he does not use the rod, they are not so miserable as might appear.

A woman of the common people prefers a man of her own class, however poor and rough he may be, to one of a higher station, whatever offers or promises he may make her. For they still preserve the traditional aversion which the creoles and native races have always felt for foreigners.

Among the Indians the violation of conjugal faith is more rare than in any other class of society; not even excepting the middle class, which, beyond question in Mexico, as in all other countries, is the most moral and upright.

When legal marriages occur, the parents make every arrangement when the young people have arrived at an age at which they are able to bear the responsibilities of married life. When such a case presents itself, the parents of the lover go to the house of the sweetheart, and take with them a *chiquihuite* (a certain kind of big basket), containing a turkey, several bottles of native brandy and other drinks, bread, ears of dried corn, and peppers of different kinds. The first time the parents of the lover go to ask for the girl's hand, they organize a sort of procession, composed of some of the relatives and friends of the family and a band of music, which plays without intermission from the house from which they start to the dwelling of the maiden.

Once there, the band and the rest of the procession are profoundly silent, while the petition is being made.

The first request is generally refused by the parents of the girl, until they consult with the relatives and ascertain the will of her who is sought in marriage. If the result is favorable, they appoint the wedding day; if unfavorable, the answer is reduced simply to returning the basket with its contents.

As soon as the news in the affirmative is received, the family of the bridegroom invite all their friends to the fandango which is given on the day of the wedding, in honor of the newly-married couple.

The bridegroom appears in pantaloons and short jacket of cashmere, white embroidered shirt, red sash, rawhide or deerskin shoes, and a highly decorated, broad-brimmed hat. Followed by his family, *padrinos* (those who are to give him away), witnesses, and those who have been invited, he proceeds to the house of the bride, where he is overwhelmed with attentions from the family.

The dress of the bride consists of a blue skirt with red sash, and a chemise with a deep yoke and sleeves elaborately embroidered with bright-colored beads, a red silk handkerchief with points crossed in front, and held by a fancy pin. The handkerchief serves to cover the neck and breast, leaving the arms free. She also wears many strings of beads, and silver hoop ear-rings of extraordinary size. Her hair is worn in two braids, laid back and forth on the back of her head, the ends tied with red ribbons. She wears *babuchas*, a kind of slipper made either of deerskin trimmed with beads or of gay cloth. The toilet is completed with a white woolen mantle, cut in scallops trimmed with blue, and hanging from the plaited hair.

Maria Graham

9

HELEN SANBORN

A Wellesley Graduate's Travels in Guatemala

On a cold New England winter day in 1885, Helen Josephine Sanborn (1857–1917), a recent Wellesley College graduate (class of 1884), left Boston with her father for Central America. As she tells us, she had learned Spanish so that her father, J. S. Sanborn of the Chase and Sanborn coffee company, would take her with him on a business trip to Central America and Mexico. The Sanborns traveled slowly by mule on bad roads from the Caribbean coast to the highlands of central Guatemala and later to Mexico via Panama, a trip Helen Sanborn described in *A Winter in Central America and Mexico.* Although she published no other books, she later served as a member of the school board of her home town of Somerville, Massachusetts, and became a trustee of Wellesley College in 1906. She died in Somerville on April 26, 1917.

Like some other educated young women of the late nineteenth century, Sanborn had been eager to travel abroad. In the introduction to *A Winter in Central America and Mexico*, she described herself as "fresh from college and longing for a glimpse of foreign lands," and undaunted by efforts to dissuade her from a difficult journey "unreasonable for a lady."* Wellesley College, which had just opened in 1875, contributed to the growth in female education in the United States. During the third quarter of the nineteenth

From Helen J. Sanborn, *A Winter in Central America and Mexico* (Boston: Lee and Shepard, 1889), 44–45, 63–64, 73, 116–17, 135–36, 172–74.

*Helen J. Sanborn, *A Winter in Central America and Mexico* (Boston: Lee and Shepard, 1889), 7, 9.

century, more women than ever before had succeeded in prying open the doors of U.S. institutions of higher education or, often with male financial backing, in founding new ones. Such colleges helped to challenge the conventional wisdom about the extent of women's intellectual capacities and the suitability of further education for females. By the end of the century the college-educated, frequently unmarried, and self-supporting "new woman" would make her appearance. When traveling abroad, such women might directly and favorably compare their countrywomen's relative freedom and autonomy to that of the women they encountered, as did Sanborn, although they generally neglected the relationship between education and class. Nellie Bly was not the only woman to declare her pride in being a "free American girl."

As did many other women authors, Sanborn took a modest approach in the introduction to her book on Guatemala and Mexico. She cited its origins in some selections printed in a trade publication, the *New England Grocer*, which led friends and strangers to urge her to publish her work in book form. However, she claimed as her primary justification for publication the lack of knowledge about Guatemala in the United States.

In that Central American nation, economic and political power remained the monopoly of a Spanish-speaking minority of European or mixed Spanish-Indian ancestry known as *ladinos*. The country was then ruled by President Justo Rufino Barrios, who impressed the Sanborns "most favorably" at their meeting shortly before his death in battle in 1885 while attempting to impose Central American political unity. Although Sanborn acknowledged the conflicting opinions about Barrios and described the dictator's harshness and use of force, she also praised his efforts to bring order and progress to Guatemala in the form of such material advances as railroads, telegraph lines, and public buildings. She even claimed that he protected the Indians. However, Barrios represented a Europeanizing process that attempted to incorporate the Indian majority of Guatemala into Western civilization whether they wished it or not. He promoted the large-scale export of coffee, dependent on the labor of Indians forced to become wage workers, and he allowed the large estates to encroach on the Indians' communal lands. According to Sanborn, Barrios was Guatemala's largest coffee exporter and invested his profits abroad.* Unlike her descriptions of members of the urban elite, Sanborn's depictions of the Mayan Indian majority of Guatemala, whom she praised as gentle and kind, tended to be more general and less personal. She portrayed their physical appearance, dress, and public activities in far more detail than she explained their economic or social situation.

The Indians with whom we were now to eat, sleep, and travel, are . . . a peaceable, honest, docile, and cleanly race; not a warlike, but an agricultural people; not nomadic, but living in villages; not savage, but semi-civilized; tilling the soil, weaving cloth, making pottery and building houses. They are of a brown or copper color, with black hair and eyes, low foreheads, but without the prominent cheekbones, and with kind, pleasant, and often handsome faces. They are noticeably small, being below medium height, squarely built, and with small hands and feet. They are so honest and peaceable that Central America is the safest place in the world in which to travel, and altogether to an American, with our idea of the Indian as a painted savage, they are quite an attractive people. But the poor things are the "beasts of burden" of the country, pack mules being so rare that almost everything is transported on Indian backs, the amount they carry being wonderful. The burden is placed in a wooden cage or basket, to which a strap is attached and passed around the head, so that the weight comes upon the forehead. In this manner, with a weight of over a hundred pounds, they trot off at a queer but rapid pace, making twenty and twenty-five miles daily, and for this arduous work they are never paid more than a "real" (twelve and one-half cents) a day. Much of the coffee is brought in this way from the interior down to the ports; thousands of dollars are entrusted to them, the merchant simply saying, "Your cargo is money," and not one dollar was ever lost or stolen. . . .

We were much interested in the Indian girl, "Candelaria," who was the busiest body in the whole house [at the German-run hotel in the Indian town of Cobán]. She waited on the table, took care of

---

*David McCreery, *Rural Guatemala, 1760–1940* (Stanford: Stanford University Press, 1994), provides a comprehensive account of Guatemalan rural society, including conditions in the countryside prior to the rapid conversion to coffee production in the midnineteenth century. McCreery also details the impact of coffee on the indigenous highland communities and the reimposition of forced wage labor on a large scale.

the rooms, brought water for the house in a jar on her head, went to the market, and in fact was doing something every moment and yet never seemed to be tired. Sometimes we heard her grinding coffee at nine o'clock in the evening, and she was always the first one up in the morning. . . .

Indian women in Guatemala at their domestic tasks, 1875. From Eadweard Muybridge, *Eadweard Muybridge in Guatemala, 1875. The Photographer as Social Recorder*, photographs by Eadweard J. Muybridge and text by E. Bradford Burns (Berkeley: University of California Press, 1986), 109.

The market, which so interested us in every town, was here a large building, the centre being occupied by the Indian women, selling all sorts of provisions, and the exterior surrounded by little booths in which were sold all kinds of fabrics made by the Indians, as well as many cheap imported articles which the Indians buy. It was always a busy and interesting scene, though we saw some curious and anything but agreeable sights; for instance, in the pauses of trade, women nursing their babies or searching industriously the heads of their children with a large, coarse, wooden comb. None of these traders ever have any paper with which to do up a bundle, but instead there are all through the market young girls with baskets on their heads, whose business it is to carry your purchases for you. There is no difficulty in having this sort of express; for there is a host of girls, and as soon as you enter the market they besiege you for a job. They will follow you about for half a day if you like, direct you where to go, advise you what to buy, and then, when you have finished, carry the whole to the hotel for five cents. One thing we learned about shopping, with everybody else who comes here, never to give more than half of what is first charged. Bartering, however disagreeable it may seem, is absolutely essential here. Indeed, if you do not do it, the Indians themselves laugh at you and call you "green Americans." . . .

At this time of the day the road [leaving Guatemala City at 5:30 A.M. bound for Antigua] was thronged with Indians loaded with all sorts of merchandise, wood, vegetables, fruit, pottery, hay, coal, everything needed in the capital, to which they were going from the little villages all around to sell their supplies in the market. They always go in groups; the men by themselves and the women by themselves, a man and a woman never walking together unless married. The men always bear the burdens on their backs; the women on their heads, their backs usually being pre-occupied by the inevitable baby, for the baby is never left at home. Whether the mother is going to market to sell goods, to church to hear mass, or to a funeral to weep in the procession, the baby always goes too; and, what seemed most strange to us, we never once, in all the time we were there, heard an Indian baby cry. They seem to be born into the world as old as their fathers and mothers. We never saw children laughing and running and playing as our children do; they were always grave and serious, as if they had the burden of years and grave responsibilities resting on their shoulders. Both boys and girls began to work as soon as they can walk, and never seem to expect or wish for any fun or play as children here do. . . .

[The condition of the Indians] seemed to us, as near as we could determine, very much like that of the serfs in the old feudal system. We were told that if a man bought a piece of ground the Indians on that land were bound to work for him. Roads are built and repaired, aqueducts made, and the government coffee plantations all carried on by "forced labor," the poor Indians working without a cent of pay. As we have shown, they do the hardest work for the smallest pay, and have but few rights. They have the power to choose, subject to the approval of the "Jefe," one of their number as "alcalde," a sort of judge, to whom they appeal for protection and justice. This is their only voice in the government.

The "ladinos," especially the lower class, are inferior to the Indians in cleanliness, honesty, and industry. Still, they regard themselves as infinitely superior, and treat the Indians with great contempt. . . .

[In Tamaju, the Indian women's] costume, like that of all the Indians throughout the country, was very picturesque. The women's dress consists of a full plaid skirt and a loose, sleeveless waist [blouse], embroidered, often elaborately, with the colors of the tribe. The hair, which is long, black, and often beautiful, is sometimes left flowing, but usually wound with a red woollen roll. They are always barefooted, and wear no jewelry except a necklace of beads and money—their necklace being their bank. The dress of the men consists of a loose jacket and trousers of a stout cloth, always white, and, what is remarkable, always clean. We never saw a dirty Indian, and seldom a ragged one. . . .

In and about the capital it is somewhat different from that of the interior, in that the women, instead of wearing a loose skirt, take a straight piece of cloth and wind it tightly about them, with an awkward effect. One tribe near Antigua dresses in black. The women of the lower class wear an embroidered chemise, a full skirt, and a bright colored "rebosa" (a single shawl), over the shoulders and head, as they never wear hats. Of the higher classes, the wealthiest have adopted the European dress; and often the costumes are imported from Paris, and are very elegant. Very few use hats, but they wear very gracefully the Spanish mantilla upon their heads, and the black shawl of fine texture over the shoulders. It is said that "when the ladies put on hats they leave off smoking." These varied costumes, so different from ours, make the streets a gay and novel scene to the traveller. . . .

The streets are full of Indian women, but one sees very few of the higher classes, and this was so noticeable that we asked, "Where are the ladies of Guatemala?" and received the answer, "In their houses." It is contrary to custom and all rules of etiquette for a lady to go on the street alone, even in the daytime. She must be attended by a servant or another companion, and it is improper for ladies, even in groups of two or three, to be out after dark unattended by a servant. Ladies and gentlemen never walk together on the street unless married.

An American girl does not half appreciate her freedom and independence until she goes to one of these countries. Indeed, the American and German ladies have found these customs so tiresome and disagreeable that they have rather broken over them, and now if a stranger walks the street unattended she is forgiven by the people, who have learned that the customs of other nations are different from their own.

10

MARGUERITE DICKINS

A Naval Captain's Wife on Tour

During much of the nineteenth century, ship captains in the U.S., as in the British, Navy could take wives with them on ocean voyages, or at least arrange their travels and meet them abroad. Like naval officers themselves, those wives might write accounts of their travels. However, Marguerite Dickins, unlike another nineteenth-century sea captain's wife, Maria Graham, was not an experienced, published author prior to her voyage to South America at the end of the century. Dickins produced only one book, *Along Shore with a Man-of-War*—which records more superficial encounters with members of local societies than Maria Graham's—and she is not even mentioned in writers' dictionaries.*

At the turn of the last decade of the nineteenth century, Marguerite Dickins spent two and one-half years sailing up and down the east coast of South America on the U.S.S. *Tallapoosa*, enjoying the scenery and visiting with local officials and their families. Although her travel account did not take the form of diary entries or letters to specific individuals, she contended that her book derived from letters home. Like earlier female authors she modestly claimed that praise of her letters published in the press led her to collect them in book form. In *Along Shore with a Man-of-War*, she described

From Marguerite Dickins, *Along Shore with a Man-of-War* (Boston: Arena Publishing Co., 1893), 225–31, 239–41.
*Madeleine Vinton Dahlgren, wife of Admiral John A. Dahlgren, commander of the South Pacific Squadron of the U.S. Navy, also wrote an account of her travels in the late 1860s: *South Sea Sketches. A Narrative* (Boston: James R. Osgood and Co., 1881).

visits to cities along the coast of Brazil, Buenos Aires and cities of the Argentine interior, Montevideo, a crossing to La Paz, and then a trip up the Paraná and Paraguay rivers to the Paraguayan capital of Asunción, to which foreigners had only limited access earlier in the century.

Long one of the most isolated nations in South America and one of the continent's only two land-locked countries, Paraguay is a riverine nation. Depending on political conditions during the nineteenth century, vessels from various nations sailed up the long Río de la Plata-Paraná-Paraguay river system to Asunción. But relatively few foreigners ever came to Paraguay to settle, visit, or trade. Under the dictatorship of José Gaspar Rodríguez de Francia, president from 1811 (Paraguayan independence) until his death in 1840, Paraguay became a more isolated nation. A controversial figure, Francia has been commonly viewed as cruel, cunning, and vengeful, with a hatred of foreigners and a fear of entanglements. But a minority of scholars has challenged this view, presenting him as an austere and honest leader who championed the poor and dispossessed and worked to achieve a self-sufficient and independent Paraguay. Francia's successor, Cárlos Antonio López (1844–1862), opened river trade with Buenos Aires and Europe. But under López's son and successor, Francisco Solano López (1862–1870), Paraguay engaged Brazil, Argentina, and Uruguay in the disastrous War of the Triple Alliance, a clash of imperialistic pretensions perhaps better known as the Paraguayan War. Only after five years of fighting (1865–1870) could the allies subdue Paraguay. The most savage war in Latin American history, it opened the Plata River network to international commerce and travel but it also killed a high percentage of Paraguay's males between the ages of fourteen and sixty-five. The population still had not recovered by the time Marguerite Dickins visited this highly miscegenated society. However, foreign trade as well as land ownership increased in this small country, which was maintained as a buffer state between Argentina and Brazil.

Some foreign visitors to late nineteenth-century Paraguay, including Dickins, appeared more interested in shopping than in investing. By then the increasing numbers of foreigners enjoying facilitated travel to Latin America could pay more attention to purchases than to personal safety. Rather than narrate encounters with bandits, stubborn mules, or poisonous snakes, they described produce in local markets. Tourism penetrated even to the center of the South American continent, and as tourists joined traverlers, souvenir hunting became another travel activity, as demonstrated in Dickins's account. However, Dickins also noted the preponderance of female venders and the predominance of handicraft industries (especially the Paraguayan lace she loved to buy and the intensive and poorly paid female labor required to produce it). She also described women's involvement in educating the largely illiterate population.

There are about 25,000 inhabitants in Asunción, and we found several good wharves, back of one of which they are building a custom-house that promises to be quite a fine one. Steamers run up twice a week from Buenos Aires to this city, and when one was in, I liked to frequent the wharves to see the bales of mate* and tobacco, boxes of cigars, ferns, palms, orchids, and other living plants; parrots, parroquets, small birds, deer, monkeys, and many small animals that were always brought down to be shipped to the lower river ports. There are two street railways, and between their tracks the ground is paved; otherwise and elsewhere the streets are full of sand, which gets into one's shoes and seems unpleasant, but I heard several people complaining that it was proposed to pave the streets, which they thought would make the city unhealthy, as all of those impurities which now sank into the sand would rest on top of a pavement and poison the air! . . .

In the sandy streets one often met the wild Indian woman with a child or two, trying to sell a few gourds or feather dusters. I bought two gourds of a woman who was so repulsive in face, form, and dirt that it seemed unnatural to see her fondle the baby she carried.

The native Paraguayans are tall and bronze skinned. The women are generally clad in white cotton skirt and manta, and the folds falling in straight lines and draping them from head to foot were very picturesque, and the burden carried balanced on the head gave them erect carriage and even gait. When we met a woman with a bundle that looked like cloth on her head we would say *Nanduti* in a questioning tone, and then, if she had any, the bundle would be

*The dried leaves of the *Ilex paraguariensis* are used to make a popular drink in the Rio de la Plata region, yerba maté—Ed.

lifted from her head and placed anywhere in the sandy street, and we all would sit down to enjoy a trade.

Nanduti is Guarani for spider's-web, and is used to specify a lace as fine as any made in Europe and more charming because of its novelty. It is made with a threaded needle, web and pattern being woven at the same time, and is generally made in wheels, hence the name, and these wheels are put together to form borders for handkerchiefs, fans, yokes for chemises, trimming by the yard, and a coarse variety for sofa pillows, bed covers, and towel ends. The thread used for fine pieces is about No. 300. The workwoman stretches a bit of muslin on a hand frame, threads a needle, and weaves her spider-web wheel, attaching it at the edges to the muslin. When finished, she cuts it loose and begins another. It is very cheap, as one can buy for $10 a handkerchief that has taken two months' labor to complete. They prefer gold in payment, as they use it to make puzzle rings and ornaments, and offering it always caused a reduction. It is said that they were taught by the Jesuit mission fathers some 300 years ago, which may be so, but it seems more likely to me that a native manufacture was improved and fostered by the fathers. In these bundles we also found table cloths and napkins of loosely-woven cotton, with bands of insertion down the center and large wheels of *nanduti* set in the corners.

Then there was a coarser knit lace, which is made of unbleached cotton threads and wears like iron; it comes in chemise yokes, edging, and insertion. There would be yokes of darned and embroidered tulle that were gems in their way, and at the bottom of the bundle would be pretty, serviceable hammocks of white cotton or striped twine and with a fringe falling along each side. When the bargain for lace or dry-goods was concluded, to touch our rings would suffice to make the vender bring from her pocket a handkerchief on which would be strung a number of gold puzzle rings made of slender chased rings, eight or nine of them, twisted so to form a solid ring when on the finger and falling apart as soon as taken off, requiring patience and dexterity to replace them. These women make the articles in their own homes all over the country and carry them to the towns for sale, but never sell to stores. If ever their fine *nanduti* becomes known in this country it is sure to become popular and take a permanent place among their finest goods on the counters of our lace merchants.

The market was a perpetual source of delight, and I went there every day of our stay. Raised two and three steps from the street was the tall, square building, occupying a square, and surrounded by a double row of columns reaching to the roof, the whole colored a deep, dark red. Crouched among the columns were groups of women and children, their bronze skins showing plainly each outline where the pure white garments parted, jet black hair falling down their backs in two braids or caught up into a careless cluster by a big comb with gold top.

These gold combs were much prized formerly, and the women divided into two classes, those who had gold combs and those who had not. These groups were guarding piles of yellow maize, yams, potatoes, and mandioca. Coming and going were numbers of white-robed figures bearing burdens on their heads, from tiny bundles to big red earthen jars filled with water. Inside was a large, square, open court filled with low tables covered with merchandise, and all, even those where meat was cut up, served by women, for the war took so many of the men that women do all the work and fill all sorts of unaccustomed places; a male child being a treasure beyond price in their eyes, the little naked fellows bare faced around as you pass that you may notice the sex and envy the mother accordingly. Here we found meat, vegetables, monkeys and other pets, breads of all kinds, and among them a crescent-shaped roll of bread and cheese baked together; lace of the different kinds and native-made jewelry stands, where we purchased gold beads, combs, and ear-rings. There were piles of native cigars—excellent tobacco they are made of—and every one smokes. The best brand is Papa Lucas and they cost $2 a hundred. Just back of the market is a large barren plaza, where one of the Presidents was once assassinated. . . .

The hotel in the city [Asunción] is on the Calle Palmas, and is a large building with nice airy rooms, but none of the modern conveniences. The dining-room is the patio and the food excellent, as well as the fruit. Not far away was the public school, as Paraguay has copied the Argentine in adopting our public school system, and has imported two United States young women to begin the work— a Miss Wales and a Miss Reid. They were furnished with a fine large house, were accumulating excellent apparatus, and were paid good salaries regularly. Of course, it was exile, but Miss Wales seemed too much interested to mind, and Miss Reid was looking forward to matrimony. The children were of the best families and attendance good, the hours of attendance being somewhat longer than with us, and a few extra branches taught.

There were a good many pretty leopard skins for sale, as the animals were numerous farther up country, and a stuffed skin was presented to us, which not only proved a thing of beauty and a joy forever, but kept the mischievous monkey out of the cabin. He first saw it when coming down by way of the hanging lamp, and could hardly believe his eyes; but when he was sure, fled with a howl of terror that brought all hands to the scene. One day, in wandering about, we found an old woman who spoke Spanish, and she invited us into her little hut of two rooms and offered milk to refresh us. Everything was neat as a pin, and in the adjoining room her pretty daughter was teaching a few little fellows their ABC's for a few cents a week each one. Doors and windows habitually stood open, and the passer-by could see plainly what was going on within, and I was struck with the cleanliness and tidiness of the poor people.

Nineteenth-Century Female Travel Accounts of Latin America

Agassiz, Louis, and Elizabeth. *A Journey in Brazil*. Boston: Ticknor and Fields, 1867.

Beck-Bernard, Lina. *Le Río Paraná. Cinq années de séjour dans la République Argentine*. Paris: Grassart, 1864.

Binzer, Ina von. *Alegrias e tristezas de uma educadora alemã no Brasil*. Trans. Alice Rossi and Luisita da Gama Cerqueira. São Paulo: Editora Anhembi, 1956.

Blake, Mary Elizabeth, and Margaret F. Sullivan. *Mexico. Picturesque, Political, Progressive*. Boston: Lee and Shepard, 1888.

Bly, Nellie. *Six Months in Mexico*. New York: American Publishing Corp., 1888.

Brassey, Annie Allnutt. *Around the World in the Yacht "Sunbeam." Our Home on the Ocean for Eleven Months*. New York: Henry Holt and Co., 1879.

Bremer, Fredrika. *The Homes of the New World. Impressions of America*. Trans. Mary Howitt. 2 vols. New York: Harper and Brothers, 1853.

Bromley, Clara Fitzroy Kelly. *A Woman's Wanderings in the Western World. A Series of Letters Addressed to Sir Fitzroy Kelly, M.P., by His Daughter Mrs. Bromley*. London: Saunders, Otley, and Co., 1861.

Calderón de la Barca, Frances. *Life in Mexico During a Residence of Two Years in That Country*. Boston: Little, Brown and Co., 1843.

Carbutt, Mary (Rhodes), Lady. *Five Months' Fine Weather in Canada, Western U.S. and Mexico*. London: Sampson Low, Marston, Searle, and Rivington, 1889.

Clemens, Eliza Jane McCartney. *La Plata Countries of South America*. Philadelphia: J. B. Lippincott Co., 1886.

Crawford, Cora Hayward. *The Land of the Montezumas*. Troy, NY: Nims and Knight, 1890.

Crommelin, May. *Over the Andes From the Argentine to Chili and Peru*. London: Richard Bentley and Son, 1896.

Dahlgren, Madeleine Vinton. *South Sea Sketches. A Narrative.* Boston: James R. Osgood and Co., 1881.

Dickins, Marguerite. *Along Shore with a Man-of-War.* Boston: Arena Publishing Co., 1893.

Dixie, Lady Florence. *Across Patagonia.* New York: R. Worthington, 1881.

Foote, Mrs. Henry Grant. *Recollections of Central America and the West Coast of Africa.* London: T. Cautley Newby, 1869.

Frances, May. *Beyond the Argentine. Or, Letters from Brazil.* London: W. H. Allen and Co., 1890.

Gooch, Fanny Chambers. *Face to Face with the Mexicans. The Domestic Life, Educational, Social, and Business Ways, Statesmanship and Literature, Legendary and General History of the Mexican People, as Seen and Studied by an American Woman During Seven Years of Intercourse with Them.* New York: Fords, Howard, and Hulbert, 1887.

Graham, Maria Dundas (Lady Calcott). *Journal of a Residence in Chile During the Year 1822 and a Voyage from Chile to Brazil in 1823.* London: Longman, Hurst, Rees, Orme, Brown, and Green, and J. Murray, 1824.

————. *Journal of a Voyage to Brazil, and Residence There, During Part of the Years 1821, 1822, 1823.* London: Longman, Hurst, Rees, Orme, Brown, and Green, and J. Murray, 1824.

Hort, Dora. *Via Nicaragua. A Sketch of Travel.* London: Remington and Co., 1887.

Howard of Glossop, Winefred Mary De Lisle (Lady). *Journal of a Tour in the United States, Canada and Mexico.* London: Sampson Low, Marston and Co., 1897.

Howe, Julia Ward. *A Trip to Cuba.* Boston: Ticknor and Fields, 1860.

Humphrey, Alice R. *A Summer Journey to Brazil.* New York: Bonnell, Silver and Co., 1900.

Jackson, Julia Newell. *A Winter Holiday in Summer Lands.* Chicago: A. C. McClurg and Co., 1890.

Jaques, Mary J. *Texas Ranch Life. With Three Months through Mexico in a "Prairie Schooner."* London: Horace Cox, 1894.

Kingsley, [Rose Georgina]. *South by West or Winter in the Rocky Mountains and Spring in Mexico.* London: W. Isbister and Co., 1874.

Kirchner, Adelaide Rosalind. *A Flag for Cuba. Pen Sketches of a Recent Trip Acrosss the Gulf of Mexico to the Island of Cuba.* New York: Mershon Co., 1897.

Kollonitz, Countess Paula. *The Court of Mexico*. Trans. J. E. Ollivant. London: Saunders, Otley, and Co., 1867.

Langendonck, Marie Van. *Une colonie au Brésil. Récits historiques*. Anvers, Belgium: Imprimerie L. Gerrits, 1862.

Layard, Gertrude. *Through the West Indies*. London: Sampson Low, Marston, Searle, and Rivington, 1887.

Lee, S. M. *Glimpses of Mexico and California*. Boston: Geo. H. Ellis, 1887.

Leland, Lillian. *Traveling Alone. A Woman's Journey Around the World*. New York: American News Co., 1890.

Le Plongeon, Alice D. *Here and There in Yucatán. Miscellanies*. New York: J. W. Bouton, 1886.

Lester, Mary [María Soltera, pseud.]. *A Lady's Ride Across Spanish Honduras*. Edinburgh: William Blackwood and Sons, 1884.

McHatton-Ripley, Eliza Moore. *From Flag to Flag. A Woman's Adventures and Experiences in the South During the War, in Mexico, and in Cuba*. New York: D. Appleton and Co., 1889.

Maudslay, Anne Cary, and Alfred Percival Maudslay. *A Glimpse at Guatemala and Some Notes on the Ancient Monuments of Central America*. London: John Murray, 1899.

Merwin, Loretta L. Wood. *Three Years in Chile*. New York: Follett, Foster, and Co., 1863.

Moore, Rachel Wilson. *Journal of Rachel Wilson Moore, Kept During a Tour to the West Indies and South America in 1863–64*. Philadelphia: T. Ellwood Zell, 1867.

Mulhall, Marion McMurrough. *Between the Amazon and Andes. Or Ten Years of a Lady's Travels in the Pampas, Gran Chaco, Paraguay, and Matto Grosso*. London: Edward Stanford, 1881.

———. *From Europe to Paraguay and Matto-Grosso*. London: Edward Stanford, 1877.

Murray, Amelia M. *Letters from the United States, Cuba and Canada*. New York: G. P. Putnam and Co., 1857.

Noble, Adeline M. *Rambles in Cuba*. New York: Carleton, 1870.

Pfeiffer, Ida. *A Lady's Second Journey Round the World: From London to the Cape of Good Hope, Borneo, Java, Sumatra, Celebes, Ceram, the Moluccas, etc., California, Panama, Peru, Ecuador, and the United States*. New York: Harper, 1856.

———. *A Woman's Journey Round the World, from Vienna to Brazil, Chile, Tahiti, China, Indostan, Persia and Asia Minor*. London: Office of the National Illustrated Library, 1850.

Poole, Annie Sampson. *Mexicans at Home in the Interior. By a Resident.* London: Chapman and Hall, 1884.

Rankin, Melinda. *Among the Mexicans. A Narrative of Missionary Labor.* Cincinnati: Chase and Hall, 1875.

Salm-Salm, Princess Felix. *Ten Years of My Life.* 2 vols. London: Richard Bentley and Son, 1876.

Sanborn, Helen J. *A Winter in Central America and Mexico.* Boston: Lee and Shepard, 1889.

Serrano de Wilson, Emília (Baronesa de Wilson). *América y sus mujeres.* Barcelona: Tipografia de Fidel Giró, 1890.

Sherratt, Harriott Wight. *Mexican Vistas. Seen from Highways and Byways of Travel.* Chicago: Rand, McNally and Co., 1899.

Smith, Ann Eliza (Brainerd). *Notes of Travel in Mexico and California.* St. Albans, VT: Messenger and Advertiser, 1886.

Stevenson, Sara Yorke. *Maximilian in Mexico. A Woman's Reminiscences of the French Intervention, 1862–1867.* New York: Century Co., 1899.

Stuart-Wortley, Emmeline (Lady). *Travels in the United States, etc. During 1849 and 1850.* 3 vols. New York: Harper and Brothers, 1851.

Tallenay, Jenny de. *Souvenirs de Venezuela. Notes de Voyage.* Paris: Librairie Plon, 1884.

Therese, Princess of Bavaria. *Meine reise in den Brasilianischen tropen.* Berlin: Verlag von Dietrich Reimer, 1897.

Tiernan, Frances Christine [Christian Reid, pseud.]. *The Land of the Sun. Vistas Mexicanas.* New York: D. Appleton and Co., 1894.

Toussaint-Samson, Adèle. *A Parisian in Brazil.* Trans. Emma Toussaint. Boston: James H. Earle, 1891.

Tristán, Flora. *Peregrinations of a Pariah, 1833–1834.* Trans. and ed. Jean Hawkes. Boston: Beacon Press, 1986.

Vincent, Ethel Gwendoline Moffatt (Lady). *China to Peru over the Andes. A Journey Through South America.* London: Sampson Low, Marston and Co., 1894.

Wallace, Caroline L. *Santiago de Cuba Before the War. Or Recuerdos de Santiago.* London: F. Tennyson Neely, 1898.

Williams, Rosa Carnegie. *A Year in the Andes, or a Lady's Adventures in Bogotá.* London: London Literary Society, 1881.

Wright, Marie Robinson. *Picturesque Mexico.* Philadelphia: J. B. Lippincott Co., 1897.

————. *The New Brazil. Its Resources and Attractions, Historical, Descriptive, and Industrial.* Philadelphia: George Barrie and Son, 1901.

Selected Titles on Women in Nineteenth-Century Latin America

Although the literature on Latin American women in the 1800s has grown rapidly in recent years, it does not approach that on twentieth-century women. Those in the colonial period have also claimed greater scholarly attention, even with the increasing interest being paid to nineteenth-century women. The expansion in research as well as its distribution across the disciplines can be seen in two major bibliographies published a decade apart. Meri Knaster, *Women in Spanish America. An Annotated Bibliography from Pre-Conquest to Contemporary Times* (Boston: G. K. Hall, 1977), demonstrates the strongly anthropological nature of works written in the 1960s and early 1970s. The volume edited by K. Lynn Stoner, *Latinas of the Americas: A Source Book* (New York: Garland Publishing, 1989), intended as an update of the Knaster bibliography, includes Brazil and Latinas in the United States. Mexico and Brazil, which are the foci of more studies on women—carried out by scholars based in those two countries as well as in the United States—than other Latin American countries, also have benefited from bibliographical publications on women: Asunción Lavrin, "La mujer en México: Veinte años de estudio, 1968–1988. Ensayo historiográfico," in *Memorias del simposio de historiografía mexicanista* (México: Instituto de Investigaciones Históricas, UNAM, 1990); and Fundação Carlos Chagas, *Mulher brasileira, Bibliografia anotada*, 2 vols. (São Paulo: Editora Brasiliense, 1979–1981).

Some of the earliest studies of women in Latin American history, as elsewhere in the world, concerned notable or "important" women left out of traditional history and their uncommon achievements. This form of compensatory or remedial history produced various accounts of heroines of the independence movements of the early nineteenth century, such as William Galván, *Minerva Mirabal: Historia de una heroina* (Santo Domingo: Editoria de la Universidad Autónoma de Santo Domingo, 1982); Alipio Valencia Vega, *Simona Josefa Manzaneda: Por patrioto, pero "chola," un infamante suplicio acabó con su vida* (La Paz: Libreria Editorial Juventud, 1978); and Vicente Grez, *Las mujeres de la Independencia* (Santiago de Chile: Zamorano y Caperán, 1945), as well as more scholarly treatments such as Evelyn Cherpak, "The Participation of Women in the Independence Movement in Gran Colombia, 1730–1830," in Asunción Lavrin, ed., *Latin American Women. Historical Perspectives* (Westport, CT: Greenwood Press, 1978), 219–34.

One of the major preoccupations of women's history in recent years has been the investigation of movements to improve women's social and legal status. Although this research tends to focus on twentieth-century events such as suffrage campaigns, a few studies include nineteenth-century activities. In *Emancipating the Female Sex. The Struggle for Women's Rights in Brazil, 1850–1940* (Durham, NC: Duke University Press, 1990), June E. Hahner traces the struggle for women's rights in Brazil from its earliest manifestations in the midnineteenth century. The studies of twentieth-century women's movements in Argentina and Mexico by Marifran Carlson, *Feminismo! The Woman's Movement in Argentina from its Beginnings to Eva Perón* (Chicago: Academy Publishers, 1988), and Anna Macías, *Against All Odds. The Feminist Movement in Mexico to 1940* (Westport, CT: Greenwood Press, 1982), begin with nineteenth-century developments. In *Del silencia a la palabra: Mujeres peruanas en los siglos XIX–XX* (Lima: Centro de la Mujer Peruana Flora Tristán, 1992), Maritza Villavicenio examines women's mobilization in Peru. Asunción Lavrin's densely textured comparative study of the Southern Cone nations, *Women, Feminism, and Social Change in Argentina, Chile, and Uruguay, 1890–1940* (Lincoln: University of Nebraska Press, 1995), includes the final decade of the nineteenth century. A broad international perspective is employed by Francesca Miller in *Latin American Women and the Search for Social Justice* (Hanover, NH: University Press of New England, 1991), which includes much pretwentieth-century material. In contrast, Maxine Molyneux focuses on a specific phenomenon, anarchist feminism, analyzing the content and social context of the anarchist newspaper, *La Voz de la Mujer*: "No God, No Boss, No Husband. Anarchist Feminism in Nineteenth-Century Argentina," *Latin American Perspectives* 13, no. 1 (Winter 1986): 119–45.

Women's legal status has received less scholarly attention. In "Changes in Mexican Family Law in the Nineteenth Century: The Civil Codes of 1870 and 1884," *Journal of Family History* 10, no. 3 (Fall 1985): 305–17, Silvia M. Arrom analyzes those codes in terms of changes taking place in the family during a period of state growth, economic expansion, and spreading liberalism. Thus, she continues the time line of her work on Mexican women in the first half of the nineteenth century, *The Women of Mexico City, 1790– 1857* (Stanford: Stanford University Press, l985), in which she studies women's legal status together with marriage and divorce patterns, challenging old ideas about female legal rights. Through such research, historians can expand the traditional realm of legal history. In "Lower-Class Families, Women, and the Law in Nineteenth-Century Argentina," *Journal of Family History* 10, no. 3 (Fall 1985): 318–22, Donna J. Guy analyzes state-family relations and examines transformations in the legal concept of *patria potestad.*

Other historical studies seek to document the daily activities of the great mass of women, concentrating on so-called common women, their lives and labor. But more attention has been paid to their "public" activities than to their domestic experiences. Various works have successfully combated the old stereotype of the passive, sheltered Latin American female, clearly demonstrating that some women among the elite have administered property or directed family enterprises. One example is the Mexican family studied by Edith Couturier, "Women in a Noble Family: The Mexican Counts of Regla, 1750–1830," in Lavrin, ed., *Latin American Women,* 129–49; other studies describe the activities of poor women, showing how the majority of females among the lower strata of society have always formed part of the labor force. Sandra Lauderdale Graham, *House and Street. The Domestic World of Servants and Masters in Nineteenth-Century Rio de Janeiro* (Cambridge: Cambridge University Press, 1988); Maria Odila Leite da Silva Dias, *Quotidiano e poder em São Paulo no século XIX: Ana Gertrudes de Jesus* (São Paulo: Brasiliense, 1980); and June E. Hahner, "Women and Work in Brazil, 1850–1920: A Preliminary Investigation," in Dauril Alden and Warren Dean, eds., *Essays Concerning the Socioeconomic History of Brazil and Portuguese India* (Gainesville: University of Florida Press, 1977), 87–117, all deal with women in Brazil. Donna J. Guy, "Women, Peonage, and Industrialization: Argentina, 1810–1914," *Latin American Research Review* 16, no. 3 (1981): 65–89, demonstrates that Argentine women did not realize the economic opportunities attendant upon nineteenth-century modernization. Working women during the Porfiriato, the well-studied period of Porfírio Díaz's dictatorship in Mexico (1876–

1910), are the subjects of studies by Carmen Ramos, "Mujeres trabajadoras en el México porfiriano: Género e ideologia del trabajo femenino, 1876–1911," *Revista Europea de Estudios Latinoamericanos y del Caribe*, no. 48 (June 1990): 27–44; Verena Radkau, *"Por la debilidad de nuestro ser": Mujeres del pueblo en la paz porfiriana* (México: Centro de Investigaciones y Estudios Superiores en Antropologia Social, Secretaría de Educación Pública, 1989); Vivian Vallens, *Working Women in Mexico During the Porfiriato, 1880–1910* (San Francisco: R and E Research Associates, 1979); and Margaret Towner, "Monopoly, Capitalism, and Women's Work During the Porfiriato," *Latin American Perspectives* 4, nos. 1–2 (Winter–Spring 1977): 90–105. Women's work in nineteenth-century rural Mexico is the focus of essays by Francie R. Chassen-López, who shows the diverse ways that women of different social classes participated in agriculture in Porfirian Oaxaca, and by Heather Fowler-Salamini, who studies women's active and changing participation as commercial coffee came to dominate the Córdoba region of Vera Cruz, in Heather Fowler-Salamini and Mary Kay Vaughan, eds., *Women of the Mexican Countryside, 1850–1990* (Tucson: University of Arizona Press, 1994).

Although the literature on African slavery is extensive, female experience often disappears in blanket histories. Studies focusing on women, such as Marietta Morrisey, *Slave Women in the New World. Gender Stratification in the Caribbean* (Lawrence: University Press of Kansas, 1989), are more commonly found for the Caribbean. However, among their selections on the United States and the Caribbean, David Barry Gaspar and Darlene Clark Hine, eds., *More Than Chattel. Black Women and Slavery in the Americas* (Bloomington: Indiana University Press, 1996), include two essays on nineteenth-century slave women and families in Brazil: Mary Karasch, "Slave Women on the Brazilian Frontier in the Nineteenth Century," 79–96, and Robert W. Slenes, "Black Homes, White Homilies. Perceptions of the Slave Family and of Slave Women in Nineteenth-Century Brazil," 126–46. More valuable information on Brazilian slave women is found in Mary Karasch, *Slave Life in Rio de Janeiro, 1808–1850* (Princeton, NJ: Princeton University Press, 1987); "Anastácia and the Slave Women of Rio de Janeiro," in Paul L. Lovejoy, ed., *Africans in Bondage. Studies in Slavery and the Slave Trade* (Madison: African Studies Program, University of Wisconsin-Madison, 1986), 79–105; and "Suppliers, Sellers, Servants, and Slaves," in Louisa Schell Hoberman and Susan

Midgen Socolow, eds., *Cities and Society in Colonial Latin America* (Albuquerque: University of New Mexico Press, 1986). Among the older writings that devote atttention to women are the now-classic work of Gilberto Freyre, *The Masters and the Slaves*, trans. Samuel Putnam (New York: Alfred A. Knopf, 1946), on slavery and planta-tion life in northeastern Brazil, and of Stanley J. Stein, *Vassouras. A Brazilian Coffee County, 1850–1900* (Cambridge, MA: Harvard University Press, 1957), which contains a section on both slave and free women on coffee plantations in the province of Rio de Janeiro (150–60). Much information on slave women in Lima is found in Christine Hunefeldt, *Las manuelas, vida cotidiana de una familia negra en la Lima del siglo XIX: Una reflexión histórica sobre la esclavitud urbana* (Lima: Instituto de Estudios Peruanas, [1992]).

Even though the growth of the history of the family in Latin America in recent years has added greatly to the body of knowl-edge about women, gender roles within the family have not been a prime concern of historians of the family, who have shown more interest in the process of familial formation and networks, and the patterns of marriage established during the colonial and post-independence periods. These authors have demonstrated the most concern with notable or elite families—the people who owned prop-erty and who left documentation supporting marriage and the transmission of property, such as wills, testaments, bills of sale, or litigation documents. Studies of elite families, frequently stressing familial strategies, include Diana Balmori, Stuart Voss, and Miles Wortman, *Notable Family Networks in Latin America, 1750–1900* (Chicago: University of Chicago Press, 1984); Dain Borges, *The Family in Bahia, Brazil, 1870–1945* (Stanford: Stanford Univer-sity Press, 1992); Billy J. Chandler, *The Feitosas and the Sertão dos Inhauma. The History of a Family and a Community in North-east Brazil, 1700–1930* (Gainesville: University of Florida Press, 1972); Guillermo de la Cuadra Gormaz, *Familias chilenas: Origen y desarrollo de las familias chilenas*, 3d ed. (Santiago de Chile: Editorial Zamorano y Caperán, 1982); Pilar Gonzalbo Aizpuri, ed., *Familias novohispanas: Siglos XVI–XIX* (México: El Cólegio de México, 1991); Doris Ladd, *The Mexican Nobility at Independence, 1780–1826* (Austin: University of Texas Press, 1976); and Larissa A. Lomnitz and Marison Pérez-Lizaur, *A Mexican Elite Family, 1820–1980* (Princeton, NJ: Princeton University Press, 1987). John Tutino has examined the question of decision-making by mothers as well as fathers in "Power, Class, and Family: Men and Women in the Mexican Elite, 1750–1910," *The Americas* 39, no. 3 (January 1983): 359–82. The dowry, one of the legal mechanisms that created and consolidated women's status, is the focus of the longitudinal study by Muriel Nazarri, *Disappearance of the Dowry. Women, Families, and Social Change in São Paulo, Brazil, 1600–1900* (Stanford: Stanford University Press, 1991), in which the author traces transformations in the functions of elite families.

The studies by Kátia de Queirós Mattoso, *Família e sociedade na Bahia do século XIX* (São Paulo: Corrupio, 1988); and Eni de Mesquita Samara, *As mulheres, o poder e a familia. São Paulo, século XIX* (São Paulo: Marco Zero, 1989), extend well beyond elite families. In her pioneering book, *Marriage, Class, and Colour in Nineteenth-Century Cuba. A Study of Racial Attitudes and Sexual Values in a Slave Society* (Cambridge: Cambridge University Press, 1974), Verena Martínez-Alier investigates the class and racial characteristics of marriage in nineteenth-century Cuba. Ann H. Johnson analyzes the impact of the market economy on lower-class rural family structures in "The Impact of Market Agriculture on Family and Household Structure in Nineteenth-Century Chile," *Hispanic American Historical Review* 58, no. 4 (November 1978): 625–48. In "Patriarchy in the Transition to Capitalism: Central Peru, 1830–1950," *Feminist Studies* 13, no. 2 (Summer 1987): 379–407, Florencia E. Mallon focuses on the complex nature of the peasant household economy in Peru's central highlands and explores the interrelationship of capitalism and patriarchy, combining gender and class analyses. *The Secret History of Gender. Women, Men, and Power in Late Colonial Mexico* (Chapel Hill: University of North Carolina Press, 1995), Steve J. Stern's wide-ranging major study of gender relations and the connection between gender and power in Mexican popular culture during the late colonial period (extended into the early nineteenth century), elucidates much in the visions and behavior of men and women of the popular classes.

Focusing on European immigrants to Argentina, Samuel Baily studies marriage selection strategies in "Marriage Patterns and Immigrant Assimilation in Buenos Aires, 1882–1923," *Hispanic American Historical Review* 60, no. 1 (February 1980): 32–48. Kristin Ruggiero investigates the role of the authorities in relations between spouses in that same city in "Wives on 'Deposit': Internment and the Preservation of Husbands' Honor in Late Nineteenth-Century Buenos Aires," *Journal of Family History* 17, no. 3 (1992):

253–70. In "The Limits of the Melting Pot of Urban Argentina: Marriage and Integration in Córdoba, 1869–1909," *Hispanic American Historical Review* 57, no. 1 (February 1977): 24–50, Mark D. Szuchman examines the functions of marriage in the socialization process of urban migrants.

The strand of family history tied to demographics that employs such sources as census and parish baptismal records has led to historical research on family structure, marriage, and fertility, successfully challenging some traditional assumptions about the family in the past, especially the old perception of the Latin American family as just a patriarchal and hierarchical institution. Work on nineteenth-century Brazil, for example, shows the existence of female-headed households parallel to the patriarchal: Iraci del Nero da Costa, "A estrutura familial e domicaria em Vila Rica no alvorecer do século XIX," *Revista do Instituto de Estudos Brasileiros*, no. 20 (1978): 17–34; Elizabeth Kuznesof, "The Role of the Female-Headed Household in Brazilian Modernization: São Paulo, 1765–1836," *Journal of Social History* 13, no. 4 (Summer 1980): 589–611; and "Household Composition and Headship as Related to Changes in the Mode of Production: São Paulo, 1765–1836," *Comparative Studies in Society and History* 23, no. 1 (January 1980): 78–108; and Donald Ramos, "Marriage and the Family in Colonial Vila Rica," *Hispanic American Historical Review* 55, no. 2 (May 1975): 200–225. As the studies on Latin American families demonstrate, family history was extremely complex, with units evolving over time to meet socioeconomic conditions and family structures taking diverse forms in different places and among various areas and societal groups.

So-called deviant behavior such as bigamy, concubinage, marital separation, and prostitution has increasingly claimed the atttention of historians. Although much of the recent research emphasizing personal relations and sexuality concentrates on the colonial period, some studies, such as that of Carmen Casteñada García, *Violación, estupro y sexualidad. Nueva Galicia, 1790–1921* (Guadalajara: Editorial Hexágono, 1989), concentrate on the nineteenth century. Infanticide in Argentina is examined by Kristin Ruggiero, "Honor, Maternity, and the Disciplining of Women: Infanticide in Late Nineteenth-Century Buenos Aires," *Hispanic American Historical Review* 72, no. 3 (August 1992): 353–73. While David McCreery, " 'This Life of Misery and Shame': Female Prostitution in Guatemala City, 1880–1920," *Journal of Latin*

American Studies 18, no. 2 (November 1986): 333–53, studies regulated prostitution in Guatemala City, William E. French, "Prostitutes and Guardian Angels: Women, Work, and the Family in Porfirian Mexico," *Hispanic American Historical Review* 72, no. 4 (November 1992): 529–53, focuses more on questions of moral reform and social symbols, education, and class differentiation. Prostitution in nineteenth- and early twentieth-century Brazil has been investigated by a number of historians, including Sandra Lauderdale Graham, "Slavery's Impasse: Slave Prostitutes, Small-Time Mistresses, and the Brazilian Law of 1871," *Comparative Studies in Society and History* 33, no. 4 (October 1991): 669–94; Magali Engel, *Meretrizes e doutores. O saber médico e a prostituição na Cidade do Rio de Janeiro, 1845–1890* (São Paulo: Brasiliense, 1990); Marta Abreu de Esteves, *Meninas perdidas. Os populares e o coitidiano do amor no Rio de Janeiro na Belle Epoque* (Rio de Janeiro: Paz e Terra, 1989); Margareth Rago, *Os prazeres da noite. Prostituição e códigos da sexualidade feminina em São Paulo (1890–1930)* (Rio de Janeiro: Paz e Terra, 1991); Luiz Carlos Soares, *Rameiras, Ilhoas, polacas. A prostituição no Rio de Janeiro do século XIX* (São Paulo: Editora Atica, 1992); and Lena Medeiros de Menezes, *Os estrangeiros e o comércio do prazer nas ruas do Rio (1890–1930)* (Rio de Janeiro: Arquivo Nacional, 1992). Although Dona Guy's *Sex and Danger in Buenos Aires. Prostitution, Family, and Nation in Argentina* (Lincoln: University of Nebraska Press, 1991) centers on the twentieth century, it contains material on prostitution in the late nineteenth century.

Since the scholarship on female religious has focused on the colonial period, information on nineteenth-century nuns is difficult to find. Hence, works on colonial convents, nuns, and religion by Asunción Lavrin should prove useful to readers, including: "Unlike Sor Juana? The Model Nun in the Religious Literature of Colonial Mexico," in Stephanie Merrim, ed., *Feminist Perspectives on Sor Juana Inés de la Cruz* (Detroit: Wayne State University Press, 1991), 61–85; "Women and Religion in Spanish America," in Rosemary Radford Ruether and Rosemary Skinner Keller, eds., *Women and Religion in America*, Vol. 2, *The Colonial and Revolutionary Periods* (San Francisco: Harper and Row, 1983), 42–78; and "Women in Convents: Their Economic and Social Role in Colonial Mexico," in Berenice A. Carroll, ed., *Liberating Women's History: Theoretical and Critical Essays* (Urbana: University of Illinois Press, 1976), 250–71. Two of Lavrin's early publications did deal with nineteenth-century Mexican nunneries: "Problems and Policies in the Administration of Nunneries in Mexico, 1800–1835," *The Americas* 28 (July 1971), 58–77; and "Mexican Nunneries from 1835 to 1860: Their Administrative Policies and Relations with the State," *The Americas* 28, no. 1 (January 1972): 288–310.

Relatively little has been written on women's education in nineteenth-century Latin America. But some aspects are discussed by Cynthis Jeffress Little in "Education, Philanthropy, and Feminism: Components of Argentine Womanhood, 1860–1920," in Lavrin, ed., *Latin American Women*, 235–53; and by Silvia Arrom, briefly, in *The Women of Mexico City*. Mary K. Vaughan, who has dealt extensively with education in Mexico, focuses on women's education in "Women, Class, and Education in Mexico, 1880–1928," *Latin American Perspectives* 4 (1977): 135–52. In "Children and Schooling in Guanajuato, Mexico, 1790–1840," *SECOLAS Annuals* 22 (March 1992): 36–52, reprinted in John A. Britton, ed., *Molding the Hearts and Minds. Education, Communications, and Social Change in Latin America* (Wilmington, DE: Scholarly Resources, 1994), 19–36, Angela T. Thompson discusses children's education and the development of public policy in Guanajuato.

Information on women writers and their publications in nineteenth-century Spanish America can be found in Diane E. Marting, ed., *Women Writers of Spanish America. A Bio-Bibliographical Source Book* (New York: Greenwood Press, 1987); and Doris Meyer, ed., *Re-Interpreting the Spanish American Essay. Women Writers of the 19th and 20th Centuries* (Albuquerque: University of New Mexico Press, 1995). The Baronesa de Wilson, Emília Serrano García del Forel, described the leading women writers she met on her travels through late nineteenth-century Latin America in *América y sus mujeres* (Barcelona: Tipografia de Fidel Giró, 1890).

Most of the formal sources historians have used in focusing on women in nineteenth-century Latin America, such as trial records, wills, census returns, law codes, official correspondence, and newspapers, have not been written by those women. Before the late nineteenth century, very few Latin American women ever learned to read and write. Even literate ones kept diaries and wrote fewer letters than North Americans or Europeans. A rare published diary is that by a lively Brazilian schoolgirl growing up in a town in the old diamond-mining district of Minas Gerais in the 1890s, Alice Brant [Helena Morley, pseud.], *The Diary of "Helena Morley,"* trans.

Elizabeth Bishop (New York: Farrar, Strauss, and Cudahy, 1957). A twentieth-century diary by a Brazilian woman from Rio Grande do Sul is that by Cecília de Assis Brasil, *Diário de Cecília de Assis Brasil: Período 1916–1928* (Porto Alegre: L and PM Editores, 1983). Since it was most unusual for a Latin American woman to write or publish a travel account, the travel diary kept by Augusta do Faro Fleury Curado recording her family's two-month journey—initially by train but mostly by horseback—from Rio de Janeiro to Brazil's far western state of Goiás, published by her daughter, Maria Paula Fleury de Godoy, some seventy years later, is a unique document: *Do Rio de Janeiro a Goiás—1896 (A viagem era assim)*, 2d ed. (Goiânia: n.p., 1985). The valuable collection of letters edited by Sérgio Vergara Quiroz, *Cartas de mujeres de Chile, 1630–1885* (Santiago de Chile: Editorial Andrés Bello, 1987), contains mostly nineteenth-century letters by Chilean women.

Brief portraits of individual women penned by late twentieth-century historians are found in Judith Ewell and William H. Beezley, eds., *The Human Tradition in Latin America: The Nineteenth Century* (Wilmington, DE: Scholarly Resources, 1987). The life and times of an Indian woman who sought to encourage her people, the Caiapó, to adapt to Portuguese life and religion in early nineteenth-century Goiás are presented by Mary Karasch, "Damiana da Cunha: Catechist and *Sertanista*," in David G. Sweet and Gary B. Nash, eds., *Struggle and Survival in Colonial America* (Berkeley: University of California Press, 1981), 102–20.

Latin American Silhouettes
Studies in History and Culture

William H. Beezley and
Judith Ewell
Editors

Volumes Published

(1995). Cloth ISBN 0-8420-2556-1
Paper ISBN 0-8420-2557-X

Silvia Marina Arrom and Servando Ortoll, eds., *Riots in the Cities: Popular Politics and the Urban Poor in Latin America, 1765–1910* (1996). Cloth ISBN 0-8420-2580-4 Paper ISBN 0-8420-2581-2

Roderic Ai Camp, ed., *Polling for Democracy: Public Opinion and Political Liberalization in Mexico* (1996). ISBN 0-8420-2583-9

Brian Loveman and Thomas M. Davies, Jr., eds., *The Politics of Antipolitics: The Military in Latin America*, 3d ed., revised and updated (1996). Cloth ISBN 0-8420-2609-6 Paper ISBN 0-8420-2611-8

Joseph S. Tulchin, Andrés Serbín, and Rafael Hernández, eds., *Cuba and the Caribbean: Regional Issues and Trends in the Post-Cold War Era* (1997). ISBN 0-8420-2652-5

Thomas W. Walker, ed., *Nicaragua without Illusions: Regime Transition and Structural Adjustment in the 1990s* (1997). Cloth ISBN 0-8420-2578-2 Paper ISBN 0-8420-2579-0

Dianne Walta Hart, *Undocumented in L.A.: An Immigrant's Story* (1997). Cloth ISBN 0-8420-2648-7 Paper ISBN 0-8420-2649-5

Jaime E. Rodríguez O. and Kathryn Vincent, eds., *Myths, Misdeeds, and Misunderstandings: The Roots of Conflict in U.S.-Mexican Relations* (1997). ISBN 0-8420-2662-2

Jaime E. Rodríguez O. and Kathryn Vincent, eds., *Common Border, Uncommon Paths: Race, Culture, and National Identity in U.S.-Mexican Relations* (1997). ISBN 0-8420-2673-8

William H. Beezley and Judith Ewell, eds., *The Human Tradition in Modern Latin America* (1997). Cloth ISBN 0-8420-2612-6 Paper ISBN 0-8420-2613-4

Donald F. Stevens, ed., *Based on a True Story: Latin American History at the Movies* (1997). ISBN 0-8420-2582-0

Jaime E. Rodríguez O., ed., *The Origins of Mexican National Politics, 1808–1847* (1997). Paper ISBN 0-8420-2723-8

Che Guevara, *Guerrilla Warfare*, with revised and updated introduction and case studies by Brian Loveman and Thomas M. Davies, Jr., 3d ed. (1997). Cloth ISBN 0-8420-2677-0 Paper ISBN 0-8420-2678-9

Adrian A. Bantjes, *As If Jesus Walked on Earth: Cardenismo, Sonora, and the Mexican Revolution* (1998). ISBN 0-8420-2653-3

Henry A. Dietz and Gil Shidlo, eds., *Urban Elections in Democratic Latin America* (1998). Cloth ISBN 0-8420-2627-4 Paper ISBN 0-8420-2628-2

A. Kim Clark, *The Redemptive Work: Railway and Nation in Ecuador, 1895–1930* (1998). ISBN 0-8420-2674-6

Joseph S. Tulchin, ed., with Allison M. Garland, *Argentina: The Challenges of Modernization* (1998). ISBN 0-8420-2721-1

Louis A. Pérez, Jr., ed., *Impressions of Cuba in the Nineteenth Century: The Travel Diary of Joseph J. Dimock* (1998). Cloth ISBN 0-8420-2657-6 Paper ISBN 0-8420-2658-4

Guy P. C. Thomson, with David G. LaFrance, *Patriotism, Politics, and Popular Liberalism in Nineteenth-Century Mexico: Juan Francisco Lucas and the Puebla Sierra* (1998). ISBN 0-8420-2683-5

June E. Hahner, ed., *Women through Women's Eyes: Latin American Women in Nineteenth-Century Travel Accounts* (1998). Cloth ISBN 0-8420-2633-9 Paper ISBN 0-8420-2634-7

James P. Brennan, ed., *Peronism and Argentina* (1998). ISBN 0-8420-2706-8

John Mason Hart, ed., *Border Crossings: Mexican and Mexican-American Workers* (1998). Cloth ISBN 0-8420-2716-5 Paper ISBN 0-8420-2717-3

Brian Loveman, *For la Patria: Politics and the Armed Forces in Latin America* (1999). Cloth ISBN 0-8420-2772-6 Paper ISBN 0-8420-2773-4

K. Lynn Stoner, ed./comp., with Luís Hipólito Serrano Pérez, *Cuban and Cuban-American Women: An Annotated Bibliography* (1999). ISBN 0-8420-2643-6